Tricks of the Trades

by Bruce Van Sant

Stratagems for cruising the tropics.

Ploys to stay healthy and prosperous in the islands.

Dodges to duck thieves, con artists and venal authority.

Ruses to thwart the ceaseless winds and wild seas.

Tactics and maneuvers in navigating the islands.

Feints around boat brokers and outfitters.

Devices to get the jump on weather.

Wiles for the single hander.

in short,

Tricks
for successfully cruising the islands of the trades.

Distributed by:

CRUISING GUIDE PUBLICATIONS

P.O. Box 1017

Dunedin, FL 34697-1017

Phone: (727) 733-5322 • Fax: (727) 734-8179

There exist no warranties, either expressed or implied, as to the usability of the information contained herein for any purpose whatever.

Other books by Bruce Van Sant

The Gentleman's Guide to PASSAGES SOUTH
A Cruising and Water Sports Guide to the SPANISH VIRGIN ISLANDS

First Edition

ISBN 0-944428-62-2

Printed in the U.S.A.
Written in E-prime

CRUISING TRICKS 1

CRUISING IN THE TRADES 2
  CRUISING VS. SAILING 2
  GETTING STARTED 3
  CRUISING STYLES 4
  CULTURE SHOCK 7
  LANGUAGE 11
  SELF RELIANCE 12
SECURITY 17
  PERSONAL SECURITY 17
  BOAT SECURITY 19
  DINGHY SECURITY 21
  INSURANCE 24
  FIREARMS 24
OFFICIALDOM 26
  TIPS ON CLEARING CUSTOMS EASILY 26
  POLICE AND MILITARY 27
  THE UNOFFICIALS 35
A CRUISING HEALTH PLAN 36
  PRIMARY PHYSICIAN 36
  TOOTH TALES 37
  PUBLIC CLINICS 38
  MEDICAL LABORATORIES 39
  FINDING YOUR MEDICINE 40
  COSTS 40
  AN OPEN MIND 41
  PREVENTION 41
ECONOMICS 45
  BEERONOMY 45
  PROVISIONING 46

TRICKING THE TRADES 51

KNOWING THE WEATHER 52
  WEATHER FEATURES 52
  WEATHER WINDOWS 54
  HURRICANES 65
  PREDICTING STORMS 69
  USING HURRICANE HOLES 72
PLAYING THE ISLAND LEES 74
  UNDERSTANDING WIND 75
  ISLAND EFFECTS ON WIND 80
  ISLAND EFFECTS ON SEAS 85
  ISLAND LEES 89
  INTEGRATING EFFECTS 92
  FIRST PRINCIPLES 93
TRADES STRATEGIES 94
  WAIT FOR WEATHER 94
  PLAN YOUR ROUTE FLEXIBLY 97

  LANDFALL DETERMINES DEPARTURE 100
  STAGE YOUR DEPARTURE 102
  DON'T FEAR THE DARK 103
  HUG THE SHORE AT NIGHT 104
COPYING THE WEATHER 107
  THE WEATHER REPORT 107
  MAKING SENSE OF NWS REPORTS 108
  SHORTHANDING OFFSHORE REPORTS 110

TRICKS UNDERWAY 113

SINGLE HANDED TRICKS 114
  THE BOAT'S WAY 114
  ANCHOR DRILL 115
  LINE HANDLING 115
  SPEED 116
  EXHAUSTION 116
  HALLUCINATIONS 117
  PICKING WEATHER WINDOWS 117
  WHEN DO YOU? 118
  GETTING OFF GROUND 118
  THE AGING CRUISER 120
MOTORING & MOTORSAILING 121
FISHING 128
  SKIN DIVING 128
  SCUBA 130
  TROLLING 131
  BOTTOM FISHING 132
  A GOOD FINISH 132
ANCHORING 133
  LAYING ANCHOR 134
  WEIGHING ANCHOR 137
  OPEN ANCHORAGES 137
  ANCHORS AND GROUND TACKLE 138
USING THE RADIO 141

FINDING THE BOAT 145

PROJECT PLANNING 146
PROJECT MANAGEMENT 149
DANCING WITH BROKERS 153
SEA TRIALS 156

OUTFITTER'S TRICKS 157

EQUIPMENT RELIABILITY 158
WHAT YOU REALLY NEED 167

GLOSSARY 179

Foreword

This book means to show high latitude seafarers how to weather living aboard in the tropics while teaching them a knack for playing the trade conditions found there.

An American in his fourth decade of living foreign *and* living aboard, I have accumulated an heroic stack of tricks for sailors going abroad, specifically to sailors of the trade winds. Not how to survive, but how to live well, and to navigate safely and comfortably.

Trade winds flow like rivers, from the subtropical high-pressure belts at latitudes 30 north and south toward the relatively low pressure areas of equatorial regions. They rarely get above 22° or below 10° latitudes on the western halves of the oceans. This belt of trade winds girdles islands which sustain, of course, quite insular cultures and, almost without exception, poor economies. You can and should fare well in them.

Islands big and small, even reefs and banks, change the trade winds and currents which pass through, over and around them. They alter the forecast conditions in a predictable manner. Playing these effects in concert, a sailor can make safe, comfortable and pleasant progress even against normally impenetrable trade winds and seas.

Since 1979 I've racked up well over 60,000 sea miles, mostly single handed. Not hard to do on long ocean passages, but most of my miles wound through the islands on the route called the *thorny path*, playing the island lees from the Bahamas to South America. With my long-keeled, 6½ half foot draft ketch, *Jalan Jalan*, I easily took the windward chain of islands seven times to South America, 40 to 50 times between the Bahamas and the Virgins, at least a hundred passages on the coasts of the Greater Antilles.

I have added all the lessons won from my Caribbean sailing to tricks I learned the hard way in Asia and Europe. The sum of these tips can make every passage, every harbor hop, an unalloyed pleasure. Year after year I watch people senselessly bang into the trades and otherwise run afoul in the tropics, sometimes losing everything. This little book shares my lessons with you, so you can get it right on your first cruise.

Forty-five years of sailing ended grudgingly. The signs piled up: skin cancers, a stroke leaving me with bouts of vertigo and missteps at night while single-handing a big ketch around the Caribbean. Clearly, to stay on the water, and to continue running the island chain, I had to get out of the cockpit, under cover and into something I couldn't easily fall out of. I transferred to an unmasted motorsailer, a Schucker 440, upon which I continue

my peripatetic cruising. I've named her *Tidak Apa*, my fifth Malayu boat name. *Tidak Apa* means "it doesn't matter anymore" and "it doesn't make any difference". And I have found in my years of trawlering that, indeed, it really doesn't. The same tricks apply.

Bruce

aboard *Tidak Apa*
Luperón
Dominican Republic

CRUISING TRICKS

Though perhaps useful elsewhere, these tips particularly apply
to the island strewn trade winds belts between the tropics.

CRUISING IN THE TRADES

Degrees of Difference Between the Tropics

Much miscommunication comes from the word "cruising", since we talk with our points of view from different cruising styles. Take for example the following exchange of letters in which my candid reply to friends never got answered. I suppose I unintentionally hurt their feelings, since he clearly hadn't a clue about the cruising life, and I hadn't either any idea of what he expected from it. Words have meanings. Cruising and sailing define matters of style.

CRUISING VS. SAILING

We were Imroning our boat in a peaceful mangroved lagoon near Cumaná, Venezuela, when I received a three months' batch of mail in which I found a letter from an old friend. He had retired and now taught navigation for the Power Squadron in Florida. I opened the letter, and the miscommunication began.

He and his wife, he said, "were considering trying out the cruising life". He wondered if they could visit us to try out a half day's cruise to see if they would like it. I wrote back with the truth. It might take several days of work to break camp, I told him. When we found ourselves harbor bound for more than a week the boat tended to get cocooned in sunshades, spider webbed in lines and bedecked with all manner of half done projects. I told him I wouldn't undo all that for my own mother just for a half day sail. On the other hand, I wrote, if we had to make a passage, guests aboard could interfere with the routine and safe operation of our vessel, especially in hurricane season. I proposed he visit next time we found ourselves in a short-term harbor while island hopping. That way they could enjoy staying aboard, have their half day harbor hops and get to visit nice tourist places which wouldn't shatter their vision of the cruising life. They could pick either the place or the time, I said, but not both. I meant that either notification would come extremely short, or the place might disappoint them extremely. Such as Castries, or a week in Chimana Grande lagoon, where we lay then, where they would dress with paint rollers in their hands and mosquito nets round their heads.

I thought this a marvelously honest and complete answer, as only a good friend deserved. I looked forward to his reply and to his sometime visit. After writing these sentiments to my friend, I went ashore for my Sundowner Gin and Tonic (SG&T, see Glossary). Next to me at the bar, Pedro asked if I knew of a fellow called Sparky. I waved my gin and tonic toward Sparky who just then began walking our way down the dock. "The cruiser there on the dock," I said.

"Which one?" asked Pedro. "The Carver or the Trojan?" Words indeed have meaning.

Boats differ as do the uses of boats. I did my share of racing on Lake Worth half a century ago on really fast scows. I've used my cruising boats in PHRF racing as well. But when a weekend sailor with a gofast boat asks me about cruising, I'm not so sure I can bridge the communications gap. Nevertheless, I try. I can tell them some false expectations I've known people to have while they planned to take up full time cruising.

RACING FOR THE CLUB

Cruising calls to mind teenagers who piddled along Main Street in otherwise high speed dragsters to ogle the girls hanging around the drugstore. In the Navy, the same young men *cruised* the bars on East Baltimore Street, teased into lingering too long at each stop where nothing really exciting ever happened to them. Later in life, after a day at the office, they *cruised* the body exchanges until, finally snared, they moved to the 'burbs, raised kids, made the school board and joined a yacht club. Sailing tugged at their middle age like the freedom of wheels did in their teens. They finally retire and go *cruising*.

At cruising club gams and breakfasts, dockside happy hours and marine store seminars, the message gets through. You must sail far and wide. Then you may grow a downeaster beard, wear a Greek fisherman's cap, give advice rather than seek it, chair the seminar, not just attend it. They fit up and sail out. They begin their race for the finish at the club with a cupful of bragging rights. They do long laps between yachting centers where, again, nothing really happens to them. They straggle home where they grow the beard, wear the hat and sit under the umbrella at dockside handing out advice.

Others, however, have lost themselves out on the course and dropped out of the race. They piddle along in the little places. Something happens to them every day they *cruise*.

GETTING STARTED

Whatever you expect, you won't get it.

Once I imagined myself languidly cruising the Mediterranean in endless summers. Boy! Did I learn fast! My work list grew three lines for every one I struck through. I found the islands of the trades no different.

Cruisers start out with lots of man overboard equipment, and little or nothing with which to receive original source weather data. They have full game shelves and book shelves, but few engine spares and supplies; lots of yogurt and sourdough starter, but no resin catalyst; colored cloth to make courtesy flags, but no fiberglass cloth or sheet rubber. They've got shot records and pet pedigrees, but no engine shop manual.

Much cruise planning focuses on the terror of the *Ultimate Wave*.

But with the right investment in equipment and skills, even a neophyte cruiser can read the weather sufficiently to hop between Ultimate Waves. The last time anyone asked me for shot records I didn't have any. They pulled me aside in Hong Kong and gave me a free smallpox vaccination. No one has mentioned it since, nor my sloppy flag etiquette. I've always had pets on board. Officials have only petted them, not that exceptions don't exist, or one's behavior can't provoke inquiry.

Target your preparations more effectively with language lessons for the countries you shall visit. Replace thrillers and romances with references on the islands. The more remote from your experience, the more you shall need it. The differences between what you expect and what you find should liven your day, not frustrate you or cause strokes.

Don't expect to evade the recessive ills of society. They often dominate in the tropics. Ineluctable authorities, unfair taxes, irreversible poverty, rampant greed, welfare amuck, little opportunity, low wages and you name it! Everywhere in the trade belt one or all of these flourish in the tropic sun, dwarfing more temperate varieties to the north.

CRUISING STYLES

An itinerant myself for half a century I can certify the old refrains "You can't run away from yourself", "The grass always looks greener...", etc. The newcomer to life aboard in the tropics, recently unchained from responsibility's chafe, often careers along blinded by childhood's "new puppy" malady, or the adolescent "new car" syndrome. Eventually that wears thin and everyone finds their own style of cruising or they give up the game. I have drifted through several styles myself and I feel another coming on.

GLOBETROTTER

I sailed as a GLOBETROTTER for years in Europe, but I metamorphosed. GLOBETROTTERS charge about the sea testing self and boat in persistent replays of sailing magazine articles. They become instant experts and write articles as the Old Hand who has done it all. If cruising of that ilk appeals to you, go for it, but drop this book before it changes your life.

CAMPER

While rearing children I could only cruise for long weekends, vacations and summers while relocating to new jobs. Even though a liveaboard, I became a CAMPER when out cruising. When not adventuring at sea, I repaired ashore. I felt awfully alive but did not live a life. One cannot sustain long term cruising as a series of camping adventures. It won't feel anything like cruising with the kids.

TOURIST

Cruising TOURISTS rarely leave the comfort of their nautical nests. They cruise as passengers in a safari park, noses pressed against the glass, marveling at the dangers around them. They savor foreign life and lands as do Manhattan yuppies their cappuccino. These cruisers leave the boat at each rest stop from which they can fly home. They bunch up in foreign harbors and do land excursions in groups. TOURISTS need money, so I never tried it.

MINGLERS

Some cruisers enjoyed so much the weekend potlucks and raftups of their boat lives at home that, when they go out into the world for a long cruise, they continue them. MINGLERS gravitate to each other like magnets. They see cruising as a continuous 4th of July. If you like this style, you shall change venues each time the egg salad sandwiches run out, the keg dries up and the stories grow stale.

AIRSTREAMERS

I call some of my favorite couples AIRSTREAMERS. They poke around marinas and sea parks scattered along the seaways, not unlike Mom and Pop who settle into RV parks between highway excursions in their Air Stream trailers. If this laid back road gypsy life becomes you, as it does me, make the whole trade wind crescent your I-75, and you'll never come home.

Coward and Passage Maker

I sailed years like a PASSAGE MAKER in Europe, but I metamorphosed. PASSAGE MAKERS always take the long shots. They want open water. Some stay with this style for good.

Like a good friend of mine who can't abide waiting for weather. At sea he takes long passages to avoid the anxiety of making entrances and exits. In port he finds a secure hole and hangs out for months, even years. When in port, he doesn't "waste time with the weather". When he prepares a passage he has no mental data base of the weather because he lacks the patience required to carefully accumulate one. He comes unglued after just two days of waiting and throws himself and his boat into the sea to get it over with.

Because of his habit of nonstop long passages, my friend has a ferocious reputation as a great navigator, a real sailor's sailor, and I often see cruisers consulting him on weather and sailing strategies. In reality, he has seen few ports, though the ones he's seen, he knows well. He's done little sailing and navigating among islands, though he's done lots of tossing in his bunk while reading bunches of books out on the open sea. To me, he confesses he simply gets "scared shitless" near islands and while making their reefy entrances. He says he doesn't understand their currents, their effects on wind and weather, and that it "drives him bananas" to even think about the weather, let alone focus his worse fears upon it day after day while waiting for a weather window. When he feels ready to go, or some woman makes it known that he must, he screws up his courage, roars an oath and makes a banzai charge onto the hazards of the open sea.

We have traveled the same routes, he and I — he in one fierce gulp, I nibbling away at it one harbor at a time. As a consequence, we rarely meet, though we like each other well. A good beer buddy, he once confessed to me his admiration for the quality of mind which enables guys like me to face the hazards of island hopping. "It takes a lot of guts", he says. No amount of explaining of weather forecasts, of land effects, of night lees or of diurnal variations can persuade him of my cowardice. I don't even throw my tea bags overboard for fear of hearing their tiny shrieks in the night.

If you do long passages to test yourself against the sea, you have to know you shall eventually lose the test. PASSAGE MAKER or COWARD, only the COWARDS survive.

Leisure Sailor

A chance encounter in Georgetown one year brought me to this cruising style. My charter guests had all left. I sat hunched over the last of the ship's supply of Bermudez Añejo Especial, morosely considering the return trip south. A toad named Thornton, Thornton Throckmorton Thorndike the Third actually, hopped over to cheer me up. A gentleman sailor, Thornton elegantly described to me how he had discovered an entirely new method for heading south against the prevailing winds while participating in the Thorny Path race of 1933.

Skilled in the art of steering with his big toe while jigging for grouper over the stern, he and his long-keeled beamy yawl, Rose, came totally unprepared for the cutthroat competition in the Thorny Path Semifinals. The high-tech go-to-windward carbon filament keel-less burgee bearers backing and filling at the starting line awed him. Could his pokey little boat cut it? Thornton thrilled at the threat and became ever more determined.

As the only member of the leisure class to compete, Thornton had a unique advantage: LEISURE itself. He laid on capers from Exuma Market to gormandize his usually superb Nassau Grouper au Vin Blanc. He researched his Rolodex file of anchorages, fishing holes and recipes. He prepared his lists of dinner guests for each anchorage, always careful to invite each of the competing skippers on exactly three occasions, never hosting the same three twice. He underestimated his competition.

Four of the other yachts had professional delivery crews, only one of whose boat survived, but in such condition that they subsequently got scrapped for spare parts for the Tortola charter fleet. Two contestants were on one year sabbaticals to sail around the world. Two were on two week vacations. One had to meet a seaplane in St. Thomas. From this field of ten tough competitors came five DNF's, three divorces and one case of road hypnosis who eventually ran ashore on the Cape Verdes.

And what about Thornton? Thornton won! Thornton's winning strategy: how to take the thorns out of the Thorny Path with leisure sailing. After a few tries at the Thorny Path, I've spent many happy years on Thornton's Thornless Path.

LEISURE SAILORS have an old fashioned leisure class lifestyle. He or she needn't have wealth, only the mindset and the minimum wherewithal to leisurely enjoy cruising without the deadlines and hustle of the working classes. LEISURE SAILORS may work upon occasion, usually doing maintenance chores on their own yacht. They work for a wage only if it goes toward recouping the cruising kitty.

Perhaps an athlete, *never* a jock, but man or woman, power or sail, *always* a seaman.

Thornton, aboard his ketch Rose

CULTURE SHOCK

Ever look forward to October's bracing chill and the smell of burning leaves? Bottle it. The tropics offer the mosquito mugginess of the autumnal troughs and the black rain from burning sugar fields. You may have already girded yourself for nature's changes. How about the accommodations you must make to differences in mores, tact, dignity, decency, body language and much more, among the different peoples you shall encounter in those new environments?

A Tip

In a "going south" meeting on the beach one year a lady expressed concern with the informal fees versus the official fees charged for entering different countries. She wanted a tale of corruption, and I didn't bite. I addressed the group instead.

Can you find corruption in the islands? You bet; the same kind as everywhere, but to a much lesser degree. By definition a small country has only petty officials, therefore the corruption, by large country standards, has quite petty dimensions. And abuse of power in smaller countries more likely touches the individual. In the yachties' countries billions get wasted (stolen) daily, but it doesn't overly annoy them. If an island official makes a sly suggestion that one buy him a beer, however, some yachties become outraged.

The lady of the informal charges now asked about tipping. I told her most cultures I've known generally recognize tipping only when some superlative service merits it. Often people enjoy doing favors for each other to express their appreciation more than do Europeans or Americans. Taxi drivers don't get tips as a fast rule. Waiters' tips are sometimes on the bill, and one leaves the change. A driver might not understand a tip, but he might understand "Keep the change". If not tipping a waiter makes you uncomfortable, then use 10 percent, plus or minus, as the Americans use 20 percent. Over tipping wins disrespect and larger charges next time.

She looked incredulous. Not tip? Then followed a long harangue about her daughter making it through college from tips as a waitress. I worked my way through high school as a hotel bell hop. I think I know about tips: no begrudging someone who forgets, and damn any rules, you only get what you earn. She really lay into me, railing at my selfishness. Trying not to respond to personal attack, I gave the point but warned the group that tipping too much, or when not expected to, could cause embarrassment. The waiter of a small restaurant might own the place, proudly independent after a lifetime's struggle. Attempts to tip could insult. Watch what locals do, and when in Rome ...

The Price of Stress

Signs of normalcy in one culture may cause alarm signals in another. For example, many cultures like to show guns as a sign of authority. Why not? Sure makes good logic.

Sometimes, the smaller the authority, the larger the guns. Larger guns cost less. Guns from the former eastern block come cheap in quantity, and because you haven't seen them before, they look all the more sinister. Unless quite well traveled, you might suppose you've stumbled into a revolution when you see poorly clad citizens roaming the streets with Russian machine guns and rifles.

Culturally transmitted visual stimuli and their culturally correct responses don't map

7

easily from one culture to another. They can, in fact, directly conflict. The receiving organism — you — shall undergo stress depending on the extent to which responses expected by the two cultures to the same stimulus differ. If a mild and occasional conflict, you giggle. If strong and continuous you undergo a stress reaction called Culture Shock.

You may have a repertoire of cocktail stories of what happened to you on your tour of Thailand. In that case, you understand the phenomenon of culture shock, but you may never have experienced it in shock dimensions. If you lived on the local economy of another nation for extended periods, forced to use another language exclusively as, say, a member of the American Peace Corps, you know well the phenomenon at shock levels.

Roaming around the islands of the trades on a small boat gets greater exposure to local people and their customs than does jetting in and out of well protected resort complexes. If you haven't had the opportunity of experiencing culture shock before, you shall learn on your boat. When it gets unpleasant you can't simply take a cab to the airport.

Culture shock has many symptoms with which you should familiarize yourself before leaving home. Your ability to communicate with or without language, your capacity to get what you want, say an engine part, depend on your skill in cutting through the background noise of your culturally learned responses and creating a totally new set of responses which can achieve your goals.

The better your skills in creating useful new responses to confusing stimuli, however, the higher stress levels you may suffer due to the number of unsatisfied natural responses you have accumulated.

You may have success handling the customs guys, finding clean fuel, provisioning at fair prices, replacing a motor part, and so forth, but you shall build a head of steam that you've got to blow off. You pay that price for coping successfully.

I've blown my safety valve right in customs and got charged entrance fees others didn't have to pay. I've seen others air ship expensive parts from home with all the attendant hassles of telephoning, wiring funds, misdirections and delays, when they could have cut through the static of their learned responses and bought an equivalent (sometimes even superior) part locally in two days for less money.

In other words, you can buy off culture shock with money or effort, and mute it with anger: take it in the purse or in the gut. You decide how you pay the price, but pay it you shall. Unfortunately, some people get others to pay it for them.

For example, the Albert Schweitzer in you might want to enfold the entire disadvantaged population of the Third World in his compassionate embrace. You settle for inviting a couple of homeless street urchins aboard for peanut butter and jelly sandwiches. Your finer instincts may get stroked by your behavior, but watch the kids don't walk in uninvited with their friends later on. Your behavior may appear bizarre to them, remember, and they might expect you're going to adopt them and take them off to New York to pick gold up off the streets. Why otherwise would you usher them aboard a thing as foreign to them as a spaceship to your kids? Obviously you shall take them to Mars, if not New York, right?

Many years ago, I witnessed an incident that illustrates the point.

Spaceship Yacht

Two American couples moored next to me in their motor yacht. They brought some kids aboard their boat with tragic results for the children. They gave the kids a tour of the yacht, an old classic motorboat once belonging to a famous man. They then fed them peanut butter and jelly sandwiches on deck. A few days later the couples discovered the kids had come back aboard, and some costume jewelry had gone missing.

Seeing themselves as having participated directly, and with great humanity, in the work of Save The Children by their charitable invitation to peanut butter and jelly, the cruisers, justifiably outraged that the children had come back to steal, complained to the police. The officials took a serious view of offenses against tourists in their fragile tourism sector. The state security police, the dreaded *Ton Ton Macoute*, took direct charge of the situation. As a result of their investigation one child got crippled and two badly and bloodily beaten. They sent one child home with a compound fracture, to find his loot. When the police asked if she'd got all her plastic bracelets returned, one of the women from the yacht, panicked by the sight of a child holding the flesh over his bone, cried, "No, but they don't matter, just, for God's sake, please stop beating them!" The beatings, of course, went on, since she said the property hadn't got recovered fully.

The child probably didn't want to give up his bit of brightly colored plastic, a link to the goddess-mother from the spaceship. She who had him experience motherly warmth, perhaps for the first time in his life, along with peanut butter and jelly. She who seemed to promise to carry him off to another and better star.

So they broke his arm. He and the other children paid the price of the yachties' inappropriate responses. The yachties, blaming it all on the police, rushed to their boat and vroomed out of the harbor for home. I got one of the dock lines they left behind.

The Remedy

Culture Shock accounts for the flocking syndrome of expatriates in any country. Latin Americans in America, for instance, or Americans in Latin America. While living in Paris I always noticed Americans klatsching with other Americans to whom they wouldn't speak while on their native soil. Matrons from Old Greenwich would eagerly trade recipes with the wives of North Sea oil roustabouts from Louisiana. They clutched together for the sole purpose of hearing their native tongues badmouth the Parisians.

Grumbling about the environment producing your stress seems normal and even necessary. Frenchmen do it in America, Germans do it in Spain and Englishmen do it everywhere. But watch where you do your grouching. You don't idle in the private salons of Paris while sitting in a cheap restaurant. You sit on display. Bitching about the local environment while under the gaze of petty port officials, dock boys and small time secret police, doesn't rank as too suave. Doing it in a restaurant where the couple at the next table run the local grocery may get you higher prices on your veggies tomorrow.

Find your own general remedy to the stress of culture shock, and apply it at appropriate times and places. Whether yoga, expatriate kaffee klatches, or self flagellation, a personalized remedy should permit daily satisfaction of personal and boat oriented goals while increasing your enjoyment of the different scenes.

Some boaters crawl into a VCR-induced haze, not leaving their boats for days at a time. Others meet every evening for a happy hour where they massage each other's spirits with spirits. The SG&T, while a dandy motivation to lie at anchor early and safely, makes a poor remedy to the stress of culture shock. The ports of Asia and Latin America teem with besotted ex-pats who have taken this false remedy to their destructions.

Whether you go into frenzies of varnishing, practice meditation, write long letters to the kids or klatch on the SSB, your remedy should work off the stress of learning new responses. You will reduce the costs of making inappropriate responses in the future and increase your enjoyment of cruising life.

Changes in Attitude

The shift to living aboard in Micronesia or the Antilles from even the sleepiest rural town above 22° latitude may rival the move of a charged up urban yuppie ad man to a cave in the wilderness. The very basics of daily life shall change. And you won't, as you thought, relish it. Change makes for discomfort, and you've got billions of years of evolution behind you which will fight it. To paraphrase Shakespeare: which thousand natural shocks shall your flesh inherit?

Failure to wait patiently for a good weather window, in my experience, overwhelmingly contributes to unhappy cruises. Yet patience hardly hallmarks many cruisers. Most cruisers have strong independent streaks. Strong willed and self confident, most skippers tend to take charge easily. Those very traits lead some to seek the challenge and independence of life on the sea. These so-called Type A people come in both gender flavors.

I commiserate with Type A's for their jumpiness. I too still stuff time. I listen to the news while reading the paper while carrying on a conversation (poorly). Watch a Type A while waiting on weather, for an example. Getting all set to go, then having to sit at home day after day, unable to go out, unable to schedule anything — and boy! do Type A's like to schedule — just waiting on a bus that never comes, it seems. All enough to try a saint. When a window does open, most Type A's jump at it immediately. They take the first hours of a three day window, the swells still up, the winds not yet laid down. Then they sit in the next anchorage for the best part of the window. I don't wish to play psychologist, but a bit of my own experience might help.

In my first few tough trips on the thorny path, I recognized behavior in myself and others which I had seen many years ago as a full time air traveler. The first-in first-out queues of taxis, ticketing, and baggage checking drove me bananas. Waiting in line infuriates me. Shuffling along with the herd of travelers like cattle does likewise. It wasn't long before I learned to act contrary to the flow. I became the last on the plane, strolling through an empty waiting room. I sat in the plane doing some work when it came time to deplane, while most people crammed the aisles for 20 minutes. Then they rode busses crammed to overflowing, then they waited at the empty baggage carousel for 20 minutes more, while I lolled around in a half filled bus and strolled up to the carousel just in time to lift off my bag. I had a hundred other tricks to air travel then, and I'm sure you know lots more and different ones today, but does that translate to cruising on a small boat? You bet it does: Type A's can always find a useful way to pass time without waiting.

Sir Francis Bacon, father of the Age of Reason, patriarch of all modern science and mathematics, said, "Nature, to be commanded, must be obeyed." You can make Nature serve you only by knowing Nature's elements and arranging them and your purpose in accordance. To the cruiser with an education in the hard sciences, this does not come as news. To everyone else, it may come as a revelation. I have good news to these unfortunates: there exists a way out short of an epiphany in monstrous seas.

You don't have to deny your Type A nature. Use it to outflank the forces frustrating it. Get busy! Study the weather. Become a weather maven. Get a computer fax. Gather data.

Sharpen your own deck level observations. The world holds nothing quite as fine for a Type A as control of a situation through knowledge, except perhaps the payoff of the smooth passage that results.

Think weather watching takes time? During my waits I spend a good 4 hours a day on the weather. How so much? I listen to whatever weather nets I can find, while doing some fixit project. I get the Offshore Reports, then satellite views, then the Tropical Weather Discussion. Morning, midday and evening I download the Tropical Prediction Center's weather charts. Add to those 4 hours a couple for meals, a couple of hours for swimming and diving, a couple reading and varnishing, and a nap — where did the day go? After decades at it I find my wait for weather full of accomplishment, while, as I grow older, the rounds of provisioning, potlucks and happy hours demand more patience.

LANGUAGE

Don't let the myth of language barriers undo the enjoyment of your cruise.

Most of us cruising the world see local people like two dimensional cardboard cutouts, unless, with luck, a local befriends us. Cruisers seldom read local newspapers. They seem uninterested in any subject outside their immediate yachtie environment. Local language, newspapers, politics and so on, lack reality and can't interest them. Yet even while in Dubrovnik I "read" the newspaper every day. And got something out of it.

In non-English speaking countries many cruisers excuse the lack of any but superficial interest with the old language barrier. Many stay aboard waiting for weather rather than discover what's going on ashore or traveling inland. Many pay too much for everything and later whine they got "cheated". These cruisers never fulfill a good piece of their cruising goals.

With most of my adult life spent outside English speaking countries I think I have a qualified viewpoint on the matter. Simply put, you erect your own language barriers. Take my experience. I have lived or worked in many countries where I did not speak the language. I have studied 7 languages, and I came to live in 4 countries where I used the language well enough to make a living. Yet I always got along best in the countries where I didn't know the language!

If you don't do the local language, people expect less of you and help you more. They have more patience with you, going out of their way to guide you. People express more interest in you. As a visitor not able to use the language at all, you have privilege. As a visitor trying to pick up a few words, you have sympathy, and honor as well. If you speak their language fairly well, you become more of an interloper in their society, not a visitor. Yes, humans practice prejudice everywhere. Parents show great interest when daughter brings the foreign exchange student home for dinner, but the excitement really gets big when she brings one home to marry!

If you seriously want to talk well in a foreign language, go ahead and make a serious try. Prepare for a mind wrenching, personality bending experience. Languages carry culture, and learning them requires personality change. Acquiring language often causes physical pain. It takes a long time and requires exhausting effort. Yet it never becomes 100% successful, despite what you've read in spy novels where the hero goes undetected while speaking rural dialects of Upper Volta. Science has long proved that language learning proceeds most imperfectly for adults. You shall achieve great satisfaction, but it

11

shall change forever your ability to become an interesting visitor everyone wants to help.

Get out and see the world while cruising. Don't erect your own language barriers. Wiggle your eyebrows, wave your arms, point to things and words and have fun.

But don't ever say to me, "It's easy for you. You speak the language." The little I speak came with great difficulty, even agony. And using it often creates more of the same.

Finally, a word of advice from a friend of mine, a Latino criminal trial lawyer: always speak your native tongue to policemen, leaving no room for equivocation there.

SELF RELIANCE

The Emersonian requirement for self reliance, that which you always held in righteous esteem, translates to a fundamental of your biological survival on your foreign cruises. How? A wad of sour dough starter and a tray of bean sprouts? They may make you feel good, but self reliance leading to survival? Maybe after the Bomb, but not in an area of the world awash with cheap grains, organically grown (yes) fruits and vegetables and cheap tailors. Self reliance simply means to *rely only on yourself.*

TRAVELING IN GROUPS

One of the nicest parts of cruising, you see the same people again and again. Cruising in company, you can share your SG&T time with others. I've often kept company with from 5 to 15 yachts. These trips weld friendships and make a normally delightful trip even more enjoyable.

STAYING TOGETHER

My favorite togetherness tale involves four crews who up anchored to move into the protection of a reefed bay with two entrances, the lee one wide and deep, the windward one shoaly and dog-legged. The boat in the lead came to his computer chart waypoint and swung left into the deep and wide entrance. "Yowie!" he hailed to the boats behind him. "There's a solid line of breakers across the entrance". The guidebook, mine, had a waypoint for this entrance, while the DMA small scale chart he used had a one third mile latitude error. Like ducks in a file they waddled four miles farther on to the tricky entrance. Upon passing the flat calm, wide and deep entrance, not one skipper looked left.

I always make clear to sailing companions that I paddle my own canoe, do my own navigation, select my own anchorages, and when I grab a weather window and go, I've made my own decision for my own boat. I encourage everyone else to do likewise. My boat, my little universe on a savage sea, and I function as a team completely different from any other vessel and crew. Barring an emergency at sea, I neither slow down to nor catch up with other boats, thus compromising the teamwork between me and my vessel, and perhaps forcing an unnatural rhythm to her functioning at sea. I suspect many problems on the path south precipitate from this phenomenon, and by the subconscious reliance on other boats. (Well, if I miss the weather, one of the other guys must have it.) You also have a unique boat and crew. Proper respect for the sea and your vessel come first, demonstrations of camaraderie, second. Sailing in company, get advance permission to dawdle or leap ports ahead. In other words, sail alone, even in company.

BUDDY CHANNELS

Many boats sailing in company stay tuned to buddy channels instead of VHF Channel 16. I have seen one yacht sunk and many others suffer narrow escapes while the "buddy boats" blithely sailed on in ignorance of repeated warnings on Channel 16. Chatting on low power on Channel 16 while on the open sea shall not bother ships in the area. On the contrary, you both shall gladly discover that you lie within two miles of each other and didn't know it. Using buddy channels while under way in or near harbors, with dangers like reefs and funneling traffic, rates the stupid prize. If you must use them ever, for Pete's sake use the VHF's dual watch or scan feature to monitor 16. More on this later.

FLEET OPERATIONS

Try one method of group cruising by emulating a loose confederation of sovereign states. With all consultations finished, each captain must make his or her own decision, sharing it with the others out of courtesy, but not for approval. Not to say, of course, that you can't change a decision upon hearing a wiser one made by someone else. Maintain contact by radio at sea if you can, or wait to meet up in port.

If you must stay together, then emulate the fascists whose emblem became the Roman faces, or bound bundle of spars. Appoint someone Navigator and someone else Admiral. Picture a fleet of neophyte cruisers at sea, all strung out like a gaggle of geese, asking each other on the VHF whether to reef or tack while assuring each other of their like-mindedness, regardless of each vessel's differences. I see them every year. Each boat thinks another boat leads the parade. The one in the lead doesn't know he leads. He thinks he made a wrong tack and left the group. Whinnie The Pooh, off to discover the north pole, organized better than most cruising groups I've heard on the VHF. Committee decisions, without a chairman to promulgate them, wind up not decided at all. Dangerous behavior in port, preparing for a storm. Purely deadly at sea.

A palm permanently bent by the trade winds.

MEET THE EXPERTS

Freedom seems the common denominator behind most people's choice of the cruising life. But freedom bears responsibilities not known in our modern socialist societies. Among the most cherished freedoms, those of carrying water, washing clothes by hand and trudging miles to the market in the dust and the heat, and all the neat stuff our ancestors got to do. The freedoms to act as your own blacksmith, carpenter, physician, plumber, weatherman and mechanic come as a shock to most new cruisers. Americans' ancestors had to do those things and more on their isolated homesteads. So can cruisers today. Rather than face up to some of the responsibilities concomitant with remote cruising, I prefer to jury rig until I get to a phone, and I can call for parts. Then I practice component replacement, until all goes right again. Even with help at hand, I anyway handle the problem myself. Usually anything you do yourself beats turning to the experts.

Like the mule hand in the old Wagons West shows, I stand aside and chuckle at the game as people get stung year after year. Let me introduce you to some experts I see repeatedly on the Wagons South show. See if you'd rather trust them than yourself.

THE WEATHERMAN

Pained by days of waiting for a weather window, I dinghied to the town dock to buy a newspaper and spend another day at the ready. I waited to go downwind as well! I had not before waited more than a few days to go downwind. Everybody who wanted to leave the harbor wore thin in patience. As I putt-putted through the anchorage I passed a fellow jubilantly hauling at his anchor rode. An airline pilot by trade, he looked one of those clear eyed, straight toothed solid men with the great airside manner and the calm, resonant voice. ("We've lost only two of our four engines folks, but, not to worry, they designed this aircraft to glide.") He read the weather to the more timid types on channel 16 every morning. They trusted him. He became their weatherman.

"Cleaning the rode, Jack?" I asked.

"Heck no! Great window! We're off!," he exhaled between pulls. He hadn't learned to let the catenary pull the boat, he still used the coronary.

"Window? I heard there was 25 knots of wind and a gale system crossing Cuba."

"No way! Northeast 15 behind the front! A reach the whole way." he puffed. The anchor came up with a bang on the chocks, and, callused by years of gratuitous advice forcefully cast back in my face, I wished Jack a safe and happy trip. I dinghied on to town.

Back aboard, I threw aside the newspaper and reread my full transcripts of the Offshore Reports. As I thought I knew, but which Jack had made me unsure of, we had three gale systems. One pulled the front that had gone through the day before, another pulled a front down on us that should arrive the next day. A third gale center out of Cuba headed northeast right over the Turks and Caicos to our north. I searched my reports for the words "northeast 15 knots behind the front". I found them. They referred to the front that had passed us two days ago and now lay hundreds of miles away.

Three boats pulled out with Jack. One blew ashore in the Raggeds. The Bahamas Defense Force pulled off the mate who flew home to mother in Toronto from Deadman's Cay. The skipper of that one dragged himself into Georgetown three weeks later severely dinged. I left two days later. I had 10 to 15 knots at the most, clear skies, full moon, and I anchored every night without going to shore. I had 12 days of the finest fishing and sailing days of my life. I had waited 11 days, and I got a window for the records.

I found Jack and his wrecked boat beached up islands, where he worked building a new rudder out of construction scraps. A gaggle of tourists and a few yachties surrounded him to hear his tales of the *Ultimate Wave*, and how cleverly his master seamanship and knowledge of the weather saw him safely through. He had a genuine old salt manner. You just had to admire him. When he finally reached Georgetown, he taught courses on celestial navigation to crowds of admirers on the beach.

Do you think you need Jack for your weatherman?

THE MECHANIC

Ace looked like a "cruiser down on his luck", as people say. He ran a marine electronics fixit shop from his boat, which looked way down on its luck. Ace did pot. His girlfriend did other things. They got by. I call these guys dirt baggers, but what do I know? Ace did fast work. In fact, he could get a rebuilt unit faster than Fed Ex could fly. He simply went to his warehouse, the fleet of boats he "boat sat", cleaning, and odd jobbing. He always found a replacement part somewhere among them. He eventually got caught and spent a few days in jail. The police told me his boat had $50,000 of stolen electronics tucked away.

Once a cruiser asked me if I could recommend Ace. "No," I said, "he's a thief."

Now, con men can convince and charm. If they couldn't, they wouldn't have the job. The cruiser liked Ace anyway. He went to Ace and told him what I said. Next day I had 20 gallons of water in my fuel tank. I found it while crossing the path of an incoming cruise ship. The motor quit with a clogged high pressure pump. The Judas cruiser got his, though. The cops took the GPS Ace had "fixed". Now he had none.

Do your own work. And don't expect me to recommend anyone but yourself.

THE SAILING MASTER

Many folks who think they know all about sailing may know nothing about the sea. In the old days of sailing they had a position of Sailing Master aboard ship. The captain looked to him to provide expert instruction to effect the maneuver he wanted to make.

For three years Dashing Dan darted all over the Caribbean. To the Med and back, in and out, up and down, damn the torpedoes, he played the star of the weather net every night. If it blew 40 knots and he had to sail more than 200 miles, Dan blew away.

I take the south coast of Puerto Rico a few miles a day in morning calms, rather than wait out a 20 to 25 knot forecast looking for longer windows. Anchored for the evening at Gilligan's Island one year, I heard Globetrotter Dan calling a cruising couple anchored a few harbors behind me. They had a small child aboard. While Dan glided down the west coast in the island's lee, he cajoled the other boat to join him on a night run to Ponce.

"You've got a well found boat," he hammered, "you're a sailor," he challenged, "I know this coast. It's not bad at all." Dan said he only had 11 knots of wind in a flat sea. Of course he sailed south down the big island's west coast and had not yet turned the corner to the east into full trade winds and seas. Thoroughly intimidated, the father agreed to come out and play. I thought of the little girl aboard. I called repeatedly on the VHF, but he couldn't hear me. I stayed tuned hoping to get his attention.

Within 5 hours Dan stood ankle deep in motor oil, feeling the bilge for a dropped bleed screw without which he couldn't start his engine. "Comes with the territory," he croaked on the VHF. The smaller boat's skipper left the air for 15 minutes, then came back on groaning. He'd got tossed across the saloon. Luckily, he only suffered a few contusions. Wife and child had packed themselves between mattresses on the stateroom deck. Both boats crept into harbor at 8 a.m. after a 12 hour run of only 9 miles. Earlier that morning I had eaten up my usual 10 miles in the normal dawn calm.

Dan disappeared from the Caribbean scene some time ago, but new Dan's arrive every season. Don't listen to Dan. As the song says, "he's a devil, not a man".

THE LOCAL

A magazine article appeared detailing the drubbing the yacht *Argonut* took. Early in the article the writer made clear that he had discarded my sailing directions in favor of local knowledge from a tired cruiser named "Sam" who had stayed at the same spot for 5 years.

I knew Sam well. A nice guy who, tired of cruising, took a local job and moored in that harbor for good, never to go farther. He had a simple theory. Forget the forecasts, just take your chances. Each time Sam had ventured out he went in forecast trades over 15 knots and against swells from distant gales. He never found a night lee along the coast in those conditions. In the daytime, he couldn't make headway against the winds accelerated by his own island. Every time he moved he got hammered. Over the years "Sam" had collected stories at the bar from passing cruisers. In other words, all Sam's local knowledge came from anecdotal evidence assembled from beginners passing through who made tragic errors. He passed on those errors as sage counsel.

While my advice to the crew of *Argonut* came from dozens and dozens of my own successfully safe and comfortable passages, they went with advice from Sam, the local, who must know. They got hammered. But they had an epic tale to tell in the article, they won many admirers for their manly deeds, and they passed on lots of Sam's bad advice. If you have an addiction to cruising and sailing magazines, beware such articles. They can poison your well of knowledge with misconceptions of newbies.

Some local cruisers remind me of the rednecks around the bait box on a fuel pier in Florida. "How deep is it at the dock?" I hailed. "Lossawada, lossawada!" they chorused. "Yes, but how many feet?" I persisted. "Big boats come in here allatime," they assured me. Probably Morgan OI41's, I thought. "I draw 6.5 feet!" I hollered. "LOSSAWADA!" they yelled, getting belligerent now that their expertise came into question. I spent the next 8 hours 14 feet from the fuel dock, hard aground. I got no fuel, but I got "lossa" dings from all the really big but shallow draft boats that came to fuel up beside me.

Consult local knowledge cautiously. The same goes for American delivery skippers who make their living smashing other people's property from point A to point B, oblivious to sea conditions.

The SG&T: lime over ice, then gin, then tonic. Stir with finger.

SECURITY
A state of mind in the trade winds belt

Tales of Caribbean rape and pillage have titillated youngsters since the 1600's when the marauding of L'Olenois, the Corsaire, and Morgan, the Privateer, first hit the bookstalls. Most long distance cruisers have adventurous and, to some extent, childish hearts. Their titillation runs wild upon occasion, and their stories of piracy and skullduggery lie on your course among many false dangers. Like cloud shadows on coral banks, if you spend your time trying to avoid them you risk running into a real hazard.

PERSONAL SECURITY

One encounters bad actors all over the world. Pirates, just bad guys potting at targets of opportunity upon the wastes of the sea, or in the alleys of the waterfronts. These really do exist. However, the Sulu and the Red Sea, lie outside the trade belts, where your chances of running into a pirate runs even less than your chances of stumbling into one in Florida. Ask any European and you'll discover that most of the civilized world knows America as among the most violent nations on the planet. Unfortunately statistics substantiate that opinion. Islands in the trades expose you to personal assault, on your boat or ashore, less than almost any yachting center in the United States. Having said that, I yet have some caveats which make for a more pleasant cruise.

AFLOAT
Avoid pickup crew. The tropics crawl with hitchhikers, especially in the yachting centers. Some simply do what they used to call *Le Grand Tour* between college and the start of a career. Others simply want to do you. If, after thorough investigation, you do take someone aboard, hold the person's passport and enough of his or her money to fly them back to their native country from your boat's destination. An even better filter of their real intentions: do as some Europeans do and charge the crew for their room and board and the trip. Let the leeches pay or go get their own boat. Cruisers have met unbelievable folly with pickup crew.

AN EXAMPLE
In the Canaries a young couple approached us for a ride across the Atlantic. They had spent a European summer, and the time had come to return home. This handsome, adventuresome young pair, blonde, blue-eyed, straight white teeth, obviously raised as the scions of wealthy suburbanites, spoke well and appeared educated. But to ask us, they had hopped uninvited onto our boat and trod aft with their hiking shoes to where we sat with our SG&Ts at sundown. Asymmetric behavior. They didn't have a clue to boat etiquette. We politely told them we couldn't accommodate them.

In Antigua a month later, an elderly English gentleman of our acquaintance, who normally sailed single handed, told us this harrowing tale. He had said yes to the kids' request to crew for him across the Atlantic. He welcomed them onboard, since he could use both the company and the extra watch keepers.

Two days out they locked him out on deck while they did drugs down below. For three

17

weeks this good soul blistered in sun and wind while the brats below taunted him and fed him like a dog, but only when he did tricks for them, and when they had left their drugged haze long enough to entertain themselves with him. He reported the abuse to the Antiguan authorities when they landed. The malefactors had cleaned up their act as soon as land came in sight. The authorities said their "hands were tied". Don't they always? They had no jurisdiction over what happened at sea on a foreign flag vessel, they said. And by the way, our friend had to buy their tickets to the U.S. and board them at a hotel until the plane left. He could find only first class tickets to buy.

Visitors

Don't let anyone board your boat at any time for any reason unless they present indisputable documentation of their right to do so. Even if they have uniforms, or if they have ID, but no uniform for a position usually requiring one. This holds especially true for official boarding parties: do not allow more persons aboard at one time than the number of the boat's crew, and a crew member should accompany each while aboard.

Avoid casual tours of your boat. What a thrill for that nice school girl to see a yacht. But she goes to school with not so nice school boys. A yacht makes a remote concept for them. It seems as unassailable as the homes of the local rich. Innocent talk at school, God forbid they should hold a full blown *Show and Tell*, may make your snug little home all too familiar and nakedly assailable.

Beware of *asymmetrical* cruisers: hustlers cruising without apparent resources and with hollow stories that don't fit neatly with accent, age, physiognomy, the appearances of themselves or their boats.

The Guy Everybody Likes

Yachties took turns inviting to dinner a good looking young fellow who had run out of funds. "And just imagine!" they gushed at me, "He's off around the world with no charts, no navigation aids and hardly a dime. What spirit! A real nice guy." He looked like a leech to me. After he'd sailed off for the wide world, a rash of burglaries occurred while everyone attended a potluck dinner. They blamed it on the locals. One yacht claimed a $10,000 loss and quit cruising. Mr. nice guy turned up in Central America fully equipped, saying he'd got the stuff cheap in Manzanillo. *Manzanillo*? I met rafts of cruisers down islands who still thought of him as a great guy, and they sincerely delighted in his finding the right equipment to go round the world. Remember, all con artists appear trustworthy, or they wouldn't have the job.

Ashore

It hasn't always looked grim. Times change. In the early 1980's in Puerto Plata and Belize City, a naked sixteen year old virgin with fistfuls of dollars would attract only admiration. And you should have seen the alleys of Belize City at night in 1981. Times have changed here and there. Skullduggery rises with tourism booms and falls with police busts. Until you know for sure, act as prudently as you would at home. No more nor less.

Dress

City waterfronts everywhere lie close to rundown sections with poorer, sometimes desperate, inhabitants. Even though your buddies assured you that "the locals were warm and friendly" there, don't walk alone down unlit streets with flamboyant tourist garb, a bulging hip pocket and half a bag on from some happy hour. In Cumaná, Venezuela, or Port of Spain, Trinidad, you may turn to dead meat. And I consider Cumaná my favorite port in Venezuela. Leave behind bracelets and necklaces. You may know you only wear costume jewelry, but does a 12 year old gutter snipe with a razor?

Travel light when out and about. Dress plainly and inexpensively, and not like a yachtie. Use flapped pockets, and sew in body pouches under clothing.

FANNY PACKS

If you have to carry a lot of cash, don't flash a roll. Keep it in separate pockets, and pay beers, meals, transport, and so forth, out of a "petty cash pocket". Don't use purses, backpacks, "fanny packs" and "belly bags" where they might get ripped off with a straight razor. I know of one man who lost a kidney in Caracas when two kids dodged through the crowd, one slashing the strap to his belly bag, the other catching it as it fell. The slasher went deeper than he needed to. These packs may get snatched elsewhere, like from under your table while you eat. Instead of a wallet or purse, carry a "data sheet", a sheet of paper with every number you ever needed, credit cards, telephones, citizenship, clearances, passports, whatever. Then wrap your folding walking around money over your credit card and slip it into a flapped pocket.

PASSPORTS

A stolen passport can make a royal mess. Don't carry yours. On the other hand I've known respectable senior citizens who have spent a night in the pokey because they couldn't show a passport to the police. Instead you can carry a photocopy of your passport and visa stamp on the flip side of your data sheet.

BOAT SECURITY

You can count as few anchorages in the islands of the trades where you feel you must lock up your boat as you can count towns in America where one can leave one's doors open. Also, most places that a local breaks through your locks he'll cause more loss through damage to joinery than he shall through the trinkets he likely walks off with.

Only boaties take boaty things. Remember this when you anchor next to the dirt bag boat full of hippies in a lonely cove. Such "cruisers" do exist in the tropics. Avoid these boats and their crews. If they need a snatch block they'll snatch yours. Unfortunately for world unity, some nations more than others tend to spawn boats like these.

In countries with acute economic stress petty theft by locals can occur. How and where you moor the boat shall give you more insurance than any company can offer. During extended absences, put up in a guarded marina. Otherwise, securely anchor the boat in a weather safe anchorage, far enough from young swimmers from the shore, but in amongst other yachts whose owners you know and trust. Leave them instructions for access to the boat, for charging the battery, feeding the parakeet or what-all else.

ALARM SYSTEMS

You can install a foolproof alarm system for your boat much easier than you think. You only need some sensors, usually small 12 V switches that a thief can trip. For a passive system, one that uses no current until tripped, you can buy the push switches used for car doors quite cheaply at some automotive stores. Place these 'normally closed' switches where closed hatches, washboards or doors keep them compressed in the 'open' position, yet where you can open the hatches enough to let air in but not a thief. When the hatch opens enough to relieve pressure on the spring loaded switch, it releases to its 'normally closed' position and closes the circuit, activating an alarm.

Otherwise, a variety of 'normally open' magnetic switches work well. If the tiny switch has its magnet mate nearby, it closes. When the mate moves away, it opens, the active circuit drops, and the control unit recognizes a trespass. You can use esthetically prefer- able ¼ inch cylindrical magnetic switches. You simply drill out holes into which you glue the switch and its mate, and they disappear. These make active circuits, and they use tiny wires that you may easily hide but which carry insignificant current.

Alternator winding, a super fine varnished wire available in most alternator shops for pennies a hundred feet, makes a fine passive circuit trip wire. Wire it to the ground side of a piezo alarm, or to a relay controlling a siren or lights. String it such that the free end will dunk into the sea if disturbed, thus completing the circuit to ground.

SENSORS	SWITCHES	Control Box	SWITCHES	ALARMS
Hatches & Doors series wired switches (n.o. active n.c. passive)	none	automotive alarm control directly connected to battery with several inputs and outputs, time delay function and digital key	secret inhibit switch below decks	external siren out of reach
				area flood light on mast
Dinghy & Motor n.c. passive	secret inhibit switch below decks			spreader lights with flasher
On Deck infrared motion (active) trip wires (passive)			none	piezo alarm buzzer below decks

Read table left to right with the flow of control from sensor to alarm.

One boater I know has a neat switch over his bunk. When he throws it, a brilliant flood light mounted high forward in the saloon blinds anyone in the cockpit, the companion way, or messing about inside. Like a stun grenade: effective, yet simple.

If you have a system installed, do not show it off, do not discuss it in public places nor discuss it with fellow cruisers likely to talk about it at the bar.

GETTING HELP WHEN YOU NEED IT

Solid statistical evidence shows that cruisers who counter a threat with noise and light almost always drive the threat away. You can:
- Blow a horn, whistle or burglar alarm as long as possible, and fire flares.
- Scream and keep screaming while waving your arms or, say, a towel.
- Get on channel 16 and holler bloody murder.

Cruisers in an anchorage or marina should respond by illuminating the distress scene and by getting to the person in distress immediately. Keep a light on any bad guys and make noise — beat on pots and pans if you have to.

In the case of theft and boardings, making noise up the bureaucracy also works: coast guard, police, newspapers, tourism and business groups. Scream and keep screaming. Make them do their jobs. Wringing your hands — "It's not my country, what can anyone do?" — guarantees more attacks. Nothing impresses officials more than a passel of arm waving, angry yachties milling about their office, shouting in foreign tongues. Wakes 'em right up.

> **In an anchorage without much VHF traffic, leave your VHF on at night. Your neighbor may frantically call warnings you need to hear.**

> **Have inside deadlock bolts below, and lock yourself in when you feel you need to.**

DINGHY SECURITY

If you haven't learned dinghy security in your home waters, these tips shall help you in the trades. Locals won't steal a yacht dinghy or motor where it would stand out like a dugout canoe in a Connecticut yacht club. Theft occurs where the thief has a ready market, or the thief can stuff it aboard his own boat and take off. Also, ports near to a wealthier border require special care. Many will see your dinghy or motor as a sure ride to paradise. As you would take extraordinary precautions with your car in Tijuana, raise your dinghy and stow your motor in these ports.

TROUBLE AVOIDANCE

If you have big motorized davits, use them to haul up your dinghy and motor every night. Another method: arrange a three point bridle with its lifting ring centered to keep the raised dinghy and motor level as you haul the rig up to the rail with your halyard. Make the bridle out of stainless cable, or it may readily get chopped with a machete.

Plaster your dinghy and motor with reflective tape so you can find it when it drifts away at night. It also becomes a less attractive target for thieves. An inflatable becomes less attractive to thieves (other boaters) when you plaster it with multicol-ored patches and caulk. A flawless Avon RIB that looked

like it had gone through the battle of Trafalgar became the best dinghy trade I ever made. I never had to lock that one up.

> **Beware: a yacht name on the dink may advertise your absence from the yacht.**

Finally, at crowded dinghy docks, leave your dink anchored well off with thirty or so feet of painter run to the dock. Neophyte cruisers often snug their painters to the dock and tip their motors up. As the tide changes their props become bucking and slashing scythes which will cut your bow section to ribbons. I usually approach a dinghy dock with a stern anchor out, actually an undeployed grapnel. A rock can do as well. I land perpendicularly to the dock, with my anchor already deployed, a distance down from where I want the painter tied. The dinghy then lays off nearly that same distance, well free of the crowd. You can retrieve it at any point by dragging, since the anchor, or rock, doesn't grab hard.

Locks

First, use chain, minimum length twelve feet. Padlock or permanently secure the chain to a permanent steel fitting attached to a hard surface of the dink (transom, for instance), not the towing eye of an inflatable dinghy — thieves will simply cut them off. I know of one case in which the thieves took the dinghy and later cut off the transom to get the motor. Even if you lock your motor securely onto the transom, run the chain through the motor handle as well. Finally, lock the chain to your boat, or ashore, to some permanent fixture with an eye to tide and current. You may want to put an anchor out to keep from sawing against a pier or going under one at low tide. You don't want to come back to a crushed motor after the tide rises.

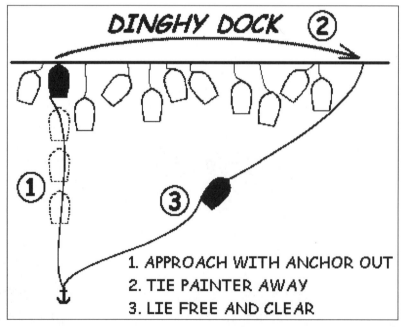

DINGHY DOCK ②

1. APPROACH WITH ANCHOR OUT
2. TIE PAINTER AWAY
3. LIE FREE AND CLEAR

Combination padlocks work better than key locks, simply because you can't lose the key. The ones with the brass hasp and brass bodies work better than steel ones because of corrosion. Don't worry that a thief can cut a brass hasp easier than a steel one. With either one he has to lug a significant tool to the site and spend some time and make some noise fiddling with it. If your fully brass padlock does seize up with salt, you simply boil it in fresh water a few minutes and follow-up with oil.

Lock your dinghy to the boat, coiling excess chain in an overturned bunch on deck, so it doesn't go overboard unless pulled upon. The thunk, thunk, thunk of the links going over the rail makes an alarm system and enables you to catch the varmint in the act and while still in the water. Depending on the sternness of your response, you won't have trouble at that anchorage for the rest of your stay.

> **Thieves can silently cut security chain which you let dip underwater.**

RESPONSE

Make noise and light. Avoid personal confrontation with a thief at all costs.

Cornered rats have an amazing strength and will do you in for sure. Nonetheless, a well produced *sonn et lumiere* show shall chase away a thief as well as a rat.

I've found flare guns neatly scare everyone in the anchorage as well as the varmint, and they certainly light up the scene of the crime well and call the attention of any law enforcement around pretending not to notice. Flares also continue to burn in the water, catching the crook in a ring of light. Don't actually hit the rascal with a flare. When he sees that it really bounces off him, he'll next see that you live to regret it.

You can separately wire your stern light so that it illuminates your dinghy as it trails behind the boat at your anchorage. A dinghy thief shall prey on somebody else's that night. You can also leave a cockpit anchor light on. I have a cutlass and a flare pistol handy. Once I squeezed intersecting streams of muriatic acid and ammonia from their squirt bottles. The effect of the corrosive gas devastated the machete wielding bandit in the water. A friend prefers a "wrist rocket" sling shot with ball bearings. One fellow I know brought back a blowgun from South America with some pretty serious darts. I've thrown rocks from the cat toilet which double the insult.

Paragua, for playing dominos

23

INSURANCE

Insurance helped me when I rammed an uncharted subsurface rock in the Skagerack. It came through when hurricane Elena took off my bowsprit and taffrail. Then, after many years of self-insured bliss, I went with the Seven Seas Cruising Association's recommended agency. Despite A.M. Best and the SSCA ratings, platoons of government inspectors and $1100 of my financial support, the underwriter went belly up 3 months after I signed up. That accounted for 11% of my net income that year. I went self-insured again.

Like the stock market, invest in insurance only what you can afford to lose. With all the boats around, and all the scams the insurers let by, rates have gone through the ceiling.

The companies increase profitability by policy restrictions only a New York actuary could come up with. Some refuse coverage between latitudes 12° and 22 ° during hurricane season. Others demand you get below 16° before the start of the hurricane season. I asked several to refund the 6 months not covered, or to stop their policy clock from ticking between June and November, if I stayed in the forbidden zone. Each company I queried said, "No." Doesn't sound legally defensible for a regulated industry, but one can't challenge big government's big businesses.

I do, however, challenge the wisdom of chasing Mom and Pop through the islands and across the sea to places with little storm protection and crowded harbors. Feeling pressed to get there, many cruisers bust their gear and propulsion systems, if not themselves. One fellow made it 30 miles into the *safe zone* only to die of a heart attack the next day. His *risk* amounted to a doubling of his deductible if he got totaled by a named storm. I estimate he had a risk of 0.00012 probability of losing $3000. All because he let an accountant in a Manhattan tower do his navigation for him.

FIREARMS

Firearms aboard can offer a major hassle while clearing in and out. Not all nations have the constitutional guarantees for citizens to bear arms. Some get downright paranoid about it and assume evil intentions of anyone who has one.

All countries can hold onto your arms and other bonded stores while you use their port. They may decline to check your arms depending on their own criteria such as the length of your stay, the length of your hair, security of your bonded locker and so on. The U.S., where military assault rifles get hawked on every street corner, doesn't bother.

You should ensure the accuracy of your clearance-in papers with respect to serial numbers and ammunition counts. They may check on your way out. If you miscounted on the way in, you shall have a major bureaucratic nightmare. Bullet counts can get off by one, and corroded serial numbers get misread easily. Get it right on the way in.

If you sit long at a dock where gun-checking goes on, you shall see how some yachts carry enough arms to look like mercenaries out to overthrow the local government. Some places boats have their fancier weapons turn up missing when they go to clear out. The best insurance against such official piracy? Don't carry firearms. And if you do, check in at ports of entries which cater mostly to yachts.

If you have firearms, train in their use and know when to use them. Never brandish a firearm. If you take one in hand, kill with it immediately. Pretty serious stuff. The problem lies in threat assessment. You need sober, non prejudicial judgment. But you rarely have it in a strange, poverty stricken land, where people speak a different language with excited jabbers and seemingly ominous overtones. Hardly possible in a dirty town where they all stare at you, point and whisper. It makes you paranoid. It turns more difficult when you get roused out of a sound SG&T induced slumber after a long, hard, adrenaline drenched beat to weather by someone who looks like a Huk guerrilla. Impulsive resort to a firearm invites tragedy. Probably yours.

Look what nearly happened to me years ago.

INTRUDERS

On two occasions nighttime intruders have roused me from my bunk while I lay in a remote anchorage. The first time it happened I had not slept in two days.

When I finally made harbor, I doused the adrenaline level with a couple of SG&Ts, then dropped like an anchor into my bunk. At four in the morning an unshaven, red-eyed, dirty and, except for old and holed jockey shorts, naked man shook me semiconscious. The hand not rousing me held an AR15 automatic.

In my befuddlement, I suspected that only a Huk guerrilla, a dope smuggler or an official of a banana republic, even naked, had a weapon like that. Smugglers can afford clothes. I hadn't heard about any revolution. The Philippines had all the Huks.

Fortunately for me, I sleepily guessed that he had a permit for the gun and that he represented some authority who had bought it for him, he not appearing to have the resources to buy one for himself. I mumbled, "Buenos dias". And so my day began.

The intruder identified himself as the local part-time representative of the Navy who had the responsibility to inquire at the boat which had surreptitiously slid into the bay that night. Out fishing all night with buddies in his little log canoe, he returned to port with the dawn. Finding my boat, they had knocked on the hull to no avail. A serious man, he went the next step and stepped aboard. Still no sign from me, he stepped inside.

Good thing I didn't grab my gun, a hand-sized automatic on the shelf over my pillow. Had I done so we would both have drowned from water pouring through the holes he could make in my hull with his machine gun.

Instead, we had an amiable beer together the next day and he warned me again not to go sneaking up on his beach like a Cuban fifth columnist. He suggested that if I really wanted a special reception, I might try night anchoring unannounced in Cuba under Fidel. Then I might spend the rest of my days in one of the *galeras* at *La Cabaña*.

The second incident took place in a moonless remote anchorage at 2 a.m. with a charter guest aboard. A skiff with four men came by looking for a drug drop. They discussed in hoarse whispers if we had their shipment. They decided we didn't, and they rowed off in the dark. By their belligerent talk and hostile carelessness we supposed they had more than alcohol in them. My guest, a Viet Nam vet, took my recently acquired Ruger Mini 14, and I took my little .22 automatic. We lay flat behind coach roof and taffrail bulwarks. They came back. They argued again. We could see several hands holding onto our rail. These gesticulated angrily from time to time. We had earlier decided that if they boarded us they might kill us to cover their mistake. We intended to shoot first. Luckily they again decided not to board us. Still muttering angrily, they rowed on home. And I sobbed in relief.

I since sold the Mini 14. Doubtfully. More about guns aboard later.

OFFICIALDOM
Verdigris grows on coppers as well as brass.

TIPS ON CLEARING CUSTOMS EASILY

I am convinced the customs and immigration officials of the world meet every February in Den Hague to attend seminars in changing procedures rapidly. They change every ten boats that enter. If someone tells you, "Here's how you clear customs in Gerfunknik, better do the opposite.

Nonetheless, I can tell you something from experience which can ease the pain.

Your experience with clearance officials generally depends on you. Have your boat and yourselves presentable. Have your papers in order: ships papers, passports and clearance out from your last port. Crew lists help in non English speaking countries, or if you use agents.

Smile, answer honestly, friendlily and courteously. Don't ever ask questions. Look bored. Never bribe. It may get you into trouble, and once started, it never stops.

The customs guys all over the world get trained to use their sixth senses. If the trip tired you, and the hassle of mooring got you all harried, you may give odd responses to them. Anchor around the corner with your yellow Q flag flying, and get a good night's sleep before entering.

> **Always try to clear at ports which specialize in yachts. Never allow more officials aboard than you have crew members to follow and watch them.**

In places where they don't have many yachts you must realize that you intrude on their management of a port, and you give these low paid working men a pain in the neck. If you think a poor country direly needs your big time cruising kitty bucks, and they should receive you like a major relief to the national debt, then think again. Real tourist economies bring in billions from vacationing factory workers, not a few penurious cruisers. Small ports often have only one man each from the Customs, Port Authority and Immigration Services. You may have to wait for them to get themselves together. Some places you may have to go in search of one or the other of them, if not all.

POLICE AND MILITARY

You may have heard tales of abuse by officials. I have a few which involve me and my friends. Remember that while honorable troops deploy world round to defend civilization in the terrorist wars, the people in these tales still creep around in their shadows.

Once a not so funny thing happened to me on the way to promote Puerto Rican tourism. State sponsored terrorists attacked my boat. They drive Cigarette looking vroom-vroom boats and wear Darth Vader suits while they do wheelies around your boat at some quiet anchorage. Just to check you out, understand. Just normal patrol.

This time they checked me out, all right. Drug sniffing dogs and all. Though close to mental collapse, my cat survived the canine search. The boat, on the other hand, got eradicable scars from the attack: a spawled hull, cracked bulwarks, split teak doors and carpet that won't walk down over floorboards incorrigibly disarrayed.

WHAT HAPPENED?

I finally took a fall in the triangle trade wars, the oil-guns-drugs reincarnation of the old evil of slaves-sugar-rum. Just as then, only bystanders and consumers get hurt in this war, while both traders and governments prosper. I had successfully ducked the drug wars crossfire for 21 years. But now the U.S. had unleashed a new contender in the fight: the *Puerto Rican Marine Police.*

Equipped to the teeth and blundering about the field like Barney Fife in search of noncombatants to terrify, they often call themselves FURA, for Forces United for Rapid Action. *Hey, kid, wanna see my gun?*

The United States had given Puerto Rico full jurisdiction over all its waters. And doubled its offshore enforcement limits. Puerto Rico Marine Police can board any flagged vessel to make any search they wish within 6 miles of their coast and without presence of U.S. officials who, if around at all, shall stand off. This has baleful meaning to yachts of all nations transiting the area.

It seems I had sailed through a field of floating cocaine the night I arrived to Puerto Rico. The newspaper accounts that I read days later said the smuggling operation left a cocaine slick spread for 45 miles, a dubious number. But like most articles on Puerto Rican drug busts, the last sentence read, "No arrests were made". Makes you wonder.

I had sailed for Puerto Rico from the Dominican Republic, the purpose of the trip to research the next edition of my *Cruising and Water Sports Guide to the Spanish Virgin Islands.* With my yellow quarantine flag flying, I set course for the first rest stop enroute, intending to clear into Puerto Rico the next morning at Ponce on the south coast. Work aside, I looked forward to spending Christmas with my many old friends there on the south coast.

Severe gales far to the north brought in an 8 foot swell, long enough for comfort between the islands, but sure to get short and troublesome once I'd rounded the southwest corner of Puerto Rico. I planned a badly needed rest stop at Mona Island before approaching the coast.

The usually snug anchorage at the wildlife refuge on Mona Island looked extremely uncomfortable with seas breaking over the reef and a bad chop inside. Not one boat lay inside, not one person strolled the beaches. I later learned they began watching me here as I backed and filled in front of the reef, deciding whether to enter. *What's he up to?*

27

I decided against chancing the surf and, despite my fatigue, carried on to a night landfall at the little cove under Cabo Rojo, on the mainland, where I could get some sleep. On the way around Mona Island I also jilled about for a good while talking on the VHF with the big school schooner Harvey Gamage which rolled heavily in the ship's anchorage on the island's south side. All this nosing around the island must have looked interesting to the watchers. *Hey! We got ourselves a suspect.* Or a fall guy.

Eight hours later, when I groggily poked into the Cabo Rojo anchorage on the mainland of Puerto Rico, it must have gotten really interesting for them. I had to screw around for nearly an hour in the dark getting the boat bedded down out of the swell.

What's he doing now? Not seamen themselves, marine police can never figure why you maneuver as you do, but as policemen they shall always attribute it to something wicked.

I upped anchor in predawn blackness in order to avoid punching into the trade winds which always come back to the coast with the rising of the sun. Suspicion must have hardened into incrimination when I did that. *Aha! Now he's sneaking away.*

Two miles offshore of the Puerto Rico south coast, and still an hour out of Ponce, the Cigarette boat began to shadow me. A cruiser anchored inshore told me on the VHF that her husband had had a stroke. She needed local information for the emergency, and I remained busy on the VHF passing it to her. I hadn't noticed the patrol dogging me in my blind spot. Suddenly, seeming out of nowhere, the Jedi warriors swooped abeam and, coming off plane, snowplowed a 4 foot wake over the existing 5 foot swell.

The wave knocked the autopilot into alarm mode and the cat off her chair. The vroomer's crew shouted in Spanish for my identification. I gave them my name and document numbers. I told them I sailed alone, but for my cat, who had climbed back to her perch, insulted. I told them I came from Hispaniola, bound for Ponce to clear in, and I pointed to my yellow flag which declared the same. They didn't know anything about quarantine flags they said. Did I have a disease?

I gave them the name of an old friend in U.S. Customs drug enforcement in Ponce with whom they could check me out. Darth Vader put the pedal to the metal, and they disappeared while the cat again bounced off her chair, and all the stuff on the chart table fell to the deck in a heap, something the higher swells in the Mona Passage could not accomplish.

I went back to the VHF where my caller began to fade behind the Lajas hills.

"Use the SSB radio," I called to her. Then, in order to insure she heard me, I repeated several times, "SSB 6215!" Then I disappeared below to crank up the short wave radio. At this point the stalkers surely thought they saw me change radios in order to make secret contact with my confederates. They had their case, or their fall guy. With their kind of police rules, no action you take can look innocent. They put about and caromed off the swell in hot pursuit.

I came topside just as the larger boat drew down on my starboard quarter. Two flak jacketed men, unsteady in the swell, put out lines and fenders to tie off alongside for a boarding. They threw their arms about in bossy gestures that basically meant "You're toast!" They spoke no English. They could not or would not understand my Spanish. They refused to talk with me by VHF. *Junior G-men maintaining radio silence.*

The high, short swell made lashing two vessels at the beam sure to cause damage or injury. I requested in English, Spanish and Body Language that we instead maintain controlled parallel way to the seas and they step aboard. I also offered to follow them to port, or they could follow me to Ponce. No response. On they came, swinging lassos.

I called on the VHF to the U.S. Coast Guard in San Juan. I asked the operator to do a land line relay for me to the marine police communicators, wherever they might bide, to make clear my request that they kiss gunnels to step aboard and not try to lash up in the swell. The Coast Guard replied with a non sequitur formula message that the police had a right to board me.

"Not the issue!" I said. "I fear broken boats and broken bones." I reminded the coasties of their obligation to protect American vessels and seamen from harm, and that I merely requested a phone call from them, something they could do enroute to the coffee machine. I guess he didn't have a dime, because he repeated his little abdication of responsibility speech in a steely cold voice.

Clearly, their bureaucracy wanted to stay clear of the Puerto Ricans' bureaucracy, and damn the citizen.

THE BOARDING

I suppose the PR marine police didn't use the VHF because they didn't want U.S. agencies spoiling their fun. Or maybe all that cocaine belonged to them. Maybe they thought I had spied on them for one of the honest drug enforcement agencies, if any exist anymore. I began to think of horrible scenarios where they would hand me and my boat over to cartel enforcers. I never did find out why they wouldn't talk to me on the radio.

The drug busters now broke radio silence explosively. They chattered with a police helicopter which made sudden swoops on us like a blue jay harassing a cat. In Spanish even casual VHF traffic can sound panicky what with all the long call and acknowledge sequences they repeat with such gusto. Sort of like Sky King has had a heart attack and the tower has to talk down Jimmy and Penny at the stick.

In any case, all their jabber on the radio alerted the Federals in Ponce. Soon a U.S. Federal chase boat came out and tooled alongside. Unlike the marine police boat's grand entrance, I hardly felt these guys' arrival. They motored peacefully alongside in the swell while their leader, a Miami Cuban-American, respectfully asked me for my cut on the situation. I told him I just didn't want a lash-up in high swell. "No problem," he said, and he and his second stepped lightly aboard as their pilot briefly eased over beam to beam. This drew resentful looks from the marine police who looked murder at me.

"How many persons aboard?" the federal agent asked.

"Just me and my cat."

"Any weapons aboard?" I indicated the location of the little .22 automatic which I have had for 35 years. That tiny pistol actually had helped me to end a pirate threat off Casablanca during one of the region's civil wars. The federal officer made clear that I had a constitutional right to have it aboard, but that they needed to secure it for their own safety. Then followed a normal and uneventful boarding by the Federals, full of courtesy and respect, even good cheer, while they quite professionally guarded themselves. Their competency relative to the marine police — both in boat handling and police work — greatly relieved me. The cat, the boat and myself felt safe in their hands.

The Cigarette boat still vroomed around us like my boat had come into heat. They called for a full search with dogs, and they insisted I proceed to the refinery port of Guayanilla. There they tied me against a rusty half sunken tug boat. My dinky yachtie fenders couldn't prevent us from sawing against the rotting steel wreck. The Feds left and the Puerto Rican Marine Police swarmed aboard.

The PR M arine Police

I couldn't keep track of all the different Puerto Rican police units involved. They had distinctive and colorful uniforms. The helicopter pilot had three shades of blue and lots of piping and trim. It reminded me of the nazi Hermann Goering's operatic flair for uniforms. They only lacked the foot high peaked caps of the Paraguayan military.

The guys in Ninja Turtle Lycra had Batman utility belts with 50 pounds of special gear dripping from them. You could tell they spent their weekends reading Soldier of Fortune magazine and ordering neat stuff with your money. The Feds dressed light.

I reviewed in my mind what I knew of the PRMP, what I might expect in their hands.

They had approached me once in a lonely anchorage with 5 heavily armed men dressed in black Lycra, like commandos. I had spent the afternoon scrubbing the bottom. They woke me from a well deserved sleep as they rafted onto my yacht. They demanded to "check my papers". Old WW2 movies flashed in my mind. The uniforms, their brusqueness and my sleepiness had me frightened and disoriented, but the men seemed to understand that and quickly played it a key lower. They acted with courtesy and respect, for which they had my thanks.

That same night the same boat returned with another crew. They played a brilliant spotlight on me for 20 minutes. They did not identify themselves. With no other boat around, I began to worry the druggies had come to snatch my boat and leave me, bound and gutted, to the crabs. This they indeed do. They finally turned off the light, and I could see the boat's police markings. They demanded again to "see my papers". I told them they already had got checked in the afternoon, but they said they worked "another shift" and didn't know that. I thought of some questions of my own, such as:

- Don't your police boats have logs?
- Isn't there normally a shift turnover performed in police work?
- Do you normally brace honest and honorable senior citizens twice in the same day?

One of them shouted at me in a Bronx accent, "You're not in America *now*! You're in *Puerto Rico*! You're in *MY* town now, ass hole!" It seemed he wanted awfully much to get me alone ashore. I thought, "What kind of cops are these?"

That same year a marine police scandal broke in which 10 cops got busted for escorting drug shipments from the island of Vieques to the Puerto Rico mainland, using their guns, uniforms and chase boats as cover. The governor complained on TV at the time that one fourth of the U.S. illegal drugs came through Puerto Rico.

Shortly thereafter I read a press quote from Police Chief Toledo that the tiny island of Vieques handled half of the drug traffic through Puerto Rico. That would mean that the tiny island of Vieques, two thirds of which the U.S. Navy owns and controls, imports as much as one eighth of the U.S. illegal narcotics. A staggering statistic if true.

With this in mind, and with my boat now crawling with Puerto Rican Marine Police with screwdrivers and dogs, I rethought my position. I kept thinking I recognized the voice from that dark night three years earlier: "You're in *my* town now!"

Extrication

The wreck to which they tied my boat teemed with spectators and press. In front of such a public display the marine police Ninja warriors shuffled about uncertainly, giving each other sidelong glances. Since the Puerto Rican police had mustered land, sea and air forces for the assault, they must have felt themselves in an embarrassing bind. Latinos have a particularly hard bent for personal dignity, especially in front of a gringo oppressor from the *coloso del norte*. I tried as I might to look Latino.

My friend from U.S. Customs arrived. Of course he had no jurisdiction over the PRMP search operation, nonetheless he helped out by quietly informing them of my status as a writer who noses in and out of all their little ports to update three yachting guides of Puerto Rico. Meanwhile, the search had gone on for two hours and showed nothing wrong. They threw more embittered looks at me as the search proved fruitless. They surely saw me as cause of their loss of face in front of the Federals. I groped to find a graceful way out for them, so old '*MY* town' wouldn't break my neck when I went ashore. They held hushed consultations among themselves, screwing up their faces and pumping their fists. They too desperately needed a graceful exit.

One of the fancier uniforms left the group and began shouting that I had Puerto Rico citizenship by virtue of residency, that I had refused lawful orders to let them search the boat at sea, and that I had violated their weapons laws. I told him both he and I shared U.S. citizenship. I showed him my gun permit signed personally by the Chief of Police of Ft. Lauderdale. I showed him my U.S. Vessel Documentation. I showed him my log, a legal document, which certifies I had made only two short stops in Puerto Rico in two years, hardly enough to justify residence! I told him I come annually to his country to ensure tourists get good information for safe boating. And could I now please clean up the mess and go in peace?

He sneered at me and pocketed the little pistol. Only Puerto Rico Law applies, he said. I figured the little device could bring a couple of hundred dollars on the black market, or thousands as a throw-down gun when a bad cop needed to justify shooting an unarmed civilian. They piled off my boat full of triumph and justification.

Their Cigarette departed with another 4 foot wake. After this wave, my boat came down on the rusty old hulk, splitting the fiberglass at my bow.

THE AFTERMATH

Before starting the engine I had to screw the engine room overhead back in place and clear the air of fiber insulation debris which could suck into the engine's air intake. By the time I finished, the crowd had disappeared.

Alone and feeling quite sad and immensely soiled, I untied from the wreck and made way for Ponce and Customs amid a tangle of unloosed floorboards, cabinets and carpeting. At Ponce Yacht Club I found myself among friends again. There Jaime Colón, the head of U.S. Customs gave me efficient and courteous clearance as always.

I began to screw back in place floorboards and cabinets. As always with a 20 year old boat, generations of screws of differing lengths and thicknesses had found their personal seats in the teak. Some went missing. Others stuck out by enough to tear holes in the carpet. Many wouldn't seat at all. A lamp support got split by a heavy arm leaning on it. A fiddle got torn off by some lunk trying to move the built-in bookcase. Six and a half foot of teak door frame suffered multiple splits from rough handling.

My faith in the U.S. Coast Guard, on the rebound after those dreadful Zero Tolerance years in which only the innocent suffered, took a pounding. And my decades long love affair with Puerto Rico went on the rocks.

YOU NEED TO KNOW

Puerto Rico requires Puerto Rican registration for all firearms within their territorial limits, including the sea. Further they require all arms aboard boats to have Puerto Rican carry licenses assigned to a Puerto Rican resident aboard the boat. In other words, you must have a Puerto Rican aboard with every gun. All boats. All nationalities.

The police will confiscate any weapons failing to meet any of these demands. Even if you voluntarily surrender the weapon, they hold hearings for violation of the Arms Law of Puerto Rico. Those hearings typically take up to 6 months, during which the vessel may get impounded, and they may not permit the owner to go aboard.

The Injustice System

Not long after my experience, a professional delivery skipper picked up a cruiser I knew, a decent retired businessman, to help him deliver a boat. They stopped to rest in Puerto Rico where the Ninja marine police SWAT assaulted them in their bunks at 3 a.m. They got carted off to jail in chains where they stayed for three days without recourse to a lawyer or judge. When they got out on bond they got the boat out of Puerto Rico before the police could impound it to "prevent their escape". I have seen a yacht after 6 months impoundment in Puerto Rico deteriorate to the point the owner doesn't want it back.

It took the three days that they languished in jail for the police report to reach the in-basket of the prosecutor's office. Once that happened they stood trapped in a Justice Department process that had only two possible outcomes: either their conviction of a crime not committed, or the bench's discipline of the marine police. If convicted, eventually a Federal court would discipline the marine police on appeal. Because they lose either way, the police keep the case revolving eternally without resolution through the device of "continuances" when one or the other of them doesn't show up as a witness.

The crew caught in this bind has to fly into Puerto Rico every few months or have a fugitive felon warrant issued on them. A professional skipper can't work deliveries while under trial, and cruisers have to seek employment to pay the considerable expenses. If they get out of the PR "continuance treadmill" by a phony conviction, it couldn't wash on appeal in Federal court where the right to have arms aboard remains secure. Few have the money to weather the Puerto Rican courts to get to Federal, and the system knowingly stacks the deck that way. So much for even the vaunted American "justice" system.

After 18 months the delivery crew mentioned above luckily won a dismissal. It seemed the non-appearing police witnesses against them didn't appear that final time because the FBI had them jailed along with 31 police confederates for drug smuggling.

Weep for the Republic

As I worked on my boat's interior in Ponce the bizarre senselessness of the episode began to grate on me. The slow return to a more normal mental attitude prompted me to wonder at how fast the PRMP could destroy one's life for no reason but their personal egos. I felt I had experienced a Koestler *Darkness at Noon*, such as the Communist terrorist states used to rapidly reprogram reputable citizens into fearful, obedient creatures. And my government's troops stood aloof and let it happen to me!

For many years I had thought the drug wars a great sham which profited everyone involved but the ruined users. While it trashed the society as a whole, it didn't seem to affect me directly. Now it had.

A fellow cruiser, inured by the excess and ineptitude of the Drug Enforcement Agency during the so-called Zero Tolerance era, remarked, "Well, at least they didn't use chain saws". His reaction typified what my cruiser buddies had to say, beyond sniggers of "Finally tagged you, too, didn't they?" Long before the era of our well justified anti terrorist war, no one cared about the nazification of the U.S. in the phony drug war.

While trying to find screws that fit the scrambled teak medicine chest, I thought of Martin Niemoeller's reflection on the Nazi terror:

"First they came for the Gypsies, and I didn't speak up. Then they came for the homosexuals, and I didn't say anything. They came for the Jews, and still I didn't speak. Then they came for me, and there was no one left to speak out."

I decided then to look into just why the incident took place. I called on my lawyer and Federal drug enforcement friends to see what they could find out.

PROBABLE CAUSES

The *why* here boils down to defensible *probable causes* for a search and seizure operation. Despite other credible scenarios, the PRMP officials named the following:

1. They understood "I'm alone with only my cat aboard" to mean a Dominican prostitute might traveled aboard.
2. *Modified structure.* In an ongoing major media spectacle the PRMP had detained and accused Cuban Americans of trying to assassinate Fidel Castro. At the time I got boarded a hot debate raged in the PR media about the phrase '*modified structure*'. The PRMP had used it as probable cause in the trial of the Miami Cubans, contending they had smelled an assassin because the Miamians' boat appeared "different than normal boats". My keen PRMP sleuths justified their search and seizure operation against me with this phrase from the TV.

For the Barney Fifes of the PRMP my converted motorsailer filled the bill. An unmasted motorsailer with a long, flat roof, it might look *modified*.

The reasons I sailed with such a configuration?

1. Since a stroke had left me with vertigo, I stay clear of deck work.
2. Eaten up with skin cancers from too many years in the sun, I stay under cover.

Not for long distance tanks and secret compartments. By the PRMPs *modified structure* logic we could arrest anyone using a wheel chair or a handicapped van.

The Puerto Rican jury, by the way, acquitted the Miami Cubans in Federal court, partially due to the ridiculousness of the *modified structure* nonsense.

CAUSES NOT MENTIONED

Like Sherlock Holmes' dog that did *not* bark, the plausible probable causes might lie among those *not* named by the PRMP.

- A major drug haul went down just when I sailed through the area. *Never mentioned.*
- The frenzy of nationalism in Puerto Rico arising from the standoff between the U.S. and Puerto Rico over the Navy's use of the island of Vieques. The same month I got hassled, Puerto Rican protests turned back a U.S. Navy carrier fleet. My little boat made a piffling thing in such a war. Maybe they just accosted me for some fun.
- My occupation as a writer took me up and down the island chain continuously. Many people knew me and my boat by sight, but they didn't know what I did shuttling back and forth through their islands. Maybe it all started with curiosity.
- After much scandal in the past, some good guys may exist in the marine patrol who, overeager to prove their worth, respond with a hair trigger.

Regardless of the reasons for my and others' false arrests, one must assume certain facts about laws and so-called law enforcement in any jurisdiction in the tropics. The violation of rights and perversions of justice I have described happened to American citizens on American territory in the presence of American Federal officials sworn to uphold the American Constitution which guarantees the right to bear arms and protection against unreasonable search and seizure. It also guarantees a speedy and public trial by an impartial jury before an impartial judge, and representation by counsel, all of which got denied in the above accounts. What can one expect in Napoleonic Code countries?

The drug wars have perverted the avuncular officials of our childhoods. One can no longer expect to meet friends among the Coast Guard, marine police, navy or land police. You shall only find indifferent bureaucrats or bullies, even criminals. It shall go downhill from there as you continue going foreign in the tropics, as the following shall tell.

OFFICIAL PIRACY

The east coast of the island of Hispaniola has grown notorious for dinghy and motor theft, even occasional boardings by someone looking for a motor. The passage between the Dominican Republic and Puerto Rico has become like the Rio Grande which separates the U.S. from Mexico. A constant flood of people smuggling operations has institutionalized criminality among the officials as has the drug smuggling which inundates Puerto Rico. This increases the likelihood that the cruiser can encounter corrupt officials.

Dear cruising friends of ours ran into a situation in the Bahía de la Finca. They recounted their experience to the DR government as follows. The International Maritime Bureau Piracy Reporting Center (www.imbkl.po.my) in Kuala Lumpur also got copied.

"On May 24, 2001, my companion and I sailed in your eastern provinces. We put the anchor down at around 10:30 a.m. We needed to stop to check the starter motor which had shorted out putting 20 amperes into the aluminum hull. I also needed to inspect the propeller which was getting loose. Between us we have nearly 140 years, so after the repairs we wanted to rest before the long night trip to Punta Cana.

"Both the 1958 Convention on Territorial Sea and the 1982 Convention on the Law of the Sea guarantee my right to anchor on this coast for the purposes declared above.

"Around 11:00 a.m. two fishermen came by saying that the comandante wanted us to leave. Half an hour later a boat arrived with 3 individuals. One waved a .45 caliber automatic pistol, and the two younger ones pointed a shotgun at us.

"When asked by the leader to leave the harbor I explained that I needed to repair and inspect the propeller. This did not help, and the leader ordered the two young men to climb aboard to inspect the boat. They were very excited and pushed us aside to get into the boat. I asked them why all this aggressiveness, and I asked for identifications as I had some doubts as to their intentions. They had no uniforms and looked more like pirates than officials of the country. One had a red sweatshirt with black shorts. The other was in a white shirt and bathing suit. The leader waving his automatic around identified himself and the unit of the Navy that he represented.

"As the two younger men searched the boat I discussed with the official and got to talk to his boss via the VHF on Channel 16. His commanding officer told me that this bay was a military zone and that I had to leave. I told him I would do so but told him that I could not know this bay was a military zone as nothing was shown on my chart.

"The search lasted about 45 minutes during which time I discussed with the leader, while my crew stayed frightened in the cockpit. When they left, having found nothing, she went down to find a real mess all over the boat and salt water on the floor and beds

— the two young men were soaked in sea water when they arrived on board. She soon found that $110 — which were in a cabinet — had disappeared. I checked my own wallet and also realized that $160 had vanished.

"I immediately took the dinghy to report to the commanding officer what we were missing. He asked the two men to answer my claim, and, of course, both denied any wrong doing. One even dropped his pants, a swimsuit, to show me he had no money hidden in his genitalia. I asked the officer in charge to report the incident to his superior.

"About one hour later he asked me to climb on a motorbike with him in front and an armed soldier, this time in uniform, behind me. After 20 km. of motocross on sandy roads and on the beach at up to 80 km/h we came to town. I explained the events to the chief who told me that it was my fault that the money disappeared as I should not have authorized more than one navy man in the boat so that I could control them. I told him that it was not possible to argue with aggressive and excited guys waving and pointing pistols and shotguns at you. He finally told me that we could stay in the bay until the next morning. I had realized by his attitude that there would be no inquiry, so I gave up trying to recoup our money.

"The return motocross was as scary and dangerous as the first. We left around 6:30 p.m. where we told our story to the local Coast Guard. He appeared quite disturbed, but I don't know if he reported the incident further.

"We were very glad to depart this country, where it appears that officials of the Navy participate in armed piracy."

Newspaper accounts had once described Bahía de la Finca as a haven for people smuggling operations where Navy officials squeezed money from the passengers before allowing the illegal voyage to proceed. My friends' account indicates that blackmail had moved on to piracy. Shall it mount to full naval assault with the anti-terrorist excuse?

THE UNOFFICIALS

Throughout poor nations in the trade winds the loafers on the docks and in the harbors will hassle you for work which they may not do or errands they may not run. Some will ruin your laundry if you let them and gouge you in the bargain. The bad actors of the breed have got spoiled by "ugly Americans", mostly paid delivery crews in town for a crack at the red light district. These crews push out their absent owner's dollars like missionaries push out Bible tracts at the airport. Therefore some of the dock boys respect neither your common sense nor your wallet. So sailor beware!

Meanwhile, there are people who can do useful chores. Some dock boys want to sell courtesy flags, and I don't deny them the business if I don't have one. If you employ someone for chores or errands, especially dock boys, specify short, specific tasks with firm, fixed prices. Have each task finished and paid for before going on to the next task, assuming you still want him to work for you. Additionally, if a dock boy thinks you've agreed for a service from him, never change dock boys before you have paid and discharged the first one. You may find yourself in the middle of a labor dispute right out of Marlon Brando's and Lee J. Cobb's *On the Waterfront*.

A CRUISING HEALTH PLAN
Self Insurance in the tropics.

The Clinica de Hospitales de Caracas looked on the inside like the Atlanta Hyatt Regency or the Manhattan Marriott. I stood lost inside a many storied, enormous, air conditioned atrium whose balconies dripped greenery like Nebuchadnezzar's hanging gardens.

Uh-oh. This didn't look like the cheapest deal in South America.

PRIMARY PHYSICIAN

The surgeon who removed a tumor from my jawbone in Puerto Rico said I'd best look at the rest of my head. It just might look like Swiss cheese, he said. I had called and faxed to clinics from Miami to Caracas looking for the cheapest MRI (Magnetic Resonance Imagery) to get a picture of my head bones. So I found myself at the Clinica de Hospitales in Caracas. I pushed on into the lobby with a sinking feeling in my wallet.

A treatment disaster in Indonesia began the chain of events which put me on a cruising boat many years before plan. From that experience I had learned to act as my own primary physician. The British doctor we had contracted to take care of our expatriate families misdiagnosed malaria, and that caused me to enter a near fatal hepatic coma. In the decade of recovery that followed, I learned to use doctors and laboratories as my consultants: never self-treating, but neither ever throwing myself under the mercy of another fallible mortal.

With MRI machines pretty new at that time, they cost a bunch to use. Miami wanted $4000, and that came before the referring physician's cut, the lab, the radiologist and the hosting hospital. A dear friend in Margarita, himself dying from cranial cancer, gave me the number of his Japanese surgeon in Caracas. Eduardo's doctor unfortunately had flown off to operate on patients in Houston when I called him, but his secretary gave me the phone number to the lab with the MRI. Five minutes later the lab's administrator told me on the phone that he had an opening at Clinica de Hospitales at 10:30 Monday night if I wanted it.

Tuesday afternoon I settled up with the clinic's cashier in the 3rd subbasement, deep under the Babylonian gardens. The machine, to which I had taken a second turn when I didn't see any holes in me on its first round of pictures, cost only $99. The radiologist, whom I hired when the second picture looked as good as the first, concurred I had no holes in my head beyond the ones my wife tells me about. His part of the bill came to $25. The clinic put their burden at $8, probably to water the plants, and just like in the U.S., a mysterious 55 cents appeared from the dispensary for "sedative". I declined the 55 cents, and the cashier gladly punched up a new bill from the computer with its American software for hospital administration. I paid $132 and went back to the boat. *And they made a profit.*

Think if I had flown to Miami instead.

TOOTH TALES

I lived in Paris for many years. My dentist, Jonathan, disliked Americans in general, but he loved their dentistry. He thought medicine around the world had a sorry state when compared with dental practice. He said that dentistry, rooted in *barber-ism* to put it historically, evolved commercially whereas medical practice got bound up in mysticism by the priesthood of the surgeons. The United States, that champion of raw knuckled capitalism, he said, gave dental entrepreneurs and their equipment manufacturers several generations of unbridled development. The marketplace created standardized dental practice and equipment world wide before governments and guilds could stop it.

I have first hand experience that he spoke the truth. Dentistry world wide, I've found, looks and feels American.

In the Bahamas I lost an old three surface amalgam filling from a wisdom tooth. I repaired it with Marine-Tex™, a procedure not recommended by the establishment, nor Marine-Tex™, for sure. However, it lasted several months.

I remembered the tooth more than 3 months later in Puerto Plata while provisioning to sail back to Georgetown to pick up a charter.

As I walked into Jose Aponte's dental office a fighting rooster stumped arrogantly past me. Aponte first asked why in the world I would want to replace such a beautiful, well-fitting white filling. He loved the new epoxies, he just couldn't use them because his profession had not approved them. For the same spooky reason I had him replace it with a three sided clump of lead and mercury, not at all sure I did the right thing.

After the procedure Aponte charged me $5 and invited me across the road to share a rum with him at his expense. That took place in 1984, not really so long ago. His prices have held about the same ratio against stateside prices since then. Getting on in years, he doesn't do the rum these days, however.

Cruising buddies returning from the Rio Dulce told their friends of the wonderful treatment they got in Guatemala City from a competent dentist who himself made high quality gold and enamel crowns and bridges. As it happened, their lady friend faced quite a dental bill for work not yet launched in Ft. Lauderdale. She believed my friends' tales, and having an adventurous soul to begin with, she flew to Guatemala City and had the repairs done. She not only paid for the travel and touring with her money saved from not having the job done in Ft. Lauderdale, but she paid for the dental work itself with profits from the duty paid native crafts she brought back with her, gaining the teeth and the tour for free.

The Marine-Tex™ filling, by the way, went like this. When the epoxy stood mixed and curing I wadded gauze around the cratered tooth and dried it. I then dipped a toothpick into the near fluid epoxy and painted the inside surfaces of the tooth. This primed the surface. When the epoxy became the consistency of bubble gum I rolled up a tooth size ball of it and stuffed it into the tooth where it could bind with the primed inner surface. Next I patiently sculpted the top and sides with a dental tool from my tool box. Just before the epoxy set well I wet the teeth above it and chomped down on the filling. I held my jaw closed awhile. When all appeared set I polished away with successively finer grades of bits of wet and dry sandpapers, finishing, like on a good gelcoat job, at 600 grit.

PUBLIC CLINICS

Should you med-evac to Europe or North America? If you have the bucks, the time and the strong inclination, yes, by all means. God forbid you get surgery in the Virgin Islands.

Do whatever makes you comfortable. I met a lady who flew her cat over the Mona Passage to avoid undo trauma to pussy on a passage. But if you don't have great wealth, great health insurance or uncontrollable silliness, you shall first want to try out the locals.

Every country has its ration of incompetence and fraud, but no one has 100%. If one believes a competent doctor or lab lives somewhere around, and a genuine drug within expiration date occurs on some shelf within reach, one has an excellent chance of finding both. Having lived and worked abroad in many venues for more than half my long life, I can testify that they practice good medicine just about anywhere if you look for it.

In Indonesia a leading American epidemiologist actually wrote me a prescription to never, under any circumstances, seek counsel of an American physician for the fevers from which he saved me. They would kill me, he said. Not maliciously. Just from ignorance of what can go on in the world of parasites outside U.S. borders. Recent press reports show some uncertainty may exist inside those borders as well.

I allowed myself to get so run down once that I picked up cholera in Puerto Rico. Though most Americans don't know it, they can find cholera endemic in the Gulf States of the U.S. Yet you haven't heard of anyone who has caught it, have you? Modern public medicine and ubequitous modern sewage systems have put cholera, a 19 century bugbear, out of business. However inexcusable, one can nonetheless contract it even in American territory. I simply hied myself to the local clinic where they rapidly rehydrated me, counseled me and sent me on my way at no charge. Lesson?

Public health facilities exist everywhere just in order to stem contagion. *Use them.*

I came to the Dominican Republic from Haiti once with a strong dose of para-typhoid I couldn't shake off by myself. I found myself in a tiny fishing village of 500 or so souls, but it had a public clinic where one pays what one can. The doctor on duty told me which intravenous antibiotic to get at the pharmacy, which I did, along with a dozen syringes. Three times a day for four days I reported to the clinic's tiny emergency room where the nurses used up my syringes with the antibiotic that they kept for me in their fridge.

I got to watch them handle an old farmer who whacked himself in the leg with a machete while harvesting sugar. I sat with a needle dangling from my arm while a large rural family filled the small room with caterwauling as their grandmom passed on of a stroke right next to me.

I would have thought the nurse incapable of more caring than she gave to me while alone. When grandmom and the descendants descended on us, she doubled her solicitous-ness, embarrassing me with her attention under the circumstances. At the end of the four days of antibiotic treatment, I embarrassed them by asking how much I owed. It seemed the clinic's emergency room couldn't handle payments. They mean to prevent the spread of disease, not make money. I contributed to the box kept for incidentals.

One should never abuse public health clinics, especially in poor countries. They exist primarily, however to address just the kind of health problems most cruisers fear in foreign places: contagious diseases. The government wants it free, of course. That way it gets used early. You must not fear to use it either.

MEDICAL LABORATORIES

I need certain blood tests semiannually to monitor a serious condition acquired in Sumatra and mistreated in Java by a European doctor, as mentioned earlier. Fortunately it lies dormant, at least when I keep a close watch on it. Since I became accustomed to Swedish social medicine, where one doesn't know the true costs of one's health care, I got roundly shocked while stopping over in Florida to fill the old cruising kitty. I couldn't believe the time and money it took for my straight forward blood tests: $120 and 7 to 10 days, and that in 1981. In Sweden it had cost me only 2 days and $5. In France it took 3 days and $30 or so.

What would you suspect the poor islands in the trades cost me in time and money?

Well, in Puerto Plata I found a lab in the back of an old Victorian house. Forewarned of a long morning waiting line of expectant mothers, I came at 8 o'clock in the morning. The technician had a 3 day beard growth, smelled of rum and beer, and dangled a 2 inch cigar ash over his test tubes. The critical test, however, got done by machine, sans ash. All tests came out correctly, and everything cost only $26, which I paid in advance.

Rolling down my sleeve, I asked when I would get the results. "Two o'clock," he said. Today? "Of course!" He looked offended that a gringo should doubt his efficiency.

At two o'clock I returned for the results. The technician had gone off to his post-siesta bar. The results stood on the living room table in an envelope marked *Bruce Lee*, a name I often give in hotels and such, where it doesn't really matter, because everyone knows it, everyone can pronounce and everyone can even spell it. The critical part of the test came from the printer of the same computerized blood test machine used in Sweden and in Florida. It only took eight o'clock to two o'clock, or 6 hours, versus a whole week in the U.S. And $26, versus $120 in the U.S. *And, as a private businessman, he made a profit!*

In the United States one can not get a specific blood test without a doctor's prescription, which means paying for two doctor visits. For a cruiser, that usually means a first time visit to a strange doctor, and first visits mean more bucks. And the medical lab will not release the test, paid for by the patient, except through the doctor. If it requires a specialist to interpret, then a reference must get cut by the first doctor. What happened to the Wright-Patman or the Sherman antitrust statutes prohibiting tie-in sales in the U.S.? For final insult, in the U.S. you often have to wrestle the doctor to take possession of your paid for property, the original of the results. Often they don't want you to have a copy!

In most foreign countries one can consult medical laboratories and purchase drugs without referral from a physician. The locals don't have the resources nor the arrogance to self treat and self prescribe. You shouldn't either. Knowing this, however, a cruiser can get needed prescriptions refilled and monitoring tests done without the expense of a new doctor in every port. Just walk into a likely looking *Medical Analysis Laboratory*, *Labatoire d'Analys* or *Laboratorio de Analisis*. They want your business.

In May, 2000, I paid $21 for an EKG and a 45 minute consultation with a cardiologist. A Swiss chiropractor saw me for an hour for just $14. Full body dermatologist exam, $28. A 24-hour Holter heart monitor $42, stress test $90, both with computer evaluation and cardiologist consultation. Shoulder X-ray: $15. Orthopedist exam: $26. And a full colonoscopy with two consultations *and* delivery of the video tape for $180. I put titles on the video: *"Through the Alimentary Canal with Gun and Camera"*.

FINDING YOUR MEDICINE

If you can buy your own prescription drugs without add-on services and charges, how do you go about it in a funky place with a funny language?

You stand in front of the flyspecked drugstore counter with your prescription, or your old pill box, in hand. People mill about furiously thrusting forth wrinkled scraps of dirty wrapping paper with writing on them. Money gets unwadded, counted and exchanged for pills wrapped in clean shelf paper. No one has time for you, and you can't think of what to ask if they did.

Ask for the *pharmaceutical handbook* or *dictionary*, which every pharmacist in every country has under the counter. This fat tome has all the manufacturers, all the patented drug names and all the generics. You can find cross references to licensed manufacturers around the world and to the names they use for the drug. You shall soon discover as well that you can get many drugs beyond those available in the U.S. For example, *Stugeron*, a motion sickness cure of British origin from the Jannsen Company, has decades ago completely replaced the U.S. brands in those markets which don't depend solely on U.S. supply. I see it as a must have emergency stores item in case the skipper should go down. If you sail among islands and reefs, you may not just go below and sleep it off.

Anyway, don't they all use knockoff imitations of American drugs? Definitely no. Nearly 90% of the American prescription drugs come one way or another from Swiss enterprises functioning in the U.S. or abroad. The production of these interlocked megaliths goes roughly 80% to developing countries at 5 cents on the dollar, and the remaining 20% to the U.S. or similar markets at 95 cents. The brouhaha about pirate drugs that occasionally rocks the press originates with the pharmaceutical giants who don't want to see their 5-cent shipments smuggled back into the country for someone else to profit on.

Does drug piracy exist? Sure. Everywhere, even in the United States. Always buy unopened boxes, and inspect all the stampings and informational inserts meticulously.

Buy Hoffman La Roche products made locally, rather than the Hoffman la Roche product on the shelf right next to it which they made in the U.S.

COSTS

The underdeveloped middle class in developing countries does not have disposable income to oversubscribe to medical services. No slack exists between the suppliers of medical services and the people who need them. In the so-called first world countries a doctor-pharmaceutical-government-insurance-lawyer complex has arisen to play in the slack that exists there; what an investor would call arbitrage. In these rich countries, super developed middle classes provide good opportunity for human gain.

A poor country can't find the slack in which to play such games. Getting the medicines on the shelves gives sufficient opportunity for profiteering. Just like my childhood in the U.S., bureaucratic barriers seldom get thrown between the purchaser and the medicine on the shelf, between the examiner and the examined, between the test results and the interpreter.

What small middle class a country may have may lie close to revolution — government dares not dink with their antibiotics. Nor their beer nor rum nor tobacco, for that matter. Without slack in the system, insurance and malpractice lawyers don't occur to anyone.

AN OPEN MIND

Xenophobic cruisers see only what they want to see. With all the medical services in the world at your boarding ladder, you won't use them if you don't trust them. Blind trust may earn you an unnecessary appendectomy, badly fitted bridgework or worse. But a modicum of research and references can lead to a knowledgeable state and to spectacularly successful outcomes.

Your trust that foreign medical establishments can indeed work for you may first have to begin with distrust in the models you grew up with. Make your own first experience with foreign medicine an epiphany. Take the case of my own epiphany with Stugeron.

Even before Stugeron became popular for *mal de mer*, it had long got used to help post operative elderly patients get early on their feet with good balance, or to assist recovery from inner ear infection or surgery. My children grew up on boats in Europe in the seventies using this completely side effect free drug. In the eighties, when we realized we couldn't get it in American territory, we traded scandalous quantities of rum to European cruisers for just a few tabs. A wealth of data exists on it. Why can't Americans buy it after decades of European usage? Lack of testing? Bureaucratic backlog at the FDA? For 30 years? I don't care as long as I can buy it where I go. But I wouldn't have believed in its existence nor its efficacy if I couldn't call up a mild mistrust in the American establishment in the first place. Then the scales fell from my eyes.

Into four decades of living abroad I have a mind more than open, yet always healthily suspicious, toward foreign health care. That attitude has saved me tens of thousands of dollars and extended my life as well. To enjoy your cruise more, or indeed to even dare embark on it, consider self-insuring with local health care in your medical plan.

PREVENTION

THE CLEAN HANDS POLICY
The best way to stay healthy in the Tropics?
Wash your hands like your mother told you to.
Even if your Psychology 101 professor said it showed paranoia.
After shaking hands with someone or handling money, keep your
hands away from all bodily orifices including your eyes.

41

AIR

After a long transit in the islands of the Pacific, or a several months stay among low islands like the Bahamas, your allergic reactions have become under stimulated. After landfall at New Zealand or Hispaniola you bathe for twelve hours a day in air sliding down from the middle of a wide, high island. This air brings with it all the pollens and allergens of practically every type of flora known and then some. You haven't seen deciduous trees or grasses in several months. Keep your antihistamines handy and double your vitamin intake.

On the other hand, a cruising buddy tells me that while living in Massachusetts, he experienced asthma symptoms nightly and had to use an inhalant. After cruising through the Bahamas and living on Hispaniola for 16 months, he threw away the inhaler and hasn't used it since, even after having returned to live in the states for a year and a half.

WATER

Most maladies reported by yachties arriving directly on Hispaniola from an extended stay in the Bahamas come from effects of climatic and allergen change. But like the New Yorker visiting New Jersey in the summer, they blame everything on the water.

On the other hand, all developing countries have notoriously poor public sanitation coupled with poor or intermittent pressure in their town water lines. While the H_2O from the mountains may run pure and delicious, like in New Jersey, wait a couple of days after an outage before tanking up on the water. And, as in Florida, always treat it.

Jerry jugging can become a way of life. If you count on catching water, for sure it won't rain for weeks, so load up when you can. I have found it convenient to have several 6 gallon jerry jugs for water and diesel. Larger sizes become unmanageable and smaller sizes make for too many trips. You should equip for it. We take 1 or 2 showers a day (albeit Navy showers) and wash dishes in fresh water. That means a little more than 3 gallons a day per person, or one jug run every 2 days with 2 people aboard. If you can afford it, I have a real back saver: use a large flexible tank with a 12 volt in-line pump with which to pump water aboard via the dinghy. You can also invest in a water maker.

WASHING FRUITS AND VEGETABLES

You shall use markets most places you cruise which differ little from the kind of markets your grandparents used, and perhaps your grandchildren shall again. Fresh lettuce, cabbage and tomatoes may have the dirt in which they grew still clinging to them. Eggs can have residue of that end of the chicken from which they exit. Rural communities have no major sanitary infrastructure. Therefore, all farm products must get washed thoroughly in good water. Fruits that you must peel offer no problem.

DOING WITHOUT MR. CLEAN

American products come clever and useful and well packaged. When they sell for the marine market they come clever, useful, well packaged and expensive, and, in the trade wind belts, generally unavailable. You can port 50 bottles of each product and displace 10 cases of rum, or you can carry the following generic chemicals, refilling the product bottle with a substitute solution which may work better and more cheaply. Remember the first two principles of provisioning:

The Highest Utility for the Least Space, and The Greatest Savings First.

In other words, a boat full of small bottles of cheap, but high quality rum, and a year's supply of cleaning agents in a few chemical flasks means both a happy boat and a clean boat.

Remember also to store and handle all chemicals with the care they deserve. I use sturdy, well sealed plastic containers. I snugly wedge them into plastic milk cartons so they cannot move around and chafe. Never place plastic bottles against fiberglass mat or other rough surfaces. Stowage techniques which worked great while fattening the kitty from a mooring or a marina, suddenly can cause ghastly accidents on a passage.

Think of a container of muriatic acid leaking into the bilge together with a bottle of ammonia. You'll have a clean and bug free bilge if you survive the gas. Or how about the folks enroute to Panamá who stored their laundry soap flakes with their chlorine bleach together in the washing machine. The boat's motion caused the machine's tumbler to tumble and chafe the containers. Their luck showed when these powerful bomb components leaked together and only started a fire onboard.

Dish Soap

I carry Joy by the gallon. Others swear by other products, but I find Joy the only one to foam abundantly in salt water. Cheaper still, and as effective, you can try the non petroleum based industrial degreasers. The jug usually says biodegradable and it smells like soap, not oil. We used to make it even cheaper in chemistry class, but too long ago for me to remember how. I can't bring myself to use degreasers for the dishes, though. Dish soap or non petroleum, biodegradable degreasers will:

1. Clean the bilge.
2. Degrease the engine and engine room.
3. Prepare the deck around the deck fill for diesel spills.
4. Emulsify any spills when squirted on the surface and spread with a hose.
5. Keep dirt and grease from under your nails if rubbed in before starting a job.

Ammonia

Foaming ammonia strips the wax off woodwork with a soft scratch pad. I keep a squirt bottle on deck of 10 % ammonia, 5% Joy and 85% water. It's good for any cleanup. Even the eyes of a bandit.

Alcohol

Acts as a great astringent for skin problems, and it stuns fish for boarding and slaughter (see *Trolling*). Have gallons aboard. I used Aramis aftershave in the 1960's. When I cruised back to America and found it expensive, I changed to a mixture of alcohol and witch hazel. Eventually I settled on only alcohol. Stove alcohol, or 99% pure anhydrous (waterless) alcohol, thins epoxy beautifully, making thick roofing epoxy do jobs not worthy of more expensive stuff, and making the expensive stuff penetrate better. You find it in refrigeration and air conditioning stores (where they use it to chase water from the lines) or pharmacies.

Hydrogen Peroxide

Pour over abrasions, cuts and wounds to disinfect before applying topical antibiotics. Have gallons aboard if you ding yourself as much as I do.

Boric Acid Powder

Sprinkle or "puff" lightly in unseen areas (under drawers, beneath cabinets, or in the lazarette). The powder shall keep the boat roach free as long as it stays dry. Eggs that hatch after 6 to 8 weeks get taken care of since the little fellows take it back to the nests on their leg hair. Then they explode when they groom each other! *Usch!* Mixed with honey, boric acid also takes care of ants who carry it as a present to their Queen. You can even desiccate small pills of it to leave behind and under things.

Muriatic Acid

Ordinary HCl, the stuff in your stomach. Don't add this powerful and dangerous stuff down there, though. You get it at hardware and swimming pool stores, usually at 20% mole strength. Don't dare breathe its acrid fumes, even at 20%. Always mix it with lots of water, pouring the acid into the water, not the reverse. It will:

1. eliminate rust stains and gel coat chalking when mixed 1:10 in a spray bottle, costing a hundred times less than some chemically identical products;
2. make your corroded 12 Volt deck sockets work instantly if sprayed into them (or your brass boat horn as I once had to demonstrate to the U.S. Coast Guard).
3. keep your coolers and heat exchangers bright and new inside when mixed 1:8 (stainless and copper only, not aluminum);
4. keep your head clean and unclogged by calcium buildups when mixed 1:6 (rubber and neoprene seals only — no leathers);
5. become Part B of two part teak cleaners when mixed 1:5 with water. Plain old lye crystals and water become Part A (NaOH). You can find lye in some toilet bowl or drain cleaners. Make sure you have pure lye and not some explosive mixture! You can still readily find lye in developing countries.

Of course, you should not allow acid to react too long without flushing it away.

Chlorine

Swimming pool shock treatment which comes in rapidly dissolving granules and has only chlorine as the active ingredient will provide you with a year or more supply of chlorine bleach for:

1. treating the head
2. pouring in the bilge
3. doing your laundry
4. killing black pin mold when sprayed on teak
5. purifying your water

To get normal strength bleach put 1-2 tablespoons powder into a gallon of water.

Mineral Spirits

Mineral spirits or high quality kerosene will:

1. burn more cleanly in your oil lamps than specially concocted products,
2. thin your paints and varnishes,
3. clean and oil your interior woods,
4. start your fires and
5. run in your diesel when you're out of fuel.

Besides all of that, mineral spirits sells cheaper than most of the products whose use it can supplant.

Economics
When you can't hop in the car and drive to the mall.

Provisioning a yacht can get expensive and often difficult in smaller island communities. Larger, more industrialized ports can give you value for many items, but they usually lie at the end of your route, not *en* it. First you must have sufficient storage to not run out of stuff if, as you should, you piddle along in the little places. Second, you must know value when you get to the big places and reprovision.

BEERONOMY

I have practiced an economic theory based on beer since 1970, and it has worked all over the world. In any country in the world you can appraise the value of goods by ratioing against the price of a standard cold beer in a workingman's bar. It goes like this:

> if a beer at a tavern near the station costs a buck at home, and a good suit costs 250 bucks at home, then a good suit at your island, barring government taxes and subsidies, shall cost you 250 cold beers bought at a workingman's tavern there.

Know Value

Knowing value before you even ask the price will keep you out of a lot of trouble.

First you have to establish a known value such as your favorite bottle of catsup. Then find out what that item costs locally. You now have a percentage to apply to anything.

For example:

> Victorina catsup costs the equivalent of 40 cents U.S. and you paid $1.00 in the U.S. for Heinz. Ergo: 40/100= 40% of U.S. prices for local food products.

> If you got a beer and a pizza in the U.S. at a not-too-swank place for $8.95, then you should expect the same to cost a Victorina Catsup percentage locally, or, 40% of $8.95 = $3.58 equivalent of the local currency.

Use more or less this percentage in pricing almost anything of local origin. Restaurants, pizzas, Coca-Cola, etc., but not car rentals. Cars on islands may cost more than double the U.S. price because of import limits.

You can learn a lot from the window of a shoe store, too. A retired English sailor told me one can establish the going rate for ladies of the evening in any port in the world by going first to a shoe store and surveying the prices from the shoes in the window. The models, he said, would range from open-toed beachwear to high class and formal. So, said he, would the services, and at the same prices as the corresponding class of shoes.

I enlisted help from friends in verifying the technique, and they reported that it worked in Sao Paolo (Gurarjao for the beach sandals), Tokyo, London, Madrid and Milan. One must treat Milan, my agent reported, as the designer capital it truly has become, especially with leather. I can't say for the trade wind belts.

PROVISIONING

You can save a lot by provisioning large scale whenever you can. I always meet skippers kicking themselves all the way down islands because they didn't make room to buy case lots when they could.

TRANSPORTATION

Steer away from the group of yachties who charter a bus or a van to provision. The guys talk sea stories and repairs while the girls talk grandchildren and gossip. Nobody looks out the window as you pass the really neat warehouses. The driver may dump you at his kickback spot or to his idea of where swish yachties would like to go. If you haven't reconnoitered the markets and tried individual brands, you need to take a private shopping tour on public transport. You can explore on your own, without having to go with the group consensus. You shall find unbelievable bargains the group never does. And what you want, not what attracts the least common denominator of a group.

GETTING CASH

You really can get cash from credit cards through automatic teller machines outside banks and shopping centers in most major ports and tourist centers in the world, especially if frequented by European tourists. If getting a cash advance from a commercial bank, inquire about any fees they might charge. You may not know what rate you got until months later. Never exchange on the street, where you may run into fast change artists.

Review the counsel in the chapter on security. Most importantly, go back to the boat before shopping, and by a devious path. Only after banking most of it on the boat, go back to your shopping. Keep your shopping roll in a deep flapped or interior pocket, and your petty cash, or transportation and meals kitty, in a handy front pocket.

FUEL AND WATER

Take on water whenever available. Always bleach water with one tablespoon bleach per 30 gallons of water. An activated charcoal filter in the line you use to drink or shower out of removes the chlorine. Never tank water after a recent loss of pressure in the town.

Always filter the fuel with a Baja Filter (see Glossary) if you can get it, tee shirts if you can't. One year I had FIVE motor stops at sea due to clogged fuel filters. In harbor I bucketed out all the fuel from the tank and gleaned 4 pounds of sand and gravel by filtering it through tee shirts. Microbes also gum up the works admirably.

Private yacht clubs usually keep their fuel clean for their members. Otherwise you can jerry jug clean fuel from the town's service station, ferry it aboard and siphon it through your filters into your tanks. I always tank up as soon as I reach a sit-down harbor, and I treat the fuel with Biobor or its equivalent. A full tank decreases the area of the garden in which the fuel microbes grow, the interface between water condensation, air and fuel on the walls of the tank. You should never leave harbor with less than a full tank.

SAMPLING BRANDS

You may get the itch to move on before you've sampled the local goods. You should therefore forego restaurants for a couple of days early in your stay and shop single items to find out what you like before you shop for case lots. Make a separate buying trip to get individual items to sample for both quality and price.

Buy locally made labels. Occasionally you'll find good prices due to trade concessions on imports, some of which get bulk shipped and bottled locally (wine, olives, mushrooms). Local products may differ dramatically between brands. Try them all.

> **Sample several individual products before deciding what to buy by the case.**

Buying Individual Items

You must ask for what you want. One fellow complained to me that a local store had no bacon. Not knowing the local name for bacon, and too shy to ask, he couldn't find what he assumed it looked like. He assumed it would come in a vacuum packed package like Oscar Mayer's, with the slices of bacon splayed out like a poker hand. In the smaller villages meats may get wrapped the way they did it in my mother's time. They wrap them in white butcher's paper and stick them among a bunch of amorphous packages in the cooler. Bacon usually comes whole and needs slicing by the guy behind the counter. For that reason, it usually also tastes better.

Ask to taste everything. Always sample cheese and salamis before buying. If you don't like any of it, at least you've had a free lunch.

Buying Case Lot Goods

After you have tried out different brands, make a list of what suits you and what can save money with power purchases. Many wholesale warehouses give you the same prices they give the grocery stores. Take a look in any walk-in coolers. They may have a furious trade with the fancy foreign tourist hotel up over the hill. You may get surprised by fresh asparagus and artichokes for dinner.

Usually you can find a broken case lots section. Here you can buy items which you won't want in full cases and at the same time you get to see pretty much what they have in all those cases stacked outside. If you don't see what you want, crawl back into the alleys of the boxes and look. If you don't know the contents of a case, ask them to break it open and show you. If you can't find something, ask. Port provisioners usually prorate case price by the unit. And look for the provisioners who specialize in Filipino, Korean or Malay crew. You'll think you died and went to Chinese restaurant heaven.

What to Buy

First of all, only you know what you want. I love French cut green beans and I use them with mushrooms, onions and mayonnaise for great salads when I can't get fresh veggies. You may hate French cut green beans and mushrooms.

Have a dictionary handy to find what you want. Here you have a list of local products which usually represent high quality at low price: dried milk (NIDO), espresso grind coffee, Worstershire sauce (local), vanilla extract (real), all kinds of fresh spices, raw shelled peanuts, soy sauce, jams, preserves or marmalades, Rum (8 years or 12), Gin, local Scotch (*caveat emptor*), liqueurs, cooking wines, cigarettes and cigars, chocolate bars (for watch snacks), salamis, large loaves of cheese, and red ball cheeses which you can warm store. And smoked and salted cod, which Scandinavians exported as sailor food for hundreds of years. They still do, since it stuck to the seaport cultures along the trade routes, even though demand long ago dried up at home.

47

Foreign products get displayed alongside the local products, such as Dutch Gouda cheese, but try the local brand first. Coffee comes in vacuum packed tins, in 10 oz. bags or in small sealed packets good for several cups of coffee each morning. Buy a *greca*, the hourglass shaped aluminum (or stainless) espresso pot, to make the coffee with. No paper filters. Control the strength by controlling the amount of grounds.

CANS

I have fished cans out of the forward bilge after 3 years aboard in the tropics and found them still legibly labeled and delicious inside. Don't waste your time varnishing cans if you have a basically dry boat.

EGGS

I've had unrefrigerated eggs aboard as long as 2 months and found them delicious, although they don't foam as much when whipped if you don't turn them. Of course, you must buy only unrefrigerated fresh eggs; refrigerated eggs go bad faster. You can easily spot unrefrigerated eggs. They have chicken poop on them. Instead of waxing your eggs, try turning them once in a while to keep the yolks centered.

FRESH FRUITS AND VEGETABLES

I can say the same for fresh veggies as I said for fuel and water: buy them whenever you see them available. And wash them in bleached water before putting them aboard. Take away all cardboard. Cardboard brings aboard cockroach eggs.

All down islands you must get to the fresh produce markets early. In small places vegetable and fruit trucks make the rounds 2 to 3 times a week. Try out the different root vegetables that fed our ancestors before the Idaho white potato and intensive farming methods drove them from North America. Europe never had them in the first place.

DRY STAPLES

You can find rice, sugar, flour, beans, meal, and so on, readily available almost everywhere and at reasonable prices. Have smallish dry staple containers aboard. Trying to store too much flour or rice will have you throwing it away when the insect eggs hatch, unless you have pounds of laurel (bay leaves) to put in your canisters. Parboiled rice should have no eggs. You may need to clean the rice and beans of small stones and stems. When visiting Florida I found myself cleaning a bag of beans, still in my tropical habits. After discarding more than usual the amount of small dirt clods and sticks, I realized I had bought the beans in the U.S. So much for superior food standards.

You shall find that flour does not always come "enriched", rice not always "polished", sugar not always "refined", and not much says "new and improved". But it just might favor your health and taste good as well.

BREAD AND DAIRY PRODUCTS

You find bakeries nearly everywhere, and they make fresh bread twice a day. You may not like the product however, except if made in the French manner. It shall pay you to have aboard a bread maker if you have the AC zaps. The presence of middle eastern populations, from the great exodus at the turn of the last century, ensures that much of the tropics have excellent yogurt, cheap and by the gallon! Ask for yo-GOOR.

PHARMACEUTICALS

Refurbish your medicine chest without prescriptions, often cheaply. Most countries don't tie disease curing drugs to doctors' prescriptions, nor can the people afford to buy drugs abusively. Therefore you'll find your pharmaceuticals available without prescription, if you know what you want. The pharmacist will gladly show you his book with which you can translate your antibiotic, or whatever, to generic, and back to the product name as available locally.

Drugs needed commonly for public health might get subsidized. Exotic items can cost more than at home. But if you need to replace drugs used up during treatment aboard, then do it. Also, pharmacies in developing countries traditionally handle dangerous chemicals as well. It may surprise you to find acetone, muriatic and stove alcohol available in quantity only through certain pharmacies.

STREET FOOD

I know I've got it coming to me, but living abroad since 1969 in the strangest of places, I've rarely got ill from street food. Once I got sick at the grand restaurant of the Palace hotel in Biarritz, not once on street food. In India, one would expect to become ill from the nazi balls (rice balls) the peddler rolls in his hands and pops into ancient hot grease. Not so. Perhaps the super hot oil does it.

Latin street vendors have superb little puffed, stuffed pastries (*empanadillas, pastelitos* or *empanadas*). I know of a baritone vendor who sings his wares. He says that the meat filled ones have "mice meat" in them. But he means "mincemeat", I'm sure.

TRICKING THE TRADES

(Both Wind and Sea)

Sir Francis Bacon, father of the Age of Reason, patriarch of
all modern science and mathematics, said,
"Nature, to be commanded, must be obeyed."

KNOWING THE WEATHER

Islands in the trades create their own weather systems.

WEATHER FEATURES

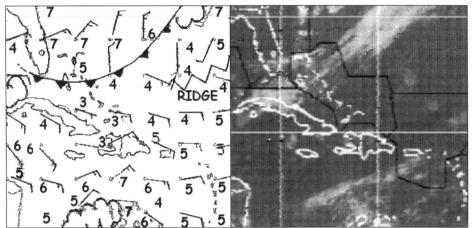

Tropical Prediction Center charts show a stalling front killing the trades.

WINTER COLD FRONTS

Many northern yachties arrive in tropic waters still applying the term *norther* to a cold front. A cold front which ventures into the belt of the trades has little similarity with blue northers up north. Don't let use of terms such as 'norther' inhibit you from seeing cold fronts, when they ever penetrate the trade wind belt, as useful friends.

Unlike western European and North American waters, the building grayness of wind and sea during the passage of an occasional front in the trades never builds to storm conditions (Force 10 Beaufort), and they rarely build to a Gale (Force 8). More likely they collapse on their southern ends, exhausted into several minor frontal lines or a broad, weak trough. Don't always run for shelter. On a mild, dying front get out your dividers and plot your progress. It rains warm if it rains, and you can sail with or without a bathing suit, though you may need a sweater when the front passes and it blows clear and cold. A poncho perhaps, never a slicker!

If a front doesn't stall north of you, but continues through your position, it typically veers the wind from southeast through south, all the way around to northeast. When the northeast wind has blown itself out it will soften and dip a bit below east before strengthening again to normal trade conditions; a very useful fact to know. When it begins to soften and dither below east, you can jump upwind to another island. That strategy sure beats holing out, then beating out into it after the front passes completely. Late in the season, on a mild front, a sailboat can trim for a broad reach and leave her there, scribing a long arc down islands with the wind's veer. A trawler can similarly plan for the needed head seas. Early in the season the northeast winds may persist for several days after passage of a strong front. South of 22° latitude fronts rarely fully clock the winds.

If you want to go only in sunny weather, take a plane. Clear weather in the winter usually means 20 knots on the nose and hobby-horsing into 6 to 8 foot short seas. By including fronts in your winter strategy you can cut your trip time while ensuring yourself a good 3 days to a week of leisurely fishing while doing waits for weather.

BETWEEN SEASON TROUGHS

October to late November boats go up on the beach practically every year in Bonaire from unexpected west winds. They should expect them. Fronts begin to make it as far as Central America in the fall, albeit weakly, and tropical waves (see Glossary) still make it there, albeit old and frail. The combination of stalled, weak fronts and stalled, dying waves often become troughs (see Glossary) which can stretch from the Andes mountains in South America to Georges Banks off Canada. Imbedded storm cells, if not the troughs themselves, can spawn west winds at the unprepared anchorages which protect you from unending easterly trades. The reversal even caught me more than 200 miles to the east at Blanquilla one October.

In the other 'tweener season, May to June, the dying fronts and early weak waves can create similar troughs. Learn to see these as opportunities, not necessarily threats. (Just invert the 'tweener months for the Southern Hemisphere.)

You can use these giant systems to make progress down islands when you have a settled period of yucky weather but predictably mild conditions. East and south of these between season troughs the trade winds get quashed, and you have opportunity for easy upwind easting should you want it.

DANCING WITH STORM CELLS

Spontaneous storm cells commonly arise in settled trades. Microbursts of upper level air, perhaps triggered by local turbulence in the Jet Stream, can inject cold air downward through the warm river of trade winds. When this happens, a vertical temperature gradient forms around this downward thrust spike. Warm air begins to spiral upward around it. Clouds develop and give birth to a small storm cell. If the column of air persists long enough, a full cumulonimbus develops and the upper winds blow its top off in typical anvil shape. Conversely, random turbulence at the surface, perhaps caused by upwelling of water either colder or warmer than the surface water, or, in the daytime, the mixing and stumbling of winds near the surface, can create a chimney of warm air around which a circulation begins.

When these short-lived storm cells approach you on passage don't panic. You can use them to better your speed and course. I think of the chimneys of rising hot air as vacuum cleaners which suck warm moist air from the surrounding sea surface, and the cells that blow cold air down as leaf blowers you use to clear the yard in autumn.

Think of a cell with cold air at its core as a high pressure center, and the cell which surrounds a rising column of hot air as a low pressure center. The first has a clockwise rotation, the second counterclockwise. If the air turns muggy you probably have a chimney cell. If, on the other hand, a spike of cold air caused the cell to form, you shall feel its cool air on your cheek as it spreads under the doughnut shaped ring of squally fractocumulus at the base of the cell. The surface air for miles around these storm cells shall spiral one way or the other. Cutting across the trades in the Caribbean, the Pacific or the Atlantic, you can gallop from one of these dancing partners to another, getting a crack-the-whip acceleration ahead or behind each one, depending on which direction it

53

spirals the wind.

Without knowing this trick you shall no doubt spend hours and miles handing sail or sailing around each system, when you could find yourself in a joyful, course-shortening *dance with storm cells*.

SUMMER TROPICAL SYSTEMS

In the summer and fall months of the northeasterly and southeasterly trades, the skipper must hole up for the season or have a storm anchorage to easily make downwind. You may have little warning as tropical systems can develop overnight, and they can change direction like a flying saucer. Keep a good hurricane hole in mind, but nonetheless, you may look for opportunities to use these systems in your navigation.

In the summer months one watches the east for a variety of tropical systems, the nomenclature of which may sound randomly chosen to the cruiser new to the trades. The nomenclature used follows a simple progression of severity, and therefore, of great interest to the cruiser, especially if uninsured.

Rather than continue to confuse these terms, refer now to the Glossary for the definition of each. Learn about these weather features and know how to use them, rather than confuse and dread them all. First on the scene you'll find the troughs and tropical waves, which come across the ocean. A *tropical wave* may spawn a *tropical disturbance*. These may begin to whirl from Coriolis to become a *tropical depression*, which can become a *tropical storm*, which often becomes the dreaded *hurricane* or typhoon. So it goes.

WEATHER WINDOWS

The word *window* got applied in the manned spaceflight program to indicate a favorable conjuncture of complexly interacting variables, the solution to which required detailed analysis and great precision. It began with familiar concepts of windows for launch, orbit insertion and reentry, but soon spread to all the esoteric disciplines of that great endeavor. I may have aided its currency in the cruising world, and it annoys me to find it most often used with shallow understanding, handling only one or two factors.

In or near the trade wind belt, weather becomes cyclic and regular. Periods of low, or altered, activity in the trades create windows of escape from normally strong windward weather. Weather windows, therefore, need the conjuncture of favorability in the cyclic wanderings of four different elements:

1. wind strength,
2. wind direction,
3. height of wave and swell, and
4. direction of swell.

How do you cruise to windward without beating your brains out or performing marathon stunts when any of these elements go against you? Wait for a miracle.

Miracles come in the form of certain weather features which upset the status quo of trades conditions. In combination with these weather features, a window may both widen in favorability and lengthen in time. Short windows accommodate short hops. Long windows can harbor several short hops. Reserve long hops for windows both long and wide. And don't quibble at crumbs and scraps of short ones. They get you there too.

This comes when winds lighten up and veer off your nose. If you must beat, do so in trades moderated to less than 15 knots maximum and seas 4 feet or less.

A weather window starts only after swells have abated, but when it starts, take the leading edge of it and don't delay. If you really want to attend one more beach bonfire, or one more potluck dinner, or you already invited the boat next door for cocktails, then enjoy yourself and wait for the next window so you can sail in leisure. Don't drink up half the window in harbor and bank on the second half holding up for you. Take a new window rather than risk getting the current one slammed shut on your tail.

> **Depart only when favorable conditions prevail and shall sustain for a day longer than you need to make safe harbor.**

A wait for weather means taking advantage of the periodic switching of the prevailing easterlies between northeast and southeast as the trade winds wander, in winter, by the passage of a front, and in summer, the passage of tropical waves.

If you feel you haven't got time to wait for an appropriate weather window, if you feel pressed to make your next cruising ground as soon as you can, closely examine your motivation and play it off against your reasons for cruising, and more importantly, your safety. If you press on in 20 knot trades and 5 to 8 foot seas in a 35 to 40 foot boat with a small auxiliary engine, you beg disaster to overtake you. When it doesn't, you haven't cheated it, but you've got that much more of a disaster next time.

Some waits may last longer than a week, but rarely. It may seem that a window will never open. Both in 1991 and 1994, for example, the Christmas Winds came as they should, but they stayed into hurricane season. Even in those tougher than usual years, cycles of moderation appeared regularly, if less frequently, than usual.

Even in those years the Offshore Report showed 2-3 day windows of 15-20 knots, 4-7 foot seas at least twice monthly. More usually windows of 10-15 knots, 3-5 foot seas, come twice a month, more often in the summer. In 1997, a vintage year for weather windows, many went unrecognized. I found myself alone more often than not.

The weather you wait for may not always look that good to you at first glance. Good sailing days come around like good lovers, I guess. My mother used to say: "They're like buses. There's another one right around the corner if you're looking for it." And if you don't look for it, or worse, don't know what to look for, you'll spend your life getting neither. You must *know* what to look for.

KNOWING THE WEATHER

The path traveled through the islands of the trades, the anchorages selected, the safety and comfort of the crew, each singularly depend on the skipper's knowledge of, observation of and use of the effects of wind and wave at the margin of land and sea.

Can you identify the wind and weather features around you, such as the *sea breeze*, the *nocturnal wind*, the *land breeze*, the *gradient wind*, the *surface wind*, the *inshore wind*, the *coastal fronts*, the *troughs*, the *ridges*, the *depressions*, the *tropical waves*?

Do you know all the ways the observed *surface wind* can differ from the forecast *gradient wind* at sea? How much it can differ in inshore waters, and why? Do you know all the reasons why the wind in harbor differs from the inshore wind? Do you know how banks affect the weather? Do each of the italicized phrases or words above seem familiar old friends? You shall never find weather windows threading a chain of islands without taking advantage of island effects, which you must know cold.

Harbor Telltales

You should not try to guess the weather from harbor almost anywhere. Even harbors sheltered by small bits of land may have massive banks and land areas to weather of them, preventing you from feeling the real wind. For example, on the north and south coasts of large islands, in prevailing conditions, the harbor wind can blow at times greater (i.e., gustier) and at times much less than the wind just a half mile offshore. In west coast, or leeward harbors, it can blow 15 knots from the west, while only five miles away on the north or south coasts, it blows 20 knots from the east. The wind may go to zero at night, while outside the reef, only one mile away, it will still blow 20 knots. Each anchorage and harbor has unique and complicated variables which contribute to its diminishing, increasing or changing of the direction of the real wind.

Ignore all harbor wind except for known telltales of the cycling of the trades.

Watch the cycling of the trade wind's direction and strength and take your exit only on a down-tick of a cycle, taking advantage of reduced wind speeds and southerly trends (northerly trends in the Southern Hemisphere). On the north coast of a large island, for instance, moderated prevailing conditions means less than 15 knots and south of east, to ensure you get shielded by the bulk of the island from the eye of the wind . Even then, you need to go with the *night lee*, more about which later.

To watch the winds, you can construct a decision table to track them and establish a baseline from which to discern "up-ticks" and "down-ticks" in the strength of the trades.

DAY	WIND DIRECTION	WIND IN KNOTS	SEA CONDITION IN FEET	CHANGE IN Wx REPORT	GO/ NOGO
1	E	10 to 15	4 to 6		
2	E	10 to 15	<5	better	go
3	E to NE	10 to 15	4 to 6	worse	nogo
4	E to NE	15 to 20	5 to 7	worse	nogo
5	E to NE	15 to 25	6 to 8	worse	nogo
6	NE to E	20	6 to 8	same	nogo
7	NE to E	15 to 20	5 to 7	better	nogo
8	E	15	4 to 6	better	go
9	E to SE	10 to 15	3 to 5	better	gone

A Go/Nogo Decision Table for Leaving Port to Windward

Always use the winds forecast by the experts (e.g., U.S.: Offshore Report; British: Shipping Report). Average the forecast winds for both zones if you find yourself on the borderline of two forecasts, or near a significant weather feature in one of them. For example: if you lie near 73° with a forecast of —

W OF 73W WINDS E 15 TO 20 KT and E OF 73W WINDS E 20 TO 25 KT.

— then assume you shall have winds of E 20 knots. You shall not normally lie so simply equidistant from different forecast segments. Normally you'll have to use weighted averages, favoring the nearer segment but, as in billiards, giving *English* to the farther one. Though a little complicated with three or more segments at play, you can still do it, more or less the way you do it by eye when studying up to four differing wind arrows around your position on a surface analysis chart. Always, of course, leave harbor on the beginning of a downtrend in the wind strength cycle, never at the middle or near its end.

Some examples follow of harbor telltales I've found to work. The additional information you receive from these telltales indicate your position on a cycle. By them you can confirm both *when* your weather window opens and for *how long.*

In normal trade weather, and in the absence of perturbing weather features such as fronts and waves, the daily progression of the time at which the morning winds rise in harbor indicates the trade cycles.

You can monitor a mountain for formation of a crown of clouds as the land warms up. It shall grow larger earlier, or smaller later, each day. You may watch the clocking of your spreader flags from landward to seaward in the morning. It will start earlier (or later) each day and take shorter (or longer) to finish clocking.

Observe the clocking of the winds each day and the cycle of their strengths day to day. The prevailing easterlies may come back down to earth along about 9 in the morning along the coast, much earlier at sea, and farther out, they never lift. They reach a maximum between noon and 2 p.m., tapering off in good harbors to a calm as early as 5 p.m. or as late as 10 o'clock at night.

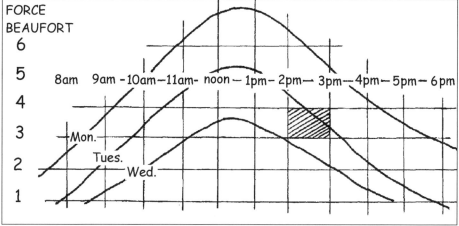

Telltale: harbor wind down to Force 3 by 3 p.m.

If you read maximum strength during the day as, say Force 5, and it goes down to Force 3 by 3 p.m. (having raised to no more than Force 3 by 9 am), get going! One rule, then, says: "Force Three by Three". .

One can also watch cycles in the endurance of the nocturnal wind over the daytime seabreeze. I constructed the following plot in Hispaniola. It clearly shows the regular cycle of the winds which become masked, but not ultimately deformed, by a front.

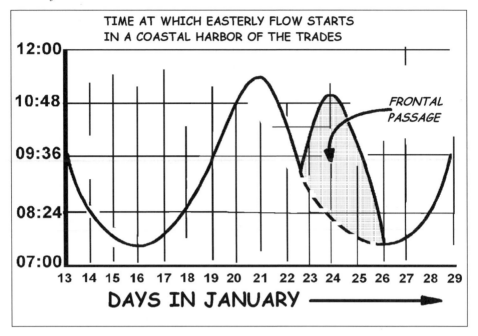

TIME AT WHICH EASTERLY FLOW STARTS
IN A COASTAL HARBOR OF THE TRADES

DAYS IN JANUARY ➡

Telltale: what time the nocturnal wind loses out to the seabreeze

You can make your own plot as simply as I did. When you hear your anchor chain rattle against the bowsprit each morning, as the boat turns to face the rising seaward wind, chunk the time into a spreadsheet on your computer. By programming a macro you can make it as simple as a single keystroke each morning! You call that difficult?

Flying Windows

The trade winds blow for thousands of miles. They amount to a river of air that bends with the Coriolis force, and sweeps through the island chains into the western oceans. Just as a river does, this fluid stream meanders a bit and eddies some. Like turbulence in a river, the trade winds have some memory of upstream events. Watch the reports closely and regularly, and you shall begin to see the stream of air switching a bit like a cat's tail: east to east-southeast, to southeast by north, then back up to east. This might happen for just a day, or even less. Often I see these switches moving toward me on the weather charts, but they don't always endure.

Then again, occasionally these slots of opportunity persist, as the following tale tells.

My waits for weather keep me busy. Radio weather schedules keep me bound to the boat for 4 hours a day at least. Not for others. Occasionally a bored Type A with nothing to do hangs on my rail during my breakfast, or worse, while I copy a weather report. He usually starts with, "Charlie says it looked pretty good today. Whatcha think?" I should answer, "I don't know because I'm talking to you instead of copying the weather!" I try to harness my tongue. I answer that I don't know, because truthfully, despite all my attention to looking for a window, I don't know for sure I've got one until I've left.

The more we know, the more questions we can think of. The more variables at play, the more confusing it can get. At the end I commit or I don't.

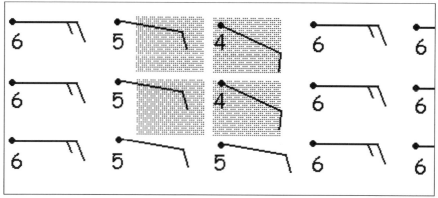

A narrow window moving in the river of air.

A Tale of Two Crossings

Not long ago I waited to cross 150 sea miles of a notorious passage. A 12 hour period of 10 to 15 knot winds appeared in the outlook section of the Offshore Report. It stayed there for 24 hours, or for 4 reports. It then moved up to the 12 hours of daylight Thursday with forecasts of 15-20 knots straddling it upwind and downwind for the 12 hour night-time periods of Wednesday and Thursday. This meant mild open sea sailing during the day on Thursday, while I could use the night effects to calm the stronger winds on either side of the passage on nights previous and following. On a chance of shooting it as it moved into the passage during daytime, I cleared out, shifted to a clean, short rode and waited for the 6 p.m. report. It still came on. I left to meet it midway in the passage.

Two skippers, experienced sailors as it turned out, dinghied up beside me while I raised anchor. (Why always then?) They wanted to know what I knew about the weather. I couldn't press my five days of study into a few minutes for them.

I told them I wanted to shoot a flying window, leading it much like you lead birds with a gun. I had to work against the sun and against a moving 12 hour window that I wanted to catch just as it moved into the passage the next day.

If the window evaporated by morning, I planned to hole up in a tiny harbor I knew down the coast at the edge of the passage. I clearly recommended they not go. They'd not done this passage before. They had no knowledge of my little reef harbor I intended to use for an escape hatch, if I needed one. They had not put away their boats. They hadn't cleared out. Nonetheless, all enthused, they raced off to get under way.

I followed my usual ploy, motorsailing the night lee of the coast. In the morning I dawdled as usual outside my escape hatch harbor until the 6 a.m. report. The window had not evaporated! I rode a truly gorgeous starboard tack, flanking the evening thunder storms west of the next island, in not more than 13 southeast knots of wind. Then, as usual, I drifted down the night lee of the destination island to a morning arrival at the port of entry, playing my favorite tapes, singing all the way, and arriving 32 hours after anchors up, all sailing. The two behind me spent 60 hours getting hammered.

Timing

When the guy a day ahead of you radios back about a strong northerly current he just named Chicken Little Gullywash, don't alter your plan. I frequently see people lose their timing crossing between islands. They either get away from the effects of the first island too late in the morning and get pinned by the trades, or they get run down by the evening storm cells drifting toward them from their destination, or, with no GPS, they just get lost. The timing of sailing tacks, even of a flat out motor passage, must take into account:

1. the island night lees on both sides of the passage,

2. the drifting coastal front from a windward island, and

3. the vigor of even light trades undiminished by island lees.

The line of west drifting thunderstorms released by the setting sun from the heat of a large island's leeward coast sometimes dissipates to squalls or showers or nothing at all within 30 miles of the coast. Other times they grow more wicked and charge like bulls. The fiercest storm cells I've seen in my life come from their ranks in the Mona Passage. And I include the North Sea and the Med. If you have satellite pictures or long range radar, you may find alleys between them, if any exist. Mom and Pop and me make a veronica-like tacking maneuver north around these charging bulls as shown in the sketches below. Power boats and strong motorsailers can outflank them to the south.

Here you have an example of what can happen. In the first half of this story the pair of yachts that followed me out of harbor, against my urging, to shoot a flying window spent 60 hours getting hammered in the Mona while I drifted dreamily in the night lee of our destination island at the end of a 32 hour delightful sail. Why?

I heard them on the VHF. They woke me up, discussing the lovely sail they had while we both tacked down the nighttime coast. They didn't *play* the night lee, they *played in* the night lee. Meanwhile, I had a serious look at my progress. To control passage timing I needed to step it up a bit. First I took shallower tacks by running the engine at a little over idle. Later, I handed the jib and escalated to a motorsail to ensure I made the end of land by dawn, so I could tack off the coast by daylight. The cape effect can murder you once the sun gets up and heating.

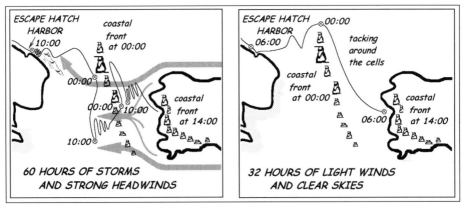

A Tale of Two Crossings

It didn't look like they'd make it. I called them and told them this. They said they understood, yet they still didn't budget their time. They got nowhere near my little escape harbor by daybreak, when according to their VHF chatter, every time they tacked out, a wedge of swift and raging water rounding the cape assaulted them, and they turned back into "smoother water". If you liken tacking in a sailboat to making zigzag stitches on the ocean, these guys did a narrowing button hole stitch inside the cape effect, getting nowhere fast. I lost them on the VHF because by then I basted a hem stitch toward the northeast in 12-14 knots just forward of the beam in 4 foot long seas. Their saga continued that night when storm cells from the collapsed coastal front drifted down on them from the island to windward. That kept them busy and pushed them back a fair bit. I saw the tops of the storms at sunset off my quarter, where my northeast tack had flanked them. Exhaustion began to worsen their case. Next they got served the roar of the trades around the corner of their destination island during the daytime.

Then came ... Never mind. You get the point.

PICKING WINDOWS

The criteria for good weather windows change for every harbor and each destination and, of course, every boat and crew. That said, I can name the conditions worse than which I won't go, as in the diagram showing Force Beaufort relative to the bow of the boat. Common sense must prevail as well. For instance, you can always choose to motor across in a dead flat calm should one come by. Duh.

Record the ever cyclic trade winds until you get a handle on the cycle. Then, remembering to weight average the different zone reports, take the first down-tick in the cycle that has sensible wind for your boat. Some absolutes do exist, however.

Like fish, large windows appear rarely, but little ones swarm in their multitudes. They get you here to there in short hops sooner than you can find a rare big one.

WINDOWS FOR INTER ISLAND CROSSINGS

Islands extend a nighttime umbra of calm around themselves which can reach as far as 30 miles to leeward and 20 to windward for the really large ones.. Knowing how this phenomenon works can permit you to make a quicker and easier passage between islands. At night, the land mass gives up the heat it accumulated during the day, while the sea, which has a much longer memory for heat, does not. Think of this as creating a "heat bubble" over the island which shimmers away from the direction of the gradient winds. More north in the component of the trades, and the bubble shimmers south and west, shrinking the north shore's night lee. More southerly component to the trades, and the bubble shimmers further off the north shore, providing sailors a larger lee there.

Additionally, the *katabatic* wind, the cooling mountain air that slides downhill after nightfall, lifts the easterly trade wind off the island's coast. The katabatic wind adds to a possible land breeze. The opposite of the day's seabreeze, the land, cooling faster than the sea, causes the night's land breeze.

All of these effects create the *nocturnal wind*, which blows lightly offshore. The island's heat loss and the nocturnal wind redirect the flow of the trade winds over and around the island like a stream flowing around a rock. The effect will start earlier (19:00) and last longer (12:00) on light wind days, and start later (00:00) and end earlier (07:00) on days with strong winds. Similarly, the effect will extend itself farther to sea on light wind days and stay inshore on hard wind days. The effect waxes greater after bright hot days and weaker after overcast days.

After hot, light wind days you may feel the warm breath of the land on your cheek, and smell the aroma of black earth, cows, and charcoal fires up to 30 miles at sea! You'll have an epiphany the first time you go through this.

Considering all the above factors, and observing the backing and veering of the winds from day to day, the shrewd Leisure Sailor waiting to lay a course for an island across the trades shall leave in less than 15 knots from the island to intersect this belt of flagging winds as far out to sea as possible. On the other hand, up to 15 knots onshore to the island makes a fine sail despite a more narrow lee from the land when you get there. This calls for some iterative course planning to handle various assumptions of the land effects. After an overcast day of moderate to fresh trades, stay in port. But after a bright hot day of light trades, consider giving it a shot.

The Equatorial Current can sometimes run as high as one and a half knots in the heart of the stream, but it usually does half to three quarters of a knot. It works for me to assume one half knot west northwest, anchors up to anchors down.

Fall Off for Pete's Sake!

> If on approaching land you find yourself bucking into it, slack sheets and bear off for the lee of your destination island. While the lee lasts you can tack back upwind in the comfort of the coast, or, when you lose the lee, bear off further for a downwind harbor. In other words, to get there faster, *go for comfort!*

If you had planned one tack to an island's lee, but for whatever reason you can't make landfall before daybreak, for Pete's sake fall off. You may beat up the boat and the crew, all the while paralleling the edge of the retreating sanctuary of the island's night lee. Fall off, and look for that lee. Even if you don't find it, you'll still have the option of slipping into some calm harbor to leeward. Then motorsail up the coast in what remains of the night's lee. The trip shall go faster and more comfortably than beating into seas that grow rougher as the sun warms up.

Use Backup Landfalls

I watch 3 out of 5 boats arriving from such passages add a 3-6 hour nightmare onto an otherwise pleasant 12-15 hour night passage. Some underestimate current or land effect. Most cruisers grossly underestimate the importance of getting in before the trades begin again in the morning. If you do, don't try to make up for your mistake by pounding into trade wind and seas. Fall off to backup landfalls and motor up in the night lee in a dead calm 5 or 6 a.m. in the morning. Some see high dark land, and they think they've come too close. Then they heave to or drift until dawn 10 miles out. They don't believe depth sounders, charts or GPS.

You can always tuck under a headland for the day if you get caught out when the trades start. Then motor up to your original destination harbor in the night lee of the next morning.

WINDOWS FOR COASTWISE CRUISING

WINDS

Hide behind the capes in the daytime and transit the bays at night, taking the wind that comes on a down-tick of a trade cycle. Go only when the forecast gradient wind blows less than 15 knots from behind the island during the day, less than 12 knots if blowing dead along the coast, and less than 10 knots if the wind has any onshore component. These winds lack the strength and direction to overcome the night lee of an island of any size. You shall have a flat calm motorsail close inshore before dawn

SWELLS

You must accept no onshore swell while coasting. Zilch. During the winter months this means you must stay aware of the lows and gales to the north. It may take them as much as three days to shed swell in your area. Ask the skippers of commercial boats from your harbor to tell you the swell direction when they come in.

WEATHER FEATURES

In mid-October through mid-December, and the spring months May through June (in the Northern Hemisphere), look for stationary troughs in the western ocean. They run up to four thousand miles long. Year round the approach of a weakening cold front can turn into stationary troughs as well. This phenomenon, shown below, opens a window for going to windward along a coast, because a wedge of relative calm gets created between the coast and some distance out toward the trough. Stationary gale systems may imbed in the troughs. They produce ferocious swells that, of course, say 'nogo'.

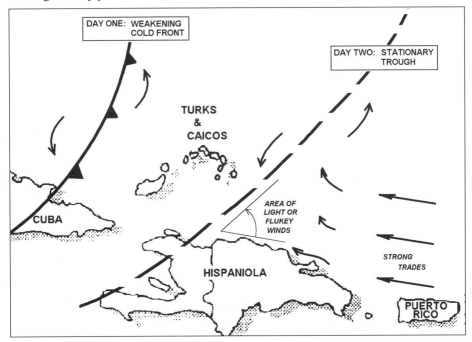

Stationary fronts or troughs developing north of Hispaniola can give protection from the trades for going east.

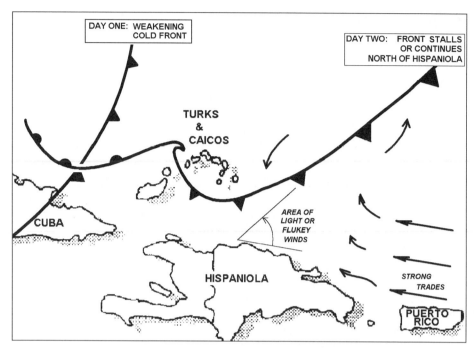

Occluding fronts also may provide a window as the belly of the otherwise strong front slides on by to the north.

PREPARATION

Some harbors leave your ground tackle a mud and growth encrusted mess. You shall have a cleanup job on the ground tackle that will leave you exhausted and in an ill mood for a bad start to sea. You'll need a night's sleep after your labors. The day before leaving, get anchors unfouled and clean the rodes. Lay to a single fresh hook, make ready for sea. Scrub prop and bottom for the motoring ahead. If you need to leave after dark, stage to a headland or reef anchorage near the sea, especially if you leave from a mangrove harbor where one finds good holding but yucky mud.

DEADLINES

Customize your departure to the weather window available. No fixed rule can calculate a fixed departure time for every window possible, but in many years of island hopping in the trades, most of my departures to windward have come either at the crack of dawn, at dusk or near midnight. Always have anchors down or get well free of land by 8-9 a.m. when the next day's trades shall hit.

Rugged seas can build during the day. If up, wait for them to subside. Also, the remnants of the day's coastal front, untethered from the land by the setting of the sun, may float down hill to their destruction ahead of you. If you leave before sundown because you want visibility in clearing the harbor, hang back a bit to miss these squalls.

When strong daytime coastal winds stay too long, probably because of an *island low* (see *Playing the Island Lees*) conditions may not lay down until some hours after sunset. Dawdle a few hours. You want to let the seas flatten out and the squalls to fall off the mountain and go out to sea.

Each departure plan may call for a new escape hatch harbor, for while you may change the departure time, the trades shall nonetheless wake up at the same old time.

In one sentence, using key words defined in the text of this book, and in its glossary, how do you coast in the trades?

> **"On a downtick of the trade cycles, and when harbor telltales favor, motorsail the night lees with a forecast gradient wind less than 15 knots behind the island and no onshore swell, staying close to shore to meet deadline waypoints in a window larger than needed".**

Obey each constraint and you shall have delightful trips as do I.

HURRICANES

One should definitely dread hurricanes (typhoons). Some caveats rule here as well, however. Consider the fellow who died of a heart attack the day his insurance company chased him across the magic barrier of 12° latitude by the first of June. Not only can fear of hurricanes incapacitate you when you most need your wits, it seems it can kill as well.

Fear of the systems which run up to a hurricane can cause you to linger just where and when you ought not. One season I took advantage of the weak circulation around a north bound tropical depression well to the east of us. The words *tropical depression* had alarmed some of the other boats into staying put. Upon the depression's passage, strong winds had returned and stayed for a while.

After my usual leisurely sail to Puerto Plata, I heard on the HAM net that one couple had got discouraged with their wait for weather and had turned back, that two more boats had given up waiting and had terrible beats to weather. Then they got cornered when the full trades came up for an extended visit.

One of them, Captain Nogo, thought a good weather window a breezy, sunshiny sailing day, like in the beer ads. Ugly looking days he stayed at anchor, regardless of wind strength and direction. Better you know when to go and when not to go. Know the promise as well as the danger inherent in tropical systems.

THE DANGEROUS SEMICIRCLE

Like jabberwocky's bandersnatch in Alice in Wonderland, beware the dangerous semicircle of a tropical storm, the half of the rotating system which has its winds moving the same direction as its forward speed. Typically, the winds in the dangerous semicircle can blow fifty percent higher than the winds in the other half of the storm. If encountering the storm at sea and caught in the dangerous half, the direction of the winds tend to sweep you into its path rather than knock you aside. For example, if you fell in the path of one of those street cleaning machines which has rotating brooms, which side of its rotation would you rather fall? The side which will squinch you forward and into its maw, or the side which will only maul you and spit you back out?

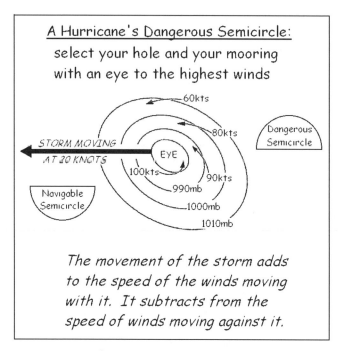

A Hurricane's Dangerous Semicircle:
select your hole and your mooring
with an eye to the highest winds

The movement of the storm adds
to the speed of the winds moving
with it. It subtracts from the
speed of winds moving against it.

The Dangerous Semicircle

Although you may watch the formation of the 'canes in the Atlantic and you may plot their probable paths two to three days ahead, they can still steer most erratically. If a storm heading west will pass your anchorage to the south, then you don't care if the anchorage lies open to the west, and you can put your nose in the mangroves of the eastern shore. If a 'cane passes north of you heading west, almost any good anchorage may do. The permutations become, of course, endless and you must choose from the holes you have available. All of these "What If?" hurricane games, like war games, must get played well in advance of a crisis. You must act instinctively when it becomes apparent an approaching hurricane may not veer. You won't have time to dither.

Draw a counterclockwise spiral on a sheet of clear plastic. Place it over a chart with your position on it. Now slide its center along various storm tracks by and through your position to see the wind rotations you shall have.

And watch those rotations of storm systems anywhere between the equator and 25° latitude for a full month either side of the June to November hurricane season (December to May in the southern latitudes).

A Winter Hurricane

We upped anchor on a bright, sunshiny morning and crept through the reef north of Providenciales in the Turks and Caicos islands. The 0600 National Weather Service's offshore report for the southwest North Atlantic had forecast a continued mild easterly flow of 15 to 20 knots with seas of 4 to 7 feet. Ideal for a fast downwind passage. Outlook for 4 days: little change. December 19th, a between seasons time of settled weather, and the weatherman seemed to cooperate with the first bluewater experience for both of my guests.

When we were in the offing I noticed a long swell coming around the end of North Caicos. Distant North Atlantic storms, I thought. As we cleared all land to the east of us, the swell became more pronounced and swung around to out of the east. I made a note to listen again to the offshore report at 1200.

We had a downwind cruise ahead with lots of anchoring and diving among the many islands in front of us. Only a nitwit could foul up the navigation with all those islands as guideposts. With that thought in mind I went below to double check my navigation.

I plotted our last land fix from Caicos. I redrew our inter island courses for the third time, taking into account current, leeway and sun-behind-you landfalls. The increasing easterly swell nagged me. I considered taking refuge at some anchorages I hadn't planned stopping at before. In hurricane season I always plot my courses to have hurricane holes within 6-12 hours sail downwind, enterable in daylight. But at Christmas time I had no need to throw the variable of hurricane holes into my calculations.

Well, nature makes mistakes as well as nitwit navigators like me, but she rarely gets abetted by the National Weather Service (NWS) as she had this time. At 1200 the NWS came back with a warning for hurricane Lilly. A December hurricane, literally out of a clear blue sky. Only a hiccup for Mother Nature, but a major surprise to small boats. They placed the small storm exactly 90 miles off my stern blowing me into the islands to the northwest.

By mid-afternoon, already reefed down and on the run before it, I surfed down ten footers with the log pegged at eight knots and me, between curses, wondering how I could have gotten there. Not only did we apparently lie in the dangerous semicircle of Lilly, but it drove us against the maze of the Bahamas Far Out Islands. It appeared we had squinch and maw in store for us.

Ahead of us were dangerous reefs and low islands which, if we could skirt all dangers, would bring us ultimately to Exuma Sound, a deathtrap in those conditions. Once in the Sound, you can't enter the cuts between the Exuma Cays in what they call a Rage, where a combination of wave over swell can catch you wrong and broach you onto the reef inside the cut when you try to make the turn. If storm conditions still prevailed by the time we got forced into Exuma Sound, we could not fight upwind to avoid the cays and reefs to leeward.

I looked for a way to slow our forward progress and wait for the storm to blow itself out. Towing warps? Long, shallow Zig-zags? We zig-zagged down breaking seas in continual darkness and horizontal rain. With all that zigging and zagging my oval of navigational uncertainty became enormous. I pondered over the chart. Just west and north of the oval I had drawn the chart showed soundings, fathom lines with which I could use the Chain of Soundings method to establish my position. To do so, however, I would have to approach lee reefs in 15-20 foot seas and a 45-55 knot wind. I rigged with only storm sail tight amidships. It cracked like a rifle shot each time I put the helm over to zig or zag.

I let each zig carry us a little farther north, and the next zag took us less far south. No soundings. I continued this game expecting to see rock and reef rear up out of the darkness under the bowsprit with each downhill surfing on the starboard tack. Afraid I might get caught in the bight between the East and West Plana Cays, I began lengthening the southward tacks.

Lilly, a small, tight, out of season hurricane bore no telltale feeder trails. She broke up early but spawned several days of gales throughout the area. The fact that the weather service reduced her in stature from a hurricane to a tropical storm, and then to a tropical depression, didn't help us.

The wind remained easterly at more than 40 knots. The seas continued to build. The sky remained black. About 10 a.m. on the second day the rain let up slightly, and some light briefly filtered through the black swirl above us, enough to spy a headland which, by process of elimination on the chart, I could identify as Northeast Point on Acklins Island. My oval of navigational uncertainty by this time included the entire southwest North Atlantic. The gates of Hell itself would have looked good, for they would have pointed toward Heaven.

I placed a triumphant fix on my chart by gouging a hole in it. It became too soggy to show pencil marks. I still don't know if we passed the Plana Cays and the surrounding reefs on the west or the east. Three months later I had a Satnav on board.

With a good fix and gradually increasing visibility, I hoisted a triple-reefed main and bulleted off to Bird Rock light where we could round up in the lee of Crooked Island for rest and recuperation at Pittstown Landing. Our rest, and the fact that the winds had gone down to only 25 knots, so cheered us the next morning that we struck off for Clarence Town, across the Crooked Island Passage, for a safe respite from possible backing of the winds later.

Mom Nature hadn't laid down enough law, though. She raised the ante in the Passage back to 35 knots and promised to raise again. Clarence Town nearly has more churches than people. Due to a long and complex history of ecclesiastic competition. But, thank God for the arrogance of his shepherds, Clarence Town makes the easiest landfall in the otherwise homogenous Bahama islandscape. When we raised the steeples of Clarence Town's warring churches it blew 35 knots with seas 12 to 15 feet, and rearing rogues of 15 to 20. The sun came in and out behind torn and scudding black fractocumulus.

The entrance normally goes straight forward, but the suddenly shoaling bottom causes tumultuous overfalls in the conditions we had. A series of reefs and islets extending across the wind defines the entrance. Brilliantly white, sunlit reefs break in a rage which, while actually 1000 yards more distant, tend to merge with the port-hand reefs until you get quite near. If approaching this entrance for the first time at 9 knots, and in such wild seas, I would have borne off. My many previous entrances notwithstanding, I had all I could do not to broach within those 1000 yards while trying to make a coordinated jibe to port. But finally, with a hard turn to port we skidded into tranquil waters and to the instant release of safety. We had more reason then ever to celebrate Christmas Eve that night.

PREDICTING STORMS

STRENGTH AND DIRECTION

If caught out without radio reception, or you just plain want to check on the old weather service, you may consider playing with the following rules to guess at the bearing, strength, direction and arrival time of a storm or hurricane. Look for the following:

- a long swell, mean period of 2 to 5 per minute (normal 10-15 per minute)
- a clockwise change in swell direction, the storm passes you from left to right
- an anti-clockwise change in swell direction, it shall pass you right to left
- swells travel from 2 to 3 times faster than the storm travels
- to find the velocity of the swell in knots, take 60% of the ratio of the crest-to-crest length of the swell, in feet, to the swell's period expressed in seconds:

$$\frac{0.6 \times \text{Length}}{\text{Period}}$$

- swell height reduces by one third for every L miles traveled, where L stands for the crest to crest length of the swell in feet, or:

    observed height = 67% of the height L miles away.
- to find the center of the storm add 115° to the present wind direction.

Neat Stuff, right? Now what do you do if you believed the drunks at the bar and actually went to sea to ride out a hurricane? Besides slit your throat, I mean. Well, you should handle direction changes in the sustained wind as follows:

- If the wind veers you stand in the dangerous semicircle:
    you should put the wind on the starboard bow
- If the wind backs you stand in the navigable semicircle:
    you should put the wind on the starboard quarter
- If a steady but increasing wind, you stand in the path:
    you should put the wind aft of the starboard quarter and pass out prayer books

STORM PATH

You can make a fairly accurate guess as to storm path knowing its present bearing, its bearing at the time it created the observed swell and the velocity of the swell.

For example, at 1200 you observe a swell from the south and you estimate the swell as 200 yards long at 4 per minute. (200 yards = 600 feet.) This means a swell velocity of

$$0.6 \times 600 \div 15 = 24 \text{ knots}.$$

Therefore, the storm moves about 10 knots, or one half to one third as fast as the swell. If you also observe an east wind while the swell came from the south, then you know the storm lies along a bearing of 90° + 115°, or 205° from your position.

69

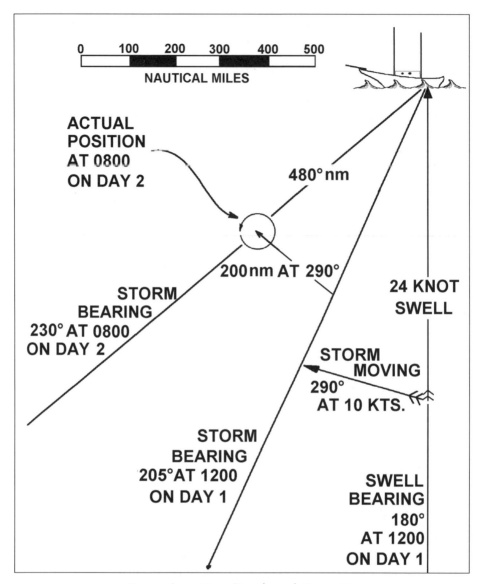

Storm Location, Track and Severity

Lay off a swell vector of 24 knots with its head on your present position. Lay off the storm's bearing of 205°. Make a storm track vector of 10 knots with its head on a line of the storm's bearing. "Slide" the storm track vector's head on the storm's bearing until you can connect the tail with the tail of the swell vector. Adjust vector and bearing until you get a fit. You now have a guess at the current heading of the storm, and you have an idea as to its bearing and velocity at 1200. In the example, the swell moves 360° at 24 knots. Therefore, the storm, which moves at 10 knots, must move in a direction of 290°.

STORM SEVERITY

What can you guess about the storm's intensity? Let's say the swell you observe has a mean height of about 10 feet. Since the swell has a 600 foot length, you know that 600 nautical miles down the swell's bearing the swell had reached 15 feet, or half again higher than now, having lost one third of its height enroute. If, indeed, the swell traveled that far.

You can estimate the force of the storm by projecting the swell height back on its path. You interpolate the original swell height at various distances off for the storm, then look at the Beaufort Scale to arrive at various storm forces for each assumed distance off.

For instance, if you assume the tails of the swell and storm vectors connect at a point 400 miles away then the original size of the swells, roughly speaking, would have to have got higher than their current height by 4 sixths of the 600 mile loss of 5 feet.

Or, $10 + (15 \over 10) \times (400 \div 600) = 13.3$ feet.

You will see the storm would have to have had a sustained strength of Force 7, and that would have occurred 400 miles ÷ 24 knots, or 17 hours ago. By which time, if it had intended to cross your position, it anyway would have overrun you, which might moot these mathematics, but you would have lost the fun of calculating it all.

LOCATING THE CENTER

Reckon the actual location of the storm through combining the results of two observations. Let's say that next day at 0800, 20 hours after the first observation, you see that the swell now comes from somewhere between 200° and 210° and the wind has veered two points (22.5°) to between 110° and 115° . This makes the storm's present bearing 115° + 115°, or 230°.

Since you think the storm traveled 290° at 10 knots you also know it covered 200 nautical miles during those 20 hours (distance = velocity × time). Only one spot on your chart exists where your dividers, spaced on the scale to 200 miles and set along a 290 degree line, will rest its points on the 205 and 230 degree lines radiating from your position. One point where the storm now lies, at 230°, and the other at where the storm lay 20 hours ago, at 205°. You now know the storm lies roughly 480 miles to the southwest traveling at 10 knots toward the west northwest and blowing Force 7 because it produces 10 + 5 × 480 ÷ 600, or 14 foot waves.

Whatever Force Beaufort you estimate, remember that gusts in a severe storm can blow 30% to 50% higher than the sustained winds. That means that even a baby 'cane (64 knots) can have gusts up to 96 knots.

If all the above discussion ruins your complacency, good! You shouldn't have any!

WHAT TO WATCH FOR

Squall lines and cumulonimbus may sweep your area. These and their high altitude cirrocumulus forerunners called feeder bands, sometimes run hundreds of miles in length, spiraling into the storm's center. If you lie directly in the storm's path, you won't mistake it's approach. The *bar* heralds the onslaught of the center of a major storm, or hurricane. It shows as a long, low, intensely black area topped by dark and chaotic cumulonimbus and with torn patches of black stratocumulus scudding in front. Prepare for the wind to gradually double in strength. If in the calm of the eye, prepare for the winds to strike from the opposite direction with sudden maximum force within half an hour. The eye *wall* shows up frighteningly apparent in its approach.

USING HURRICANE HOLES

Land must lock a hurricane hole close enough to run lines to shore against dangerous wind directions. The hole must offer unrestricted entrance at all times and tides. Unless in a bay or estuary likely to empty on the wind, look for depth a few feet under the keel at low tide. Storm surge will raise your boat, not lower it. Look for shallows and island shelving to weather of the hole in order to reduce storm surge. If in the path of the storm's right quadrant and holed up near deep ocean you may suffer the storm's full open ocean surge. Unless the mangroves grow extraordinarily high around you, your boat may rise fully exposed above reef and mangrove.

THE BEST HOLES

The perfect hole does not exist. Nowhere gives you 100% safety, but you can get close. The boat wants good holding and soft shores to wash up on. Mangroves make the softest shores. They grip the ground with myriad springy roots. The brittle dead wood snaps and breaks easily, but alive, it bends like a palm. A tight bark covers the hard wood like an easily broken skin. A thick mucous layer lies underneath. Strike the tree and it first bends, then its skin breaks. The mucous slides the striking object upward where smaller and more plentiful branches continue the same action. An impinging boat slides up the mangroves harmlessly as onto a Teflon bedspring causing no harm to the trees. Absent overwhelming storm surge, the boat slides back when wind and water abate. Sunshine melts the mangrove stains on the boat's topsides and quickly heals the mangrove's skin.

Near yachting resorts charter boats and boats with no skippers aboard plug up the harbors during a threat, making the crunch of boats around extremely dangerous.

You should seek deep mangroved rivers and bayous, far from charter fleets and megamarinas. Better still if you have surrounding land masses and mountains which defeat the winds, even with a direct hit; impenetrable mangrove bays in which hurricanes crossing the island must lift over high mountains, causing it to disorganize and produce little destruction and much rain.

WHAT TO DO

Run! Run every time, and run early. Don't dither. Don't cavil at false alarms. Don't listen to the jerks with the jokes, the hardies with their parties. Run! Getting an early jump means forsaking commitments, not letting friends or job, if you have one, distract.

Never run from a 'cane at sea as the bar myths say, unless you can do 30 knots in heavy seas as carriers and destroyers do. Run to a hole, which you should already have scoped out. Stake your claim before the 36 hour Hurricane Watch, then begin to act slowly and deliberately in order to get your nose pressed into the ground all during the Hurricane Warning, the 24 hour period before storm landfall. Stay put until the warning lifts.

Always have your boat sea ready in hurricane season. Storms sometimes rise out of nowhere, practically skipping the tropical depression stage. Have a clear plan for a hole downwind within timely reach. If you decommission your engine for any reason, do so while tied off in a hole.

Rumors and grousing to the contrary, named storms, with rare exception, tend to follow the instructions of their forecasters. With each report, plot the storm's approach and tie in another line, leaving open the most options possible. Between reports, the work of stripping the boat will loosen the knot in your guts and ease the pain of waiting.

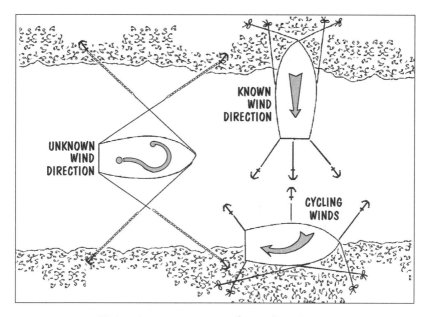

Tying into mangroves for a hurricane

STAY ON OR GET OFF?

No absolute answer exists. If you penetrate deeply into mangrove rivers for ultimate protection you can't leave the boat. To leave the boat you must use a hole within dinghy reach of a secure civilization, but not surrounded by drooling looters. If you can make the boat safe, then you can safely stay with it, can't you? But have you made it safe?

PLAYING THE ISLAND LEES
Using Island Effects to Better Your Rhumbline Time

Modern navigation often has its moments. Consider my weekend wine run from Normandy to southern England. I would bring mercy packs of wine and baguettes to my friends suffering in England, and I returned with Portuguese Madeira, Port and Sherry, of which the English have the best.

It made a good 11 hour sail in a 15 knot reaching wind dead across the English Channel. With a 6 knot peak tide running directly up and down the channel, the true wind varied from 9 to 21 knots. Since the trip took exactly a full tidal period, I trimmed straight for Newhaven, sliding sidewise 12 miles up the axis of the Channel, then 12 miles back down again, the tide delivering me exactly to the entrance bar, and I would zip across in best time.

GPS enables today's navigator to follow the dotted line straight across the Channel. Yet following the rhumbline shall ensure you that the boat puts 24 more miles under the keel, that you motor a lot and that the trip takes 6 to 8 hours longer. That's not all. You arrive at the wrong tide, can't cross the bar, you must lay off, and you get caught in a night squall as the katabatic wind floats the day's coastal front out to sea. English friends have long ago gone to bed, and the bread gets wet. All brought to you by the electronic miracle of GPS navigation.

In my home ports along the French coast, where tides ranged from 28 to 34 feet, I learned to observe the effects land has on sea and wind, as well as what tide does to rhumblines. By my fourth decade of trade wind sailing that knowledge became instinct.

New to the trade wind belt, most yachties can't shuck themselves of the idea that the wind will eventually back or haul around to get them where they want to go. Well it won't. For that reason they call it a trade wind. If you choose to bring your boat through the islands, you must use island sailing tactics. To do open sea sailing seek latitudes without islands.

All good things come with a price. If you sail the islands you must learn to play the island lees. You've got to understand and predict them. You must learn to modify official forecasts of *gradient* open sea conditions and make your own local island forecast.

Islands, reefs and banks, change the trade winds and currents passing through, over and around them. Playing these effects in series, a sailor can make safe, comfortable and pleasant progress against normally impenetrable trade winds and seas. After decades observing and using these effects under different forecast conditions. I can assure you that you can predict these effects. If, after careful study of this exposition of island effects, you still can't, I suggest you sell the boat and buy back the farm.

Good interpreters daily unravel the system of thermodynamic chaos called the Weather. They cut through its riddles using high-tech models, and they fairly accurately predict *gradient* conditions several days in advance.

Gradient forecasts assume a smooth billiard ball of an earth. But physical obstacles such as islands, atoll reefs and banks, and their thermal radiations, present upsets to these smooth earth forecasts. You have to assess the effects of a nearby headland, a rapidly shelving bottom or a strong but offset coastal front. Only you can observe these things at your position, not the forecasters.

Looking at the many effects, each of which inhibits you from obtaining an accurate local forecast, you may conclude that you just have another jumbled and chaotic puzzle. Not if you understand each of these effects, learn to predict them by your own observation and listen, with pencil in hand, to all the forecasters.

Given a settled weather forecast, you can overlay it with the effects discussed here to come up with your certain local forecast. With an unsettled, or rapidly changing forecast, forget going out anyway. Unsettled weather in the trades, which normally stay settled, should signal you to stay in port. A simple definition of *settled weather*? A weather report with the same data for each of the *today*, *tonight* and *tomorrow* sections.

UNDERSTANDING WIND

Rhumbline sailing the GPS in the trades has caused hundreds of crews to hang it up and go home after just a few hundred miles. Inadequate answers to other questions cause turnabouts as well. Weather, motor mechanics, crew expectations and boat readiness. But navigation? Come on! Haven't they solved that problem? Even experienced cruisers deceive themselves that they have — with GPS!!.

Islands give the sailor shelter from the relentless dead ahead onslaught of trade seas and winds. They also radiate special effects which the skipper can use as pivots, or hinges while threading the islands. A to C to B might take less than just A to B.

Islands change conditions in many ways. Most of these effects operate diurnally in accordance with the sun's day. These shifts from the conditions forecast for the open sea may favor or disfavor the sailor. Even in the Bahamas or the Florida Keys, where the trade winds don't quite reign, sailing rhumblines and ignoring the effects of islands and banks on sea and wind shall for sure get you there slower. And with more wear on boat and crew. Among the hundreds of low lying, light colored islands, only a relative few exhibit strong resistance to open sea wind conditions. The various banks, on the other hand, often make prime examples of the effects of daytime heating.

I used to run charters in the Bahamas, dashing back to Hispaniola between guests because I had a house going up there. With little time to waste I learned to flit in and out of the island lees in combination with forecast wind shifts. Fleets of sailboats out of Georgetown would often punch directly into it from Rum Cay to Puerto Plata. I would leave at the same time as they did, but I'd already have lain at anchor several days in Puerto Plata to watch them, broken and bent, limping into port. In my case, I had already leisurely reprovisioned, and I stood ready to up anchor and sail back again when they came in.

Before looking at how islands alter the winds and waves that the weatherman expects, you must understand the wind and wave forecasts. For instance, all but inshore marine forecasts predict the average of the upper third of wave heights. Wind forecasts give the sustained gradient wind expected 33 meters above the surface in open sea. The predictions come from quite accurate models which take input from measurements of wind and wave and air pressure at fixed points. Most weather models describe the atmosphere in terms of isobars, or the set of points of identical air pressure at specific altitudes. I shall present the case for island effects from the beginning.

AIR PRESSURE

Scientific purists will tell you that minute collisions of the atmosphere's gas molecules cause us to feel pressure from the air we breathe, kind of like adding up the impacts of a gazillion teensy billiard balls in what they call Brownian motion. But you can think of air pressure as the weight of air molecules stacked vertically above the place at which you measure it — between

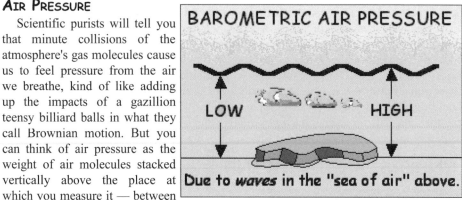

your ears. This model lets me think of myself walking around with a 400,000 foot wobbly stack of air on my head. Air, weighing only .07 pounds per cubic foot at sea level, when stacked high, presses down on you with 14.7 pounds per square inch.

Take a look at the island in the figure. As you move around on the ground, the weight of air over your head goes up and down as fewer or more molecules appear above you. The upper reaches of the atmosphere churns with molecules at the end of the collision chain. Some punch back into the mess below after a precipitous rise, others actually escape into space. The earth's atmosphere acts like a colossal sea. We really crawl around on the seabed of an airy ocean. Way up there on its surface it has waves and troughs just like the real ocean, and they stack more or less air molecules over your ears, making the weight you feel, or the pressure, lighter or heavier.

ISOBARS

If you could look at any arbitrary pressure surface above the island, say 200 millibars, it would clearly look like the surface of the sea does from your boat, but in titanic scale. Weather scientists navigate these mountains and valleys, hills, cliffs and inclines of our sea of air the same way Girl and Boy Scouts, orienteering enthusiasts, army generals and surveyors do the dry

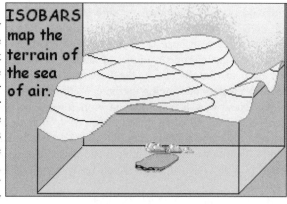

land. They use terrain maps. Instead of lines of equal altitude in feet, they use lines of equal pressure. In the diagram, the island lies under a dome of air with a long, tapering ridge leading away from a steep cliff face. Next to this ridge and across a valley lies a round dome of air almost as high. Nowadays they call the valleys troughs, in recognition of the fluid nature of the atmosphere. Until the 1950's, weathermen still used the word *valley*. Ridge has remained in use, however. I hope you didn't expect consistency from weather scientists. They call bowl shaped valleys low pressure centers, and bowl shaped mountains they call highs, of course. Now how does this help me understand wind?

WIND

A thermodynamics professor argues that wind comes from temperature differences between large masses of air as the more energetic hot mass tries to Brownian-bash its way into the cooler one. Or the heavier cool mass slides under the lighter warm one. It all starts with the sun, of course. Don't get spellbound with chicken-and-egg arguments. You need to know what the weatherman means by wind because, as

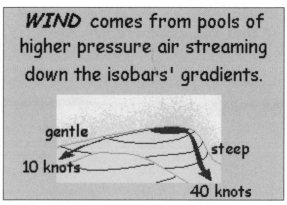

WIND comes from pools of higher pressure air streaming down the isobars' gradients.

gentle
steep
10 knots
40 knots

goofy as it may sound, you must use his definition in order to know how his forecast gets affected by your island.

The weather guy thinks those waves and troughs he describes with isobars really act as a fluid. If air molecules heap up too high in one place, they start to slide downhill to another, lower place, just like water, albeit on a much grander scale. This avalanche of air molecules starts the wind. If the hill comes with a steep grade, then the molecules really whiz on down. If the hill makes a gentle grade, then they sort of stroll their way down. As a military strategist might view the battle on a terrain map, so the weatherman watches the atmosphere's troop movements on the isobar charts. Air masses stream fast across tightly spaced isobars which show steep grades, and slow across the widely spaced ones.

Not surprisingly, the slopes depicted by isobars get called gradients, and the wind that slides down them has the moniker *gradient wind*.

GRADIENT WIND

The weather service gives the forecasts in gradient wind near the surface of the open sea. When discussing forecasts for any but local areas, you should use the gradient wind as the frame of reference. If you don't, the discussion falls into the apples and oranges class and no one knows what anyone means.

We use the word *gradient* to describe the wind whooping down

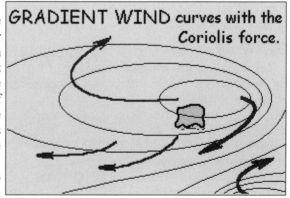

GRADIENT WIND curves with the Coriolis force.

the ridges and high pressure zones of the atmosphere, always headed toward the nearest lower pressure zone, like that of a wave, a trough or a low pressure center. Gradient wind turns always to the right in the northern hemisphere, due to the Coriolis Force, an incredibly small force around the neighborhood, but incredibly large when applied across the large distances that the wind has to blow (or *fall*). Because of Coriolis, wind wants to spiral clockwise off its mountains and counterclockwise into its valleys, though always veering to the right.

CORIOLIS EFFECT: air moving anywhere but east meets faster/slower streams and appears to turn right.

900 knots   600 knots   300 knots   0°

30°

North Pole   60°

Unless something gets in its way, gradient wind strikes your boat as forecast. But it rarely does except at night and many miles from nowhere. Why it doesn't make it to you unchanged, only the sailor at the island can know. The weatherman tells you what wind shall get shipped to you, not how it looks when it gets delivered and unwrapped.

NIGHT WIND AT SEA

Most cruisers I meet prejudice their navigation with the presumption that the night wind blows softer than the day wind. Not so. Night wind, with only friction of the sea surface to slow it down, has the nearest to max gradient conditions. Lighter gradient winds, 5 to 15 knots, can curve as much as 10° to 15° more toward lower pressure as they brush the surface. Stronger winds bend much less. The sailor

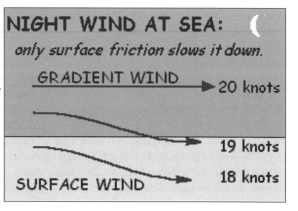

NIGHT WIND AT SEA: (

only surface friction slows it down.

GRADIENT WIND ➤ 20 knots

19 knots

18 knots

SURFACE WIND

below 33 meters of altitude may feel a light night wind which varies from the weatherman's forecast as much as a compass point. Sailors of a large boat pinching a light wind at night can get fooled by masthead instruments which deviate significantly from what strikes their noses much lower down.

DAY WIND AT SEA

The day's wind gets complex as the day wears on. As the surface of the sea accumulates heat from the sun, it gives back progressively more of it to the air it touches. This convective transfer of heat to the lower layers of the atmosphere causes a vertical heat gradient , and when pieces of air of different temperatures mix, then, as with humans of different temperament, a bit of jostling goes

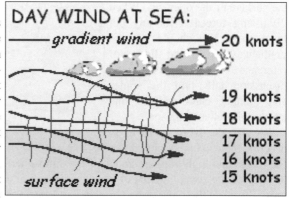

DAY WIND AT SEA:

gradient wind ➤ 20 knots

19 knots

18 knots

17 knots

16 knots

15 knots

surface wind

on. This turbulence causes the otherwise orderly troops of the gradient wind to stumble. In the ensuing riot the wind trades in some of its energy to produce water vapor, or clouds. All this energy expended to make clouds, the wind has to get slower.

SEABREEZE

Daytime heating of the land creates the seabreeze in a fashion similar to the making of the daytime sea surface wind. The sun heats the land. The land heats the air above it. The warmed air rises and gets displaced by cooler, heavier air from the sea. A circulation begins which can create wind of up to 20 knots with effects distinguishable as far inland as 10 miles and as far at sea as 20 miles,

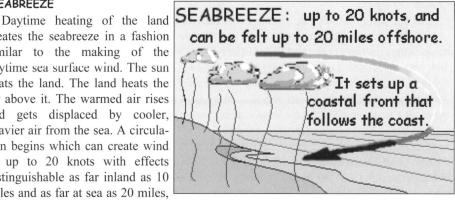

SEABREEZE: up to 20 knots, and can be felt up to 20 miles offshore. It sets up a coastal front that follows the coast.

depending on the terrain. In the tropics, seabreezes run year around, but they blow strongest in the spring and summer.

The seabreeze in the islands of the trades makes up the prime diurnal effect with which the sailor must contend. Seabreeze can reinforce a light trade wind. It can even outright cancel it. Even a strong trade of 25 knots, gusting to 30, can get significantly bent by seabreeze. A forecast breeze of 10 to 15 knots along the coast can become as much as 25 to 30 knots onto the coast by 2 p.m.. Nevertheless, I often see sailors rushing to the harbor entrance to look out at the sea in mid afternoon to correct the weatherman's forecast. They take the seabreeze for gradient wind and retire to the bar. Can't go tonight. Nor the next, nor the next. Some never catch on. They just follow their buddies out.

Clouds created by seabreeze draw an outline of the coast in the sky (a *coastal front*). As you look for an island think as an old time general had to when he lost sight of his troops in the confusion of battle. Where did he find them? Under all those clouds of dust.

NOCTURNAL WIND

The nocturnal wind begins after sundown and dies before dawn, reaching its strongest between midnight and 2 a.m. It asserts itself by combining land breeze and katabatic wind. Land breeze reverses sea breeze. It occurs at night with a much milder circulation than its daytime sister. Since sea holds the heat it absorbed during the day better than land, which quite quickly gives it up, the land becomes cooler than the sea

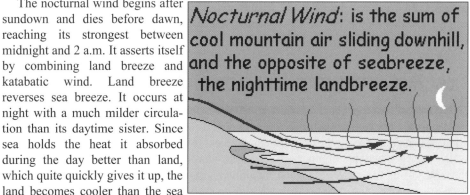

Nocturnal Wind: is the sum of cool mountain air sliding downhill, and the opposite of seabreeze, the nighttime landbreeze.

at some point. A nighttime circulation starts from the land and feeds updrafts over the warmer water. On high islands the land breeze gets an assist from the *katabatic*, a wind that flows down slope, bringing cooler upper level air which, heavier than its coastal cousins, will slide downhill.

TRADE WINDS

Gradient winds which run permanently like rivers over the earth got dubbed trade winds by the traders that depended upon them. In the trade wind belts daytime heating of the sea forms uniform ranks and files of fluffy cumulus clouds at altitudes up to 2000 feet. High level flyers see them as looking like a broad river of neatly crisscrossed city streets.

Trade winds flow as do rivers, from high pressure areas of the Tropics to the relatively low pressure areas of equatorial regions, rarely getting above 22° latitude on the western shores of the oceans. Northeast Trades bend with the Equatorial Currents, the northern ocean highs and, of course, Coriolis. Easterly by the time they pour over the Lesser Antilles into the Caribbean, the North Atlantic trades continuously swing between poles of northeast and east southeast at 15 to 25 knots in the winter, and between east northeast and southeast at 10 to 20 in the summer. Wind blowing any direction not within those limits during those seasons has bent from island effects or significant weather features in

its way, such as a tropical wave, or the rare cold front or warm front. Pacific trade winds run on average about 5 knots less than Atlantic trades do.

Islands in the stream of the trades make them appear stronger along the coasts in the daytime and weaker, even nonexistent, at night. Growing up near the beach in south Florida, I had nothing but mosquito screens between me and the wind as it soughed through the 60 foot casuarina trees above my little porch. I thought it as natural as sunrise and sunset that the night lee of the land would kill the strong sea breezes and reverse them with a 10 knot land breeze. Finding these effects and more in the islands of the trades came as no surprise. Yet most yachties I meet must hail from inland cities. After several years cruising the islands they still haven't noticed all these different breaks from wind and sea that the islands give them to employ toward comfort and safety on their passages. Let's count them.

ISLAND EFFECTS ON WIND

Islands present themselves as obstacles to the prevailing wind, whether trade winds or transient gradient winds, which sweep otherwise unhindered across the wastes of the sea. Given the prevailing wind conditions from the weather forecast, the sailor must take into account a number of often conflicting effects, mostly diurnal, with which the islands change the gradient wind. Any course plan based solely on the prevailing background conditions shall go wrong within up to 30 miles of a substantial island. The best course planning tries to benefit from these effects, not just mitigate them.

CAPE EFFECT

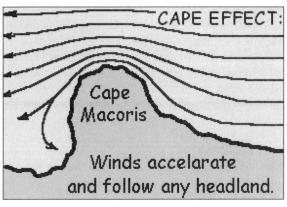

Any bay, river or lake sailor can tell you how to take advantage of wind off a point or a headland during a race. As you round the headland, the breeze always seems to come directly from the point until you get well clear of it. But sailors often forget everything they learned dinghy racing when they get into the trade winds. The sailor who rounds a headland by keeping parallel to the shore finds the wind on the nose all the way around despite nearly 90° of course changes during the beat. The mountainous capes of some islands act as the camber of an airfoil, squeezing the wind blowing by them. The same volume of air passing a smaller space must go faster, or the air behind would stack up clear back to the other side of the ocean. This occurs even in light night conditions. Don't despair, the real wind blows less than what you see at the capes themselves.

CHANNEL EFFECT

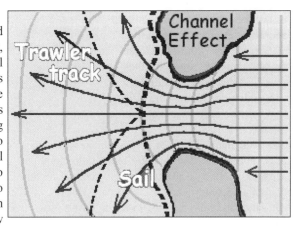

When plowing to windward through a cut in a chain of keys, or transiting a broad channel between high mountainous islands, both the wind and the sea squeezes between the ends of the two islands. The resulting effect can stymie the sailor who hadn't snuck up to the channel prepared to use the squeeze to advantage. Trawlers will have to wander a bit more offshore in order to maintain a good bow angle on the seas throughout the crossing. Otherwise they can get caught in horrendous rolls. See the two tracks in the diagram above.

The sea's parallel waves broadcast in concentric patterns on the lee side of the channel. The channel effect has a cousin in the optics business known as diffraction. In fact, a chain of islands makes up a diffraction grating, whose wave interference patterns you can see in the swell a long way off. Once I played Polynesian Navigator by ignoring my instruments and calculating my landfall by the swell patterns. Since sea and wind states gradually altered as I closed the islands, I turned off the pilot and trimmed sail and rudder to follow the pattern. The diffracted wave train brought me right to my destination island without touching a sheet for 100 miles. Once again, I found that trimming ship for *comfort*, not rhumbline, also made for a faster trip. But more on sea changes later. Let's stick with the wind effects for now.

COASTAL FRONTS

Turbulence of the seabreeze fluffs up cottony balls of cumulus clouds which mark the beach below them where the cold sea air pushes in. These mini cold fronts map the island's shoreline. Depending on the colors and textures of the land below, they can show you a mirror image chart of the coast before you see the coast itself. The island's colors and the water behind it often reflect in the lower surface of these clouds, particularly where the islands have fairly uniform colors and textures. Coastal fronts normally get pushed somewhat over the land by the trades. In the figure, the *south* coast's coastal front got set up by a southerly seabreeze onto the heated reefs and beaches. Nonetheless, a light northeast gradient wind shifts the line of convection over the sea.

A curious effect of the coastal cold front, it produces a mild convective circulation up and down its length, just like its big brothers. Perhaps not surprisingly then, the circulation runs counter clockwise as it does along a cold front. This results in the seabreeze always turning to the right as the day wears on. Its onshore vector gets rounded out by the front's circulation vector which grows as the sun's day proceeds.

The heat of the sun nails the coastal fronts in place over the coast. The seemingly tranquil pillows of coastal front cumulus in reality move inland at quite a clip, but they don't get far before evaporating. A stop action motion camera shows these clouds furiously making up on their seaward leading edges, while their trailing edges break up and drift off. When the sun sets, the front dissipates unless the island

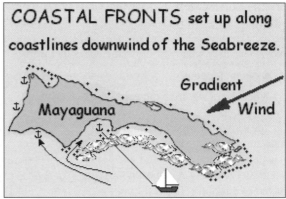

COASTAL FRONTS set up along coastlines downwind of the Seabreeze.

Mayaguana   Gradient Wind

supports the manufacture of really huge amounts of vapor. In that case they can build high enough during the day that the temperature gradient due to altitude causes an internal vertical circulation. That gives birth to cumulonimbus clouds which can live on awhile as evening thunder storms.

On large and high islands, look for strong gusts and showers coming from storm cells spawned by the large coastal fronts in the late afternoons. Don't make the mistake of forecasting sea conditions based on conditions in harbor beneath a strong coastal front, especially over an irregular coastline.

A REAL LIFE DRAMA

When I sailed toward the island of Mayaguana a while back, I encountered quite a VHF drama with two buddy boats, one in harbor behind the reef, the other in the offing, waiting to take the southern reef entrance. A light gradient wind blew from the east northeast, which shifted the southern coastal front to the south and west, where it obscured the entrance with rain. See the above figure. Bound for a short overnight on the west end of the island, I passed the bay's western entrance. I could look behind the coastal front into the clear waters of Abraham Bay where the sun shone on the buddy at anchor inside.

The sailboat inside assured the boat hove to on the other side of a curtain of rain, that he could see the "storm" on the radar, and that it should pass through in 20 minutes. Each

20 minutes he gave the same advisory to his weary friend. Both marveled at how the "storm" seemed to make up from the east as fast as it moved to the west. I finally got on the horn to tell them they sat on either side of an afternoon coastal front, and that the boat wanting to enter should go around it through the western entrance. They curtly informed me they had the "storm" on radar, that they "knew what they were about" because they had sailed the whole Caribbean, and they didn't feature going around to the west entrance. I hung up, But the VHF radio theater ran into late afternoon when the coastal front finally died, and while I soaked up some sun along with a gin and tonic.

BANK EFFECTS

Cruisers seldom understand the effects produced by shallow banks, sea mounts and even underwater ridges upon which a chain of keys may lie. These areas, more shallow than the surrounding sea, act like land. In other words, they store heat during the day and give it up almost as easily as land does during the night.

BANK EFFECT: daytime heating of shallow banks can also leave a shallow night lee to deflect the gradient wind.

Crooked & Acklins Island

ESE Gradient Wind

Atoll reefs may enclose vast banks of hundreds of square miles. Such banks stop moderate winds at night, but let it rip in the daytime. The 180 mile long sea mount between the Mona and the Anegada Passages holds the islands of Puerto Rico and the Virgins. On the east end of the big island of Puerto Rico, in the center of that long bank, light to moderate trade winds drop dead at night, even though you can look uninterruptedly east clear to Africa. Often you get a katabatic there as well.

COASTAL ACCELERATION

Gradient wind will try to follow a coastline upon hitting an island. Even a wind truly parallel to the coast will accelerate as it bunches up over land toward the lower elevation of the sea and, in the daytime, away from the warmer gradients over land. Let the gradient wind strike the coast at an oblique angle and the surface wind will accelerate even more as it bends to the coast, similar to what happens as it rounds the capes. You can't turn the wind without it accelerating someplace. An east southeast wind onto an east-west line of coast can accelerate up to 10 knots. Therefore, in a south coast harbor, a gradient daytime forecast of east to southeast 10 to 15 knots can deliver 20 to 25 knots.

The sun heats the land and the seabreeze sets up. By 2 p.m. the combined effect of coastal acceleration, coastal front circulation and seabreeze can get to 30 knots, ferocious compared to the wind forecast. Now add the acceleration on the capes ...

And I haven't yet told you about coastwise circulation you can add from island lows.

ISLAND LOWS

Mountainous islands produce their own weather systems scaled to the island's size. Trade winds lose their moisture on its slopes, a convection aggravated by daytime heating of the island's center. Late summer afternoons terrific heaps of cumulonimbus span the interior of the island creating a regional low pressure center. Check your satpics of an island from 8 a.m. to 8 p.m. and you shall see it form and die with the sun.

Significant winds can begin to circulate around island low pressure systems formed in this manner. A storm cell up to 40,000 feet may form. Talk to the captains of the big jet airliners that have to avoid them. Early evening, such towers drift westward with the trades along with the rest of the leeward coast's coastal front. Approaching such an island's lee coast can get exciting in late afternoon or early evening. On the other hand, some benefit might accrue depending on geography and where you want to go.

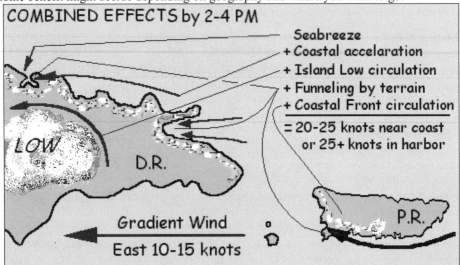

On the high cordillera in the north central part of Hispaniola a vast island low can develop. It can grow large enough to keep strong winds circulating around it and parallel to the coast long past sundown, long after the seabreeze dies and well after accelerated coastal trade winds should have abated on the night lee. In harbor it can appear daunting for yachts wanting to leave on the night lee. Before midnight, however, the low has dissipated, the coastal front diminishes and tumbles out to sea, and a belated night lee asserts itself under a star bright sky.

The mid afternoon squalls of small and high islands may unload their minor lows around lunch time, cooling the yachties in the lee harbors, but in the summer months they can stay until quite late,.

THE REED SWITCH EFFECT

Quite some time ago the Scientific American had a wonderful article by scientists who had built an air driven digital computer based on the reed switch. They used the same principle that made the reed in Glenn Miller's clarinet produce such beautiful music. Variations of wind intensity cause the reed to deflect from one side to the other, producing a non electric, air driven binary switch. With a series of tubes and reeds the scientists created a sophisticated binary digital computer operated by wind flow.

Real geographical instances of this physical phenomenon help sailors everywhere. Circulation around the *island low* in Puerto Rico's southwest corner shifts the coastal front north of the Lajas Valley, diminishing in turn the *cape effect* at Cabo Rojo.

The harbor of Boquerón, Puerto Rico provides a case. When the trades blow less than Force 6 out of the east, but not south of east, the wind forks at the keys and bayous around La Parguera. The north fork circulates around the island low up the Lajas Valley to spill out over the harbor of Boquerón. While doing this it shaves off the corner of the coastal front that builds with daytime heating. The coastal front wraps the island's western end, bypassing Boquerón. Under these conditions it rarely rains in Boquerón in the summer, but Puerto Real, just to the north gets horrendous tropical downpours.

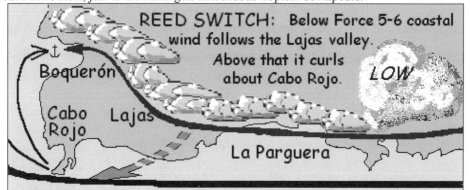

REED SWITCH: Below Force 5-6 coastal wind follows the Lajas valley. Above that it curls about Cabo Rojo. *LOW*

Boquerón

Cabo Rojo Lajas

La Parguera

Whether wind follows a coast or a draw can depend upon velocity.

Let the trades blow out of true east at Force 6 or more, however, and they stream right on by Cabo Rojo. Under these conditions the coastal front can build south to Lajas which will create a seabreeze from the west into the bay of Boquerón. The cape effect around Cabo Rojo further helps the seabreeze, and you've got 15 knots of a good fetch west wind into the anchorage setting the yachts to pitching.

At this point the yachties all shout "Hooray for a west wind!", let their genoas fly and head off for Cabo Rojo for an expected run down the south coast. If they actually try to round Cabo Rojo, some blow out their head sails in 25 or 30 knot *easterlies* before giving up the attempt. That evening, as the unchained coastal front moves out to sea, they sit back in Boquerón under a downpour, grousing about the weatherman.

ISLAND EFFECTS ON SEAS

Islands interfere with the sea's fluid dynamics as they do those of the atmosphere. You usually want to predict an island's effect on the sea in order to avoid their consequences. Salt water weighs about 850 times more than air. It should not surprise one that changing the movement of good hunks of water can have crushing results on a small boat.

When the sea vibrates in periodic vertical motion, we call that which we see waves. Waves actually reflect the minute movement of molecules of water which, acting like a jillion closely packed billiard balls, nudge each other to transfer energy put into the sea by an external event like surface wind. Or maybe by the eruption in 1883 of the volcano Krakatau, in the Samudra Straits between Java and Sumatra. When the nudging reaches the surface it goes around again to the bottom, since the air above doesn't nudge much, and the energy has to go somewhere. A wave, really a tall, oval vibration of water, hasn't much movement at bottom where great pressure gives great resistance, but a bunch at the top.

Whether from the launching of a boat, a thrown rock or the plop of a raindrop, the energy imparted to the water starts a vertical vibration of its molecules. Small energy inputs, like a child doing a cannonball off a yacht, create small vibrations that don't reach too deep nor propagate too far. A large one, like Krakatau, creates vibrations which go to the deepest bottoms. While its explosion got heard through the air in Africa, Krakatau's waves through the water created no more surface disturbance than a cannon balling child in the deeps of the Marianas Trench. However, when it reached shoaling waters it created surface waves 120 feet high. Its tsunamis, which inundated South American ports, swept some Pacific atolls with waves much higher than the islands themselves. Sounds like stuff you ought to know about if you sail through the islands.

A simplistic, yet nonetheless realistic look at island effects on the sea follows.

GROUNDSWELLS

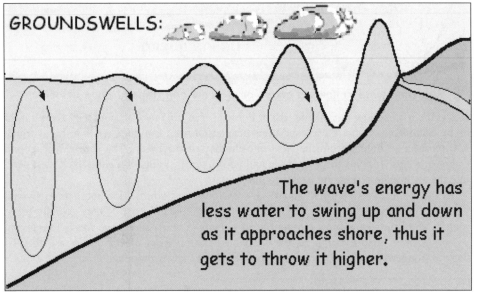

GROUNDSWELLS:

The wave's energy has less water to swing up and down as it approaches shore, thus it gets to throw it higher.

Your barcarole at sea can become your requiem near land.

Even the smallest vibration of a ripple or a wavelet, when moving into shallows shall heap the water up on the surface. Waves move great quantities of water in great depths, albeit each molecule of water gets moved only a tiny distance. When the wave enters shallow ground it has less water to move, but it still has most of the energy. The flatter trajectory of the oval oscillation now literally throws the water forward as well as up. Hundreds of tons of it in the space of your boat, whereas before, practically nothing.

SHOALS

Many cruisers don't recognize the shoals on the charts because they run several hundred feet deep and more, and that does not, in their experience, mean shoal. However, the water these shoals try to contain comes from the Equatorial Current. That means a lot of water and a lot of energy for the shoals to dissipate, and you don't want to take part in it. Pay attention to the fathom lines of your charts, even though they read in the hundreds. Stay clear of any area much more shallow than another if it lies downwind of sharp bottom gradients.

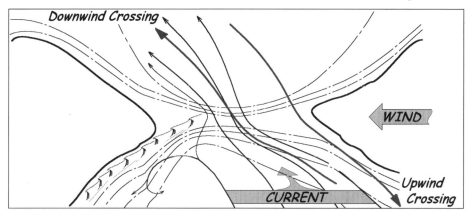

Learn to Predict Rough Seas and Stray Current from Fathom Lines

Often an undersea land bridge connects islands. Any current between the islands must climb this wall. Cross the passage so as to avoid the confused seas down current, and to get a lift from the current while it tries to slide along the contour of the bridge.

REFLECTION

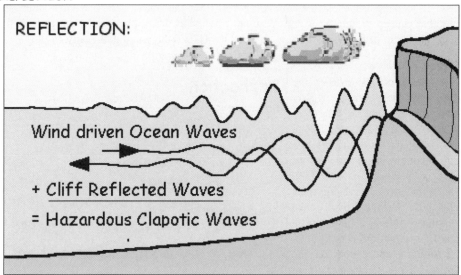

Confused waves, like those you see on an oscilloscope when you speak the word *spaghetti* into its audio input, come from waves reflecting off steep shores. The convexity of the island's shore as it lies athwart the onslaught of the seas, and the concavities of its seaward bays, cause the sea's waves to behave just as waves of light do when they hit convex and concave mirrors in the fun house. But no fun for the sailor caught in a drubbing from reflected waves.

Trench Effect

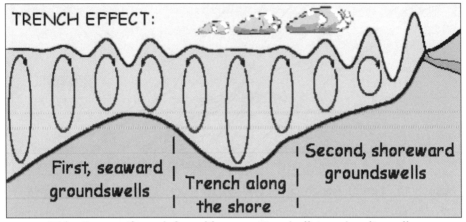

TRENCH EFFECT:

First, seaward | groundswells | Trench along | Second, shoreward | groundswells | the shore

Ride it smooth and free like a gutter ball in a bowling alley.

Many islands show on charts surrounded by elongated forms of closed fathom lines. They look like intracoastal waterways behind barrier islands sunken by the last ice age thaw. Ride these trenches like a bowling ball does the gutter. You'll have a safer and smoother ride in its quieter water. You can often find them, but you've got to look for them. Then you just slide over a few hundred yards, and the going gets really easy.

Refraction

If island passes *diffract* the seas and their coasts *reflect* them, do waves get *refracted*?

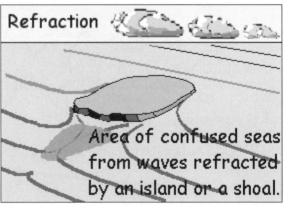

Refraction

Area of confused seas from waves refracted by an island or a shoal.

Yup. Like light through a lens, wave refraction occurs at a critical angle of incidence of wave onto shore (perhaps 37°). Above that angle, its energy gets reflected. Below, the wave continues forward, but in a modified direction. Friction of the shoaling shore acts on the wave, causing seaward parts of its train to stumble over the dragging shoreward parts, dissipating energy. These wave parts now travel at different speeds. Therefore the wave appears to turn, and it wraps the island.

Similarly, waves and current refract along the shore of island bays. In the *Bay Effect* diagram that follows a westbound sailor can get set onto the reefs east of Cape Macoris.

CURRENTS

United States Navy Lieutenant Matthew Fontaine Maury, the hydrographer who initiated the idea of sea lanes in his Sailing Directions in 1859, created a repository of data on world currents and winds which today you see in the American Pilot Charts and the British Routing Charts. This data, confirmed and refined for a century and a half, doesn't preclude Captain John Courageous of the

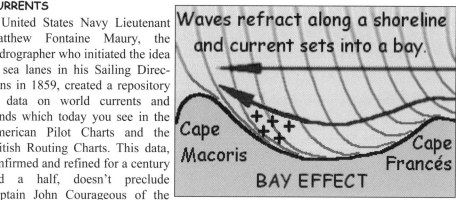

S/V Chicken Little from differencing his GPS from his speed log and announcing to the world the discovery of a new current.

One year a whole fleet of cruisers put me on the spot. They radioed me with insistent requests that I sponsor a notification to the U.S. Navy and NOAA that the Equatorial Current had reversed itself and flowed east. I put it all down to giddiness of overnighters approaching an island of the trades for the first time. They urged I act, feeling they had uncovered an incipient El Niño, and that the world must have warning. To no avail I listed the extensive variety of phenomena at play: speed logs, GPS microcode algorithms, standing hull waves playing on their impeller, tide, upwellings, eddies, hydraulic curlicues and hallucination. To end the embarrassment I asked they mail me data logs from each ship with exact times and instrument readings. I committed to forwarding the data to a disinterested Navy (after all, *ornithologists* brought El Niño to their attention).

Of course I heard no more from the cruisers. My point for course planning? If not on the Pilot Charts, it doesn't exist!

ISLAND LEES

Sailors benefit most from islands through the reduction of wind or wave by their lees. Using island lees from adjacent islands, or the cascade of diurnal effects from a chain of islands, one can navigate from the effects of one island to those of another's, much as astronauts might use the focus of the planets' gravitational force fields to swing around the solar system.

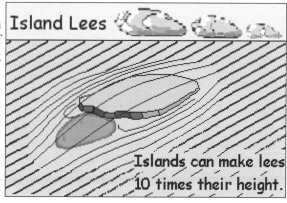

LEE OF THE WIND

The island shown doesn't have the height to trouble the wind much, nor breadth to block the seas. The seas shall meet on the lee side and some confusion shall result. But there shall exist a sweet spot up to 10 times the island's height somewhere to leeward where the seas remain regular, reduced by refraction, and wind shall favor your tack.

NIGHT LEES

AN OLD PLOY

Boats coasting against the wind hide behind headlands and capes during the day, then proceed close to shore at night, where the more moderate conditions of the night lee permit a sure progress against tranquilized trade winds and seas.

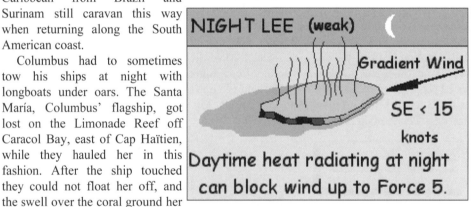

Sailors have used this tactic all over the world for longer than recorded history. Traders with the Caribbean from Brazil and Surinam still caravan this way when returning along the South American coast.

Columbus had to sometimes tow his ships at night with longboats under oars. The Santa María, Columbus' flagship, got lost on the Limonade Reef off Caracol Bay, east of Cap Haïtien, while they hauled her in this fashion. After the ship touched they could not float her off, and the swell over the coral ground her slowly to bits. Lucky you have an auxiliary engine. When the mate carps at pulling the sweeps, don't cavil at starting it.

The greatest benefit of all island effects, the night lee creates distinct calms which follow daytime heating of land, or banks (i.e., land under shallow water). Land cooling faster than nearby deep water creates a thermodynamic anomaly which lifts or deflects the trade winds.

A *nocturnal wind* blows from off the shore by combining the *land breeze* and the *katabatic wind*. This increases the shield against the trades. The bigger and higher the land mass, and the stronger the daytime heating, the more assertive the night lee. Usually the effect of the night lee collapses under assault by gradient winds at 15 knots or more. Along mountainous shores of large islands night lees can extend many miles. They block, lift and divert gradient winds up to 15 knots, and modify stronger winds.

A strong night lee shall result when trades become depressed, perhaps by colliding with weather features such as fronts or tropical waves, or by strong heating of the island

90

due to either topography, surface colorations or the seasonal declination of the sun, and even whether the atmosphere holds a dust cover. Rocket science? Not at all.

Forecasts available today by marine radio and satellite, have made gradient wind and its near term progressions known quantities. If the sailor studies them closely, he can know the rest simply by practicing good daily observation of local conditions.

EXAMPLE OF USING NIGHT LEES FROM BANKS

I got a three day leg up on a gang of boats waiting for weather at Rum Cay by using a trick I learned while sailing years before between Menorca and Mallorca. A strong stalling front just to the north of us kept everyone at bay. The forecasters agreed that the front had equal chances of moving forward again, or of stalling hard and dissipating in place. I knew that Crooked and Acklins Islands supported a good night lee in the conditions forecast for them 24 hours ahead. By sailing *away* from my rhumbline for the safe harbor at Clarence Town, Long Island, I would put myself in a position to use that lee the following night if the front stalled. If it continued to move, I had a safe harbor from which to wait for the winds to clock and weaken. I set sail for Long Island.

These same tactics would work as well for my trawler.

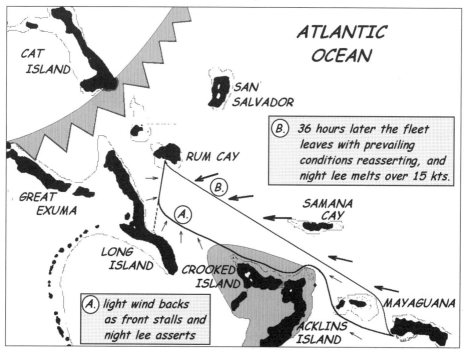

Anticipating a Night Lee

All night I watched the fireworks in the skies to the north of me, while downloading every forecast available every hour. The front did stall, and as the wind backed to its normal quarter, I tacked with it into the night lee of the Crooked-Acklins banks, skipping over to Mayaguana by morning. The gang behind me, if they chose to leave now, faced 90 grueling miles dead into the strong gradients that returned the next day. I took the longer route through the islands, but I beat their rhumbline route by three days. But more important than a faster trip, I made a more comfortable and safe trip.

TRADES STRATEGIES
Bluewater rules don't apply around islands and reefs.

I have spent half a lifetime seeking alternatives to beating my brains out into the seemingly ceaseless near gales and tumbling seas of trade wind waters.

As a mostly single-handed senior, living aboard below 20° latitude, I sought to take the thorns out of my travels by looking for the most comfortable and the safest passages.

In the tropics, where the trade winds blow, each season brings its own surprises: no year just like another, no day just like another. I learned to count on and use this constant variation in wind and wave to play tricks against the trades. With a 6½ foot draft, long-keeled ketch, and now my small trawler, I hoofed up and down the trade wind highways in any season at any direction, once I learned to give careful study to the weather — and to use patience in applying my methods.

These planning strategies of the Leisure Sailor, when inflexibly adhered to, create delightful cruises in the trade wind belt. Seemingly rules of elementary seamanship, which we all should know, all the disasters I have encountered while sailing in the trades have generated from the failure to obey any one of them.

WAIT FOR WEATHER

It always amazes me that retired cruisers, who, with nothing but time, and having piddled around in harbor for weeks, even months, suddenly break into hives if they can't go right now! Others insist on going "next Tuesday", or "on the 22nd". Year upon year, like the Tortoise and the Hare, I find myself passing them where they hole up with repairs, breathing hard.

These folks whom earlier I would watch go stir-crazy waiting for a break in the weather, give up their wait and go to sea because, as they say,

"It's rolly here."

I change to a less rolly anchorage.

Or they say, "it's best to take bad medicine all at once."

I refuse to take any bad medicine.

Seasoned salts say, "We've got a strong boat."

I've got a strong boat, but it has a weak me inside it.

The stoic downeaster usually says "We've seen worse!"

I remember all my worses all too well. I won't repeat them.

And everyone uses the "well, we sailed with a group and ..." excuse.

If you want good passages rather than good excuses, learn to interpret the weather forecasts, the sea conditions and the island effects. And, whether short or long hops, thoroughly understand the concept of weather windows.

THINK BEAUFORT

FB	knots wind	descriptive term	SEA CRITERIA	waves in feet
0	0	calm	sea like a mirror	0
1	1-3	light air	ripples, but no foam crests	$\frac{1}{4}$
2	4-6	light breeze	small wavelets with glassy crests	1
3	7-10	gentle breeze	crests begin to break, glassy foam	2-3
4	11-16	moderate breeze	fairly frequent white horses	4-5
5	17-21	fresh breeze	long waves, many white horses	6-8
6	22-27	strong breeze	extensive foam crests, some spray	9-13
7	28-33	near gale	sea heaps up, foam blown in streaks	13-19
8	34-40	gale	spindrift forms, clear foam streaks	18-25
9	41-47	strong gale	tumbling crests, dense foam streaks; spray may affect visibility	23-32
10	48-55	storm	long, overhanging crests; great patches of dense foam streaks; sea surface appears white; tumbling of sea heavy and shock like.	29-41
11	56-63	violent storm	sea completely covered with long white patches of foam; everywhere the edges of wave crests blown into froth; bad visibility.	37-52
12	64	hurricane	sea completely white with driving spray; visibility very seriously affected.	45

The Force Beaufort Wind scale

Work in Force Beaufort. It accustoms you to consider overall sea conditions including recent or pending changes.

The Beaufort Wind scale encompasses both wind and wave. The Beaufort ratings assume relatively stable conditions. For instance, you can't call a nice 10-15 knot breeze in the morning after three days of 25-30 knots a Beaufort Force Four. The wind driven waves of 3 to 5 feet roll over residual swells heaped to 8 to 10 feet!

In the winter months, the Caribbean trade winds blow between northeast by east and east-southeast at Force 4 to 6. In the summer, May through October, they run east-northeast to southeast by east at Force 3 to 5. If they forecast either a southeast or a north-east wind, look for a significant weather feature such as a tropical wave or cyclone in the summer, or a front in the winter, or an unusually strong high or low to weather of the zone. The trades hardly ever blow true northeast or southeast in the western ocean where the islands lie.

Swells from the 3000 mile fetch of the open ocean sweep through the islands. They get superimposed with swells from distant storms and, of course, waves from local wind and chop from currents. These all affect the boat's progress and make for considerably different sailing when compared with similar wind strengths at home. Cutters and spoon-bowed sloops may carve through these conditions better than clipper or schooner bows. Windward going can get extremely rough. Cutters may have their expected way cut by 20%, clippers by half. Downwind, true double-enders and squared off sterns can get tossed about quite a bit. Large rounded sterns and schooner fantails rise nicely with each sea due to their greater buoyancy, and the seas have less purchase with which to heave them sideways.

Here's a good Beaufort rule of thumb for all hull configurations in these waters, assuming settled conditions and no extraneous weather features in the forecast. Starting with a rhumb line dead to windward, add one Force Beaufort for each compass point working aft from the bow until reaching Force Six. For example, if you have a forecast for 48 hours of light airs with a few ripples on the sea, you may motor to windward. If it shall blow 17 to 21 knots aft of your beam, with a few white horses, you'll have a good sail, but not a good trawl. Trawlers need to head up or down sea for a comfortable and safe ride.

The jocks in their yellow slickers eating cold beans from cans go in Force 5 forward of the beam. The Leisure Sailor of the trades, whether power or sail, sails in swimsuit and eats pate from china (Corningware unbreakable?) plates.

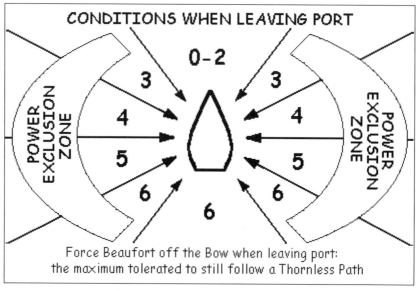

CONDITIONS WHEN LEAVING PORT

Force Beaufort off the Bow when leaving port:
the maximum tolerated to still follow a Thornless Path

Expressed in degrees (**D**) of the wind off the bow, the Force Beaufort (**FB**) you want should not exceed:

2 + D÷30, max. 6 FB, or, for the purist, **half the square root of D, max. 6 FB**.

Never start out in a Force 6-7, but if one develops on the quarter, ride it all you can. Unless you missed something major in the forecast, it won't grow stronger. Not out of cyclone season.

Finally, in the tropics, if you need a slicker and you can't sail in a bathing suit, you should not have left harbor.

PLAN YOUR ROUTE FLEXIBLY

This rule deals with the strategy for choosing anchorages while wending the islands of the trades under continuously cycling conditions. Its bottom principle: avoid the *idée fixée*, or what the French see as foolishly stubborn.

One acquaintance left a good sanctuary during the height of the cyclone season. In his mind, a yachting center two islands further on became some sort of terminus, or cusp, in his cruising plans. It became his "be all" and "end all" cruising experience. His *idée fixée* nearly did end it all for him. One of the strongest cyclones of the century wrecked him. Without detail fallback plans he dithered at the hurricane's approach. He arrived the last boat to shelter at a marginal, yet nonetheless jam-packed hurricane hole.

SAVE YOUR WINDWARD ADVANTAGE

Given a choice of routes between islands in the Northern Hemisphere, you should give weight to the northernmost to preserve any windward advantage. In order to maximize your possible weather windows you have to widen your angle on the wind. If the "collective eye" of the prevailing winds blows east to east-southeast, either you must come *over* it before sailing south-southeast, or you must get *under* it to sail northeast. Gain easting by sailing through the islands up north, before you enter the thick of trade wind and current, then spend your windward advantage by sailing south-southeast.

You play the island effects and the slight switches in the wind. If you want to make a *windward* rhumb line which you plot east-southeast, the true trade winds will never switch enough for you to lay it. So, when you choose your routes each day, have uppermost in your mind that you don't give up northing, just as you wouldn't give up easting.

I watched a 120 foot charter schooner, with English crew, leave on such a route. They chose 65 easy south southeast miles around the lee of a large island which lay just at the edge of the trades, rather than east northeast to preserve their windward advantage. Not realizing the megayacht's mistake a contingent of yachties followed. Cruising couples in their sixties with a 35 footer and a 25 hp engine, even a 50 foot ketch with 120 hp, cannot compete with a passel of temporary hires behind 1200 horses dragging the bottomless purse of some foundation. The flotsam of retiree cruisers with their jetsam of broken marriages and relationships often drift in the wake of these gin palaces. After all, didn't those big boat professionals know best? The answer?

No! They had never sailed the trades before either! After a day of easy lee sailing, they found themselves slogging directly into the eye of the trades and bucking into the mainstream of the Equatorial Current, which runs up to three knots some places.

The 120 footer began taking on water half way through the weather slog. In the onboard crisis a small fire developed which got quickly dowsed, but the atmosphere thickened with panic along with the smoke. Those yachties who had not already turned back, one with a broken boom and torn mainsail, gathered about the stricken vessel and off loaded crew. Mom and Pop slunk back to the safe lee of the nearest island with the so-called *professionals* onboard.

Just as in approaching the windward race mark, preserve every breath of your windward advantage while you trick the trades to windward.

THINK TWO MOVES AHEAD

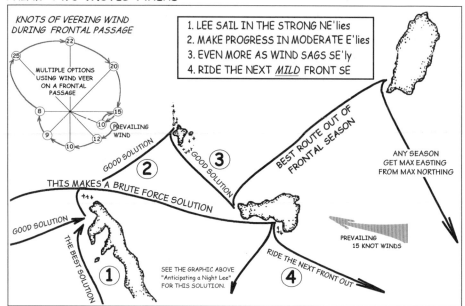

1. LEE SAIL IN THE STRONG NE'lies
2. MAKE PROGRESS IN MODERATE E'lies
3. EVEN MORE AS WIND SAGS SE'ly
4. RIDE THE NEXT *MILD* FRONT SE

Alternate routes may take longer in distance but overall less time and go easier on boat and crew.

When planning your next leg, consider not only a *staging anchorage* (see below) and multiple landfalls, but ensure you know what conditions shall prevail at each destination, and what steps you might have to take when you get there. Like moves in chess, you should thoroughly consider your maneuverability at your next position (and your next, and your next ...).

If the wind goes light to 12 knots but doesn't change to the direction you want, you may leave harbor anyway, exercising an alternate plan to go off on the other tack to a different anchorage, at a more stately pace than you had wished. Or you could motor flat-out to your original goal. Either choice shall alter your original plan. Landfall or arrival times have changed. Therefore other contingent conditions have changed: the angle of light for reading the water, the distance to the next comfortable harbor when your weather window closes, and so on.

In other words, plan flexible landfalls, even while enroute. And never, of course, ever set a schedule or a deadline. Don't hang up on a particular destination as though you had a pot of gold under only one particular rainbow.

PASSAGE ELAPSE TIMES

To estimate the time required to make a specific passage while using the island strategies in this book, you must add time underway to time spent waiting in various harbors for windows in the weather. When planning a cruise consider the time of year since winds shall vary depending upon season. Consider your mode of passage making. If a blow-boater, do you motor, or motorsail, at the slightest contretemps? Or do you follow the purist way and sail in whatever? If a stink-potter, do you blast into it or tack and wear with the seas?

I have had to whiz down islands to make business schedules associated with my ketch, *Jalan Jalan*, chartering in the north, building a house in the south, and refitting each year in South America. I island hopped down several times a season to see my girl and to work on the house between charters. Single handed and uninsured, I traveled as fast as feasible with the welfare of my boat and myself in mind. Many trips I made for pleasure, or just aimlessly wandering, which the expression *Jalan Jalan* means after all.

We tacked directly to windward only under Force 4, accepting a 3.5 knot average. Despite those that claim tacks of 35° to the real wind, C. A. Marchaj, in his definitive work, *Sailing Theory and Practice* (ISBN 0 229 64253 5), has laid this argument to rest by showing the mathematic impossibility of coming under 37.5°. With leeway and set, which the 35° crowd dismissively discounts, *Jalan* persisted in giving me a fat 50° on the passages. I consider that a 35 foot sloop with a 30 hp auxiliary and a retired couple aboard should do about the same. With 50° tacks at 5 knots, you shall put 14.4 miles under the keel for each 10 miles on a windward rhumbline. With minimum of half-knot Equatorial Current against you, make it 16.6 miles. To make 5 knots you've got to have a Force 4-5 with seas 4 to 7 feet. You will lose way with those seas. You shall lose about one degree of course for each Force Beaufort. So! A small boat with a cruising configuration should expect a factor of 1.75 keel miles to each rhumbline mile while tacking. Less than 2 knots over ground! Trawlers tacking into head seas of any height may not do much better.

Despite all this data many cruisers ask me to tell them exactly how long a particular leg will take their boat (with them at the helm, making their decisions). Well, you can calculate the speed you make under full motor, against 20 knots of wind, three quarters knots of contrary current and short 8 foot seas. To windward subtract thirty percent for leeway and optimism. Downwind subtract 10% for wearing in the seas.

If you find yourself trying to beat these times more often than not, although I wish you well in your cruising, you should closely examine your reasons for doing it. Cruising takes time. Each stop you make will require rest and recuperation, perhaps some touring or local cruising, and get-togethers with other cruisers. Novice cruisers try to make maximum mileage. Experienced crews go through all the smaller islands and count on diving lots and meeting lots of locals during their waits for the windows.

If you haven't partied out when a good weather window opens up, or your favorite serious children fly down to visit their wastrel parents fiddling their inheritance away in the tropics, and you miss the leading edge of the first window, then add more time on your total cruise. Take a new window and don't try to make up time by going when you shouldn't.

LANDFALL DETERMINES DEPARTURE

In amongst islands plan your departure to make landfall in favorable light, arriving with several hours of daylight left. The way south has many windward shore anchorages (i.e., entered to the east) where you will need the sun high and over your shoulder. A 3 p.m. landfall may dictate a 4 a.m. start. If you like to wake at 7 a.m. and have your Wheaties before addressing the world, and you don't want to break that custom, then sell the boat and move ashore. Almost every leg island cruising requires an early start, even a predawn start, in order to benefit from island effects that reduce headwinds, or to ensure a landfall in safe conditions.

Have a variety of departure plans ready for different breaks in the weather and for different landfalls. Prepare to cancel all your commitments and haul anchor at the first opening of a weather window meeting one of your plans. Similarly, never plan a last minute chore, such as one friend who wanted to buy cold milk when the store opened at 8 a.m. That bottle of milk caused him to miss an earlier departure when the situation changed. He tried to use the change in the weather despite a later start and got pinned down in the next island along. Two weeks later, while I dined in Puerto Plata, he had a window slam on his tail and suffered some delamination problems from all the pounding he took. He lay 350 miles behind. The lengths of the windows and the lengths of the legs just didn't go together for him. The morals to this story?

Plot several routes contingent on breaking weather, and

> *depart at the earliest time called for by your contingent routes so that you can make changes underway in response to changes in the weather.*

Every delay in departure creates a risk upon arrival. Reckon on 20% less speed to windward than you normally get. If you get more, great!

CONTINGENCY PLANNING

When planning your route, add in contingencies both for getting underway and for getting settled at your new anchorage. Most of us plan adequately when planning contingencies along the route. You easily recognize the contingency of over-the-shoulder light on landfall. Many other contingencies exist, for which you must leave yourself enough time. Cruisers often quote how long it took them to make a passage by talking about offing to offing, ignoring the time taken with departures and arrivals.

When comparing run times with other cruisers I find their numbers significantly lower than mine, yet we left at the same time and I arrived ahead of them. I always quote hours of a passage from ready to up anchor to anchors down and set. Offing to landfall just might take less than mooring to offing plus landfall to mooring. Discounting these takeoff and landing times may prove fatal, since most mortal errors occur in these reefy parts of a passage, not on the open sea. Dismissing it may find you motoring hard into failing light through fields of coral to make your anchorage.

Contingencies Getting Underway...

One wonders sometimes how one ever escapes some harbors. Different factors should worry you on the landfall side.

1. the office hours at the customs shack for clearing out,
2. the over-the-shoulder light needed to wend your way in or out of a reef anchorage,
3. the anchors-up drills with lots of mangrove mud to clean off oneself and the boat,
4. getting the dinghy and motor aboard,
5. .... and on and on.

Contingencies of Landfall...

1. any reefs to navigate in over-the-shoulder light,
2. time to nose around selecting a safe and shallow spot in which to anchor,
3. getting the dinghy and motor down before shoreside closings,
4. properly put the boat to bed in a new place with an eye to 2 a.m. anchor drills.

**You must consider timing of arrival at capes as well as at landfalls.
See the section on Cape Effects.**

Tally the time taken by the above lists, then add a couple of hours of safety margin. You shall discover that navigating some hours in the dark seem inevitable for most passages. I've learned to stage my departures to eliminate night dangers. I've also learned to benefit from the night to make safer passages and safer landfalls.

NEVER MISS A SUNDOWNER

A leisurely gin and tonic at sundown, with the boat all squared away and ready to move again, should end every landfall. Not a frivolous rule, to never miss a Sundowner Gin & Tonic you've got to plan your navigation with lots of margin for engine stops, adverse currents and so on. In order to make your landfall in time to get down secure anchors, square away yourselves and the ship, and make yourselves comfortable with a drink by sundown, you must make your anchorage several hours before. The SG&T (some of my friends leave out the gin) reward you for good planning. Never miss it.

IF IN DOUBT, STAY OUT

A two million dollar, 92 foot ketch got totaled only one month after its maiden voyage. They went aground early on a clear night at the foot of the light house at the *fortaleza* San Felipe. The light functioned all right, but some confusion existed as to which of the crew really controlled the helm. Each time one of the men came on deck and looked around, he shrugged and thought, "Oh, well. I guess he knows what he's doing," and went down below again. Until they powered up the rocky slope at 8 knots.

Even after scrupulously following all the rules, Murphy's Law eventually will catch up with you. If you can't make the tidy daylight landfalls suggested here, or you just feel uncomfortable with an entrance under some conditions, stand way out to sea, set the boat to an easy offshore jog in open water, or heave to with the boat fore-reaching off shore and go below in watches. Trawlers heave to with leeway and idling engine just countering wind and sea.

A properly hove to boat keeps you snug as in a baby's cradle. Of course, you make coffee your SG&T at sea.

STAGE YOUR DEPARTURE

The most common fault while planning a passage poses the gravest threat to the boat: underestimating the endurance of the crew. Not realistically estimating reserves of stamina to satisfy Murphy's Law guarantees you shall need more. We often make judgments based on our younger selves. Hardly one inter-island leg defies shortening by 10% to 30% in time, and 20% to 60% in adrenaline, by one simple practice:

> **stage to a departure anchorage the day before leaving.**

Get away from the crowd. Get near the sea. Get your dinghy up. Go to one shallow hook. Clean up all your rodes. Make sea-ready on deck and below. Sailboats should take in a reef while at anchor. You'll easier shake out a reef than tie one in later while in seas. Take a swim and a snorkel. Dine by lantern light, listen to music, read a book. Turn in early. Turn out an hour before anchors-up. Watch the dawn, or listen to the night. Hoist a cup of coffee or two. Then hoist sail, bring aboard that shallow single rode, fall back on the wind, and slide out. You'll shorten the first leg by an hour or more, sometimes much more. Why do all that work just before departure, then sail out of the inner harbor with muddy decks and sweaty crew?

In some snug harbors the afternoon winds caroming off the high coast lines just outside, and even inside, the harbor can create a heavy chop in the entrance channel which usually doesn't lay down until after dark. In these land locked anchorages stage in the morning to a lee sandy anchorage at an islet, or behind a headland, outside the harbor. There you can make a safe night exit after the seas have subsided. When threading a chain of islands across the trades, stage yourself to the harbor nearest the pass you want to cross. That shall let you leave early enough to get into an anchorage at the next island before the lunch time squalls hit.

Cleaning up and waiting for weather in a lonely anchorage nearer the sea after you've spent a while in a metropolitan port gets miles behind you, and it makes a relaxing interlude.

I could go on forever with examples, because the principle of staging applies to almost any leg you can think of, even at the place you berth your boat now as you read this. If you plan a weekend outing, suppose you get to the boat late on a Friday afternoon, square away and putt over to you local beach in the offing. Watch the harbor lights with cognac and coffee over the rubble of a two hour gourmet dinner before washing up, putting away and turning in. Up at dawn for coffee with the egrets. Hoist sail and glide off in the first wisps of morning air. Now you really enjoy your weekend.

You might have practiced the alternative method of making one more last minute run to the store on Saturday morning, and stuffing things aboard in temporary spots. Then, as the wind has already risen, you throw the lines off in a fair panic, nearly shearing the port running light on a bollard, only slightly twisting the bow pulpit before you round up to a 10:30 a.m., 18 knot breeze dead from the marina entrance. You haul up a wildly flogging mainsail whose second batten now jams in a twist of sailcloth caught in the expert rolling hitch the wind just tied tightly around your back stay with the topping lift.

That night you nurse your broken toe at the beach bonfire, while you listen to the sea stories from the gang that made it to wherever you sail to in your neighborhood. The weekend sailors around the fire brag on about wind sheer, currents, rogue waves, deck work accidents, equipment failures, sinkings and piracy. On and on about marine products and processes, cuts of sail, fuel additives, epoxies and teak oils. You wonder about the sailboat which already lay at anchor when you arrived late in the day. You saw the couple swimming and beach combing up the coast as you tacked in. Their boat lies a ways off your bonfire beach this evening. A soft yellow gleam flows from their port lights, their dinghy tranquilly rides off their stern. You think, "They must cruise full time, lucky buggers. Someday. Someday ... " But they came from your marina.

Of these two boats, one shall more likely sail into divorce court than to Bora Bora.

If you haven't started staging your departures already, spend a few years *cruising*, actually moving the boat around, not sitting long stretches in yacht harbors between marathon sorties at sea. Short legging in this fashion, you shall quickly learn to spend your last day staged at a lonely cleanup anchorage on every leg, however insignificant.

> **Staging into harbors to rest and clean up before clearing in also makes sense.**

DON'T FEAR THE DARK

Inter-island cruising usually calls for 8 to 15 hour passages and longer, anchors up to anchors down. When one considers all the conditions and requirements upon getting underway, a 6 hour sail easily becomes 9 hours, and even that short leg may cause a night landfall if to windward.

For instance, I often sail after sunset to ensure a well lit midmorning landfall. Rather than push out of a crowded lagoon or busy harbor in the dark, I stage the day before to an easy night departure site just outside, where I moor off the windward beach with a clean rode and a short scope. At nightfall I hoist sail in the gentle breeze, lift the shortened anchor aboard and, making coffee below, I ghost out beyond the island's lee where I take up my course. No rounding up in 25 knots of wind to raise sail with sheets whipping and snarling on the pinrails. No sweating and cursing over fouled and muddy ground tackle. I do the cleanup the day before leaving. Now on a trawler, actually an unmasted motor-sailer, I follow the same pattern with great success.

To sail from a reefy atoll to a high island coast, move next to the entrance through the reef. Before dawn hoist your reefed sail and fall back on the light nocturnal wind. After you've breakfasted underway, the lee from the atoll's reefs gives way and you reach in midmorning trades. That night the loom of the high island's town lights leads you into the mountain night lee where the land breeze warms your cheek and crowds your nostrils with the scents of livestock, grasses and charcoal fires. Anchor near the customs dock in a flat morning calm even before the officials arrive, and of major importance, you clear in and motor off into the mirror calm of the town anchorage before the trades come up to molest your anchor drill.

You can make many anchorages in the dark also. I have often sailed up to the beaches on the leeward side of islands by starlight. Wide open anchorages behind large headlands can also make fine night landfalls. In many, the white sand beach to windward gently slopes with a long shelf of sand without keel hinder. From a mile or more out one can luff into the mild night lee until the sounder shows just a few fathoms. From that point on you can idle dead to windward, the clear sand bottom below visible by only starlight. You creep into the wind until the bright white sand beach lies practically under the bow, lower the anchor and gently fall off in silent nocturnal wind slowly feeding out scope. A much more civilized exercise than heaving to five miles out in trade seas, or trying to make and settle into an anchorage in full daytime trade wind.

I've seen countless cases of the fear of night sails leading a cruising couple into problems. Take an inter-island crossing of 150 miles for example. Not everyone has the patience to wait for a rare calm in order to bug across 20 hours, so many cruisers try to make it in one and a half days and a full night, rather than one and a half nights and one day, because they "don't like running at night". That may compromise their landfall to late in the second day. Just one pause to replace a blown raw water pump impeller, or slowing down to coddle an overheating engine, puts them precisely where they didn't want in the first place: close to land in the dark. I've seen several incidents where crews turned back exhausted after forty eight hours jilling around in a windward passage against full trades precisely because they departed in the morning rather than in the evening. No other factors differing, they could have had a delightful passage had they drawn full advantage of night lees by taking one night on each side and a day in the middle to cross. At the end of the second night they would have a dawn arrival with plenty of time to clear in and get sorted out in a strange anchorage before the winds get up.

Besides a required cruising skill, nighttime navigation has many benefits. You make earlier landfalls, leaving more time to investigate and enjoy your anchorage. You avoid sunburn and glare. Along with quieter watches you get cleaner radio reception and better visibility at sea. Lights loom over the horizon at night, then stand out sharply while still many miles away with ship type, size, aspect and course instantly apparent. In daytime, everything blends into a vague blur on the hazy, headachy horizon. Far from a scary enemy, cruisers meet their best friend in the dark.

HUG THE SHORE AT NIGHT

The wise navigator, like Columbus, takes advantage of the night lee on the windward coasts. Modern sailing yachts sail well to windward under these light conditions and in calms they can proceed under auxiliary power instead of behind a rowed longboat like Columbus had to do. This technique applies to most large islands that have east to west stretching coastlines.

HOW FAR OFF?

My rule for sailboats coasting a hazard free coast: tack out until well off soundings, or until the boat starts to buck, then tack back in until:
  1. between 10 and 20 fathoms by day (or eyeball), or
  2. between 20 and 30 fathoms by night.

This can make for short tacks on a steep coast. If coasting to take advantage of the night lee, the strip of calm water along the coast can stretch out between 1 and 3 miles.

A Stress Test

Some cruisers find coasting at night stressful. Fight that stress with this test. Steer a good watch on an inshore tack and go below to read or catnap on the offshore tack, relying on the rougher water to shake you out of the bunk so you can head her back inshore again. One year while reading below on an outward motor tack, an incident occurred which, unfortunately, happens all too commonly among cruisers new to the islands of the trades.

I heard a barely intelligible call on the VHF. Cruisers I'd met at a beach function up islands supposedly followed my advice to hug the coast with me. I marked my book place, heaved the cat off my lap and ambled back over the upright deck to the navstation.

My friend's voice over the radio reminded me of an old Charles Laughton movie where the terrified helmsman, lashed to the wheel during a survival storm and backdropped by mountainous seas gets whipped by buckets of sea water and foam flying horizontally on the screaming wind, while the ship groans onto her beam ends with every wave.

At any rate, that seemed the condition of his vessel and crew to judge by the sound effects coming over the VHF and the strain with which he spoke.

"Where the heck ARE you?" I asked.

"A-ABOUT FOUR...MIIIILES...OOOUT!" he cried stoically from the heart of the gale.

"Why not come inshore?" I asked after rescuing my peanut butter sandwich from the cat who almost dumped my coffee cup in her backward scurry.

"We ... WE'VE ... SEEEEN ... WORRRSE!" crackled the speaker.

Earlier, this same guy had insisted on punching on through the day rather than waiting for evening with me tucked behind a headland further down the coast because "people were saying we couldn't anchor there." I had anchored there as usual for a refreshing four hour nap and a hot supper, then continued on when the seas and wind subsided in the night lee. Despite his earlier start I overtook him that night motorsailing inshore of him. And, even though I spent most of the next day anchored behind the next headland while he soldiered on, he made the island's windward harbor only a couple of hours earlier than I.

Totally zonked out, he didn't clear customs until the next day while I cleared in immediately and went out to lunch with an old friend who lived there. Later, when I asked him again why he punched on in the daytime and why he didn't sail further inshore at night to grab the lee, he told me that his wife didn't want to sail at night, which they had to do anyway. He also said he worried about the rocks along the shore, which his chart told him didn't exist. You figure it.

If you get stressed hugging a windward coast at night, then I propose you take a stress test. Convinced you motor or motorsail as close inshore as you dare? Talked yourself into accepting conditions as tolerable? Take this stress test. Nudge the boat still closer inshore, keeping the depth over 100 feet. Nudge it again, then again. With each shoreward nudge you shall discover a strange paradox. Relaxing sea conditions and better boat speed and stability overcompensate the stress of nearing shore. With a good fathometer, you can forget your fear and stay inshore once you have tried it.

Don't make cruising either an Outward Bound course or an endurance contest for retireds. Sailing coasts that stretch along the trades requires good sense and planning, not a high tolerance for pain. If you round the capes in midday, or fail to coast close inshore at night, you shall indeed have an evil trip and shame on you. Double shame if you venture out of harbor into 15 knots of forecast gradient wind, or wind which blows onshore, or into large onshore swells coming from far off storms. You hadn't a window.

Hugging the shore pays a bonus by putting you inside the boundary layer ripple outside of which most trash floats. Whether a rock in a stream or an island in the trades, the same phenomenon that makes ducks fly in vees shall fend off most of the feared flotsam. Yet how often I hear skippers excuse their offshore track with trash avoidance.

> **When hugging any coast to windward at night, don't forget the cape effects.**

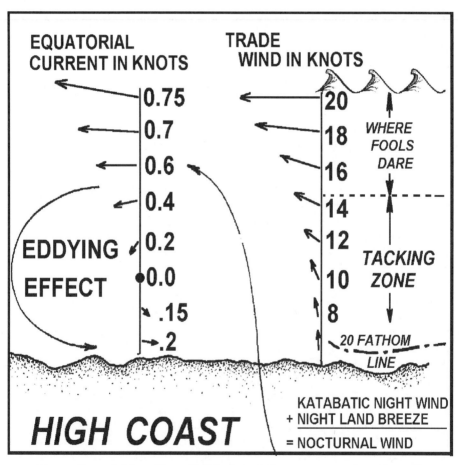

EQUATORIAL CURRENT IN KNOTS

0.75
0.7
0.6
0.4

EDDYING EFFECT

0.2
•0.0
.15
.2

TRADE WIND IN KNOTS

20
18
16
14
12
10
8

WHERE FOOLS DARE

TACKING ZONE

20 FATHOM LINE

HIGH COAST

KATABATIC NIGHT WIND
+ NIGHT LAND BREEZE
= NOCTURNAL WIND

Strength and Direction of Wind and Current as a function of the Distance Offshore

COPYING THE WEATHER
Ships don't listen to the weather, they copy it!

THE WEATHER REPORT

Offshore and High Seas Reports, transmitted by the Coast Guard on Marine SSB, get read on some standard AM broadcasts by professionals, and on VHF, Marine and HAM SSB by amateurs. Listen to *rebroadcast* weather at your peril! For Europeans, the Offshore Reports have their equal in the European *Shipping Reports*.

When near boundaries of different zones stitch the zone reports together with averaging techniques. Then, pay attention to land effects on both sides of the passage.

The Offshore Report uses an internationally standard lingo with little variance. You can easily take shorthand notes each day and compare forecasts. The changes in the forecasts should interest you. For instance, if you have a forecast of an approaching cold front with thunderstorms reaching 300 miles ahead of it, and the front moves at 20 knots, and packs 20 knots of northwest wind behind it, you better batten down for the passage of a reasonably sized front. If, on the other hand, the *previous* report of this same front gave only a 100 mile radius of the convection activity and a forward speed of 15 knots with only 15 knots of wind behind it, you now know you've got a Grand Daddy of a blow and you must make condition red preparations. That thing has grown like The Front That Ate Tokyo! The lesson here: watch the *changes*, not single report items.

YOU MUST HAVE HARD COPY

When copying verbal reports I use the 3M Company's Post-It slips that I can stick up on the bulkhead over the radio. Because the forecasts have the identical format every day my shorthand notes fill the slips in the same way, and I can rapidly scan them, showing a weather picture developing, or disintegrating, just as those still pictures you flicked through with your thumb as a kid made the lady take her clothes off.

If you didn't have that colorful a childhood you may wish to employ another method such as recording the broadcast. People who do this tend to not have it written down and can't find it on the tape when they need it. Then they play you the whole rotten rigmarole from The Bering Strait to the Straits of Magellan, while they mutter about which day's recording they've got. You can't flip cassette tapes to get the change picture. If you record, write while you listen anyway, then replay immediately to correct your shorthand. Write into a notebook you won't throw away, and erase the blasted tapes!

You can also get hard copy from your SSB radio right into your computer with various software packages. With lots of money you can even download Internet via satellite. Keeping reports on computer, you can make minor format changes that let you flick through the reports on the screen and make the Isobar charts and satellite pictures move.

DON'T LISTEN TO YOUR "BUDDY"

If you know the formats and lingo of the reports, you can separate the wheat from the chaff (nicely said) put out by some fellow yachtie on the SSB or VHF. For example, if

107

Captain Hornblower gets on the horn and knowingly declaims the Offshore Report for the Southwest Caribbean as east 15 knots with swells 3 to 4 feet and waves 1 to 2 feet, you know he's full of it! The Offshore Report does not give swells and waves, it gives sea conditions in overall heights with notable exceptions. He probably repeated a coastal report from an airport met office, about as useful to the passage making sailor as the beach report from Miami. One yacht I know crossed the Mona Passage, hearing on the NOAA VHF Wx Channel's coastal report that waves ran to only one or two feet, forget the swells. When he returned to Samaná he adamantly insisted the NOAA report had gone wrong, and Hornblower continued as an accurate source. With forecasts in the trades, you may meet your worst enemy in your best friend.

Learn to Act as Your Own Weatherman

Know your reports, the lingo and the area covered. And always listen to the same reports every day at the same time so as not to louse up your sense of progression — remember, it's the *changes* that count. Get hard copy. Get it right, get it from the NWS. In a few months you'll *smell* the weather windows.

Regular Listening

When reading the reports and weather faxes, don't confuse the map with the territory. The gradient melodies they give won't always include the themes local land effects can play. Only you can hear the terrestrial counterpoints in your neighborhood.

You might think you do a good job tracking the weather because you catch the reports *most* of the time, as when you haven't gone out to dinner, or because you listen to the reports *almost* every morning, making up with later reports. Try this: record a piece of music. Leave out one note per measure. Change the key on one chord per measure, then delete the introduction, and the refrain. Now ask anybody to name the tune.

That's exactly what 99% of cruisers do, and they wonder what happened to all the windows. Get smart. Write up the reports, or download them, every morning, and listen to the entireties of all the weather call-in shows on marine SSB.

I've seen horrendous mistakes made in choice of report to use. One professional captain I knew insisted on taking the Northwest Caribbean forecasts while in the Bahamas. He earned the nickname Captain Nogo, because he made decisions based on conditions prevailing in Jamaica. Nonetheless, he read the weather on the Georgetown net, and everybody loved it. After all, as a professional sea captain ...

Start with the Offshore Reports. Don't accept rebroadcasters such as HAM nets if you can get the official source. Then fill in details and get experienced counsel from qualified forecasters. They give forecasts and routing tips for individual yachts interactively on Marine SSB. I've used their reports for many years. They know their job, and they make great teachers, if you listen to the *whole show*. With these as a basis, you now do your job and putty up the cracks with local conditions.

MAKING SENSE OF NWS REPORTS

For following the National Weather Service reports and the various cruiser nets you must have a radio capable of receiving Marine Single Side Band, Upper Side Band (SSB-USB). A portable shortwave receiver with a "BFO" switch usually works too.

I begin listening to the offshore reports ten days before leaving harbor. That ensures my listening and my shorthand get exercised before going to sea. That also lets me develop a sense of rhythm and progression of the weather. In trade wind areas the weather ardently pursues periodicity. One develops a prescience for its cycles. I listen to the early morning report. Always aboard mornings, I never miss a report. I've seen no end of grief simply because cruisers listen to broadcasts at more convenient times like 5 p.m. Then they dine in town and miss the forecast one evening and catch up the next morning. They lack a sense of progression since they listen at different times of the day and not every day. Or worse, they rely on the guy anchored next to them. It boils down to just plain discipline.

REPORT FORMAT AND STRUCTURE

The offshore reports use a fixed format and jargon which you shall understand only by repeatedly listening to the report for the same zone at the same time of day. Warnings of tropical systems come at the beginning of the hour. Each report begins with a time stamp, the time and date at which they released the report. The release process takes place just minutes before the broadcast, but if technical problems arise, they may broadcast a report 12 hours or more old. During Hurricane Hugo this went on for 17 hours. Many thought Hugo had stalled, and they began to venture out! If a yeoman in the studio screws up badly, you may get a report from last January. Always note the time stamp.

TIME STAMP	time and date report valid (e.g., 0915 UCT 2/29/02)	
SYNOPSIS	weather features (e.g., movements of fronts, lows, highs)	
Windows	12 hour periods of decreasing predictability rolled over each 6 hours (0000, 0600, 1200, 1800 AST)	
	TODAY	the next 12 hours (e.g., 0600-1800) probability around 95%
	TONIGHT	the following 12 hours (e.g., 1800-0600) probability around 85%
	TOMORROW	the following 12 hours (e.g., 0600-1800) probability around 75%
OUTLOOK	the following several days, probability around 50%	

The forecaster begins with a synopsis of significant weather features in the zone, followed by three 12 hour periods beginning with the time given on the time stamp. Then comes an "outlook", or longer range forecast, for the 36 to 72 hour period following the 36 hours already covered. For example "Outlook for Tuesday night through Thursday" follow "Today, tonight and Tuesday:...". Reports at 1700, of course, begin "Tonight, Tuesday and Tuesday night", and so on. They describe each period with wind and sea conditions (wave + swell), including precipitation, in all parts of the zone relative to the weather features given in the synopsis.

All told, a new set of three 12 hour periods gets forecast every six hours.

BEAR IN MIND . . .

BOUNDARIES OF THE REPORT ZONES HAVE IMPLICIT COORDINATES

The analyst works as a surgeon with an opaque sheet around the square of the operating zone. Nothing outside the zone gets mentioned. An impinging front not affecting the zone at this time, shall not get mentioned except in the Outlook section. For that, you can always listen to the zones to weather of you (east in summer, north in winter).

"EAST TO SOUTHEAST" DOES NOT EQUAL "EAST SOUTHEAST"

Nor does it equal 'southeast to east'. If the analyst has gone to the trouble of telling you "southeast to east", a movement counter to the diurnal flux of the trades, you can bet he means it. He means the wind shall more likely back than veer, usually a sign of strengthening trades. A veering trade usually portends weakening of the wind. If, instead, he says "east to southeast", you don't know if he means normal diurnal veer, simple convention to start with the main cardinal point of the compass, or pronounced veering. But you listen every day just so you can tell, right?

WHICH WEATHER SOURCE GIVES THE BEST RESULT?

Answer? All of them. Navy and NWS weather faxes, and marine SSB and HAM radio forecasters. Don't miss the stereo vision value of taking all of them together. They access the same data, but weight them differently. The U.S. Navy models get high marks from most. NWS has consistency. Each reports developments at different times during the day. In any case, get the official, original source, not a rebroadcaster. Beware of yachties and net operators, who repeat "Thursday" instead of "*by* Thursday" or "*through* Thursday", losing you 8-16 hours calling a front. A 160 to 320 nautical mile mistake!

SHORTHANDING OFFSHORE REPORTS

Consider this example: "south of the front and west of 70° west, winds east to southeast 15 to 20 knots, seas 4 to 7 feet; elsewhere (meaning south of the front and east of 70° west to the end of the zone) winds east 20 to 25 knots, seas 5 to 8 feet. Scattered thunderstorms west of 75° west." In shorthand this might look like this:

$$S_F \ W70 \ E\text{-}SE \ 15\text{-}20 \ 4|7 \ \exists \ E20\text{-}25 \ 5|8 \ S\theta \ W75$$

CF	cold front	**WF**	warm front	**F**	front	**R**	ridge; remainder
Fl	frontal line	⊗	center (low)	**S$_F$**	south of front	**N$_R$**	north of ridge
2d	today	**2n**	tonight	**2m**	tomorrow	**S M T W θ F δ**	(days)
am	morning	**pm**	afternoon	**l$_g$**	late	**Δ**	little change
nr	near	**fr**	from	**bt**	between	**fw**	few
lg	large	**α**	area, along	**$\exists$**	elsewhere	**θ**	through, T-storm
stn	stationary	→	moving	**bld**	building	**bc**	becoming
v	decreasing	**∧**	increasing	**<>**	less than, etc.	**≤**	up to
W	widely	**O**	Outlook	**D**	depression	**S**	scattered, showers
G	gale	**GW**	gale warning				

Legend for My Shorthand System

RTTY NAVTEX F EBRUARY 11, 2002, NMN 0545 AST vs. S HORTHAND

OFFSHORE MARINE FORECAST NATIONAL WEATHER SERVICE MIAMI 0915
UCT TUE FEB 11 2002

CARIBBEAN SEA AND SW N ATLC BEYOND 50 NM FROM SHORE.

. SW N ATLC S OF 32N AND W OF 65W

...GALE WARNING N OF 29N E OF 73W TODAY...

.SYNOPSIS... GALE CENTER ABOUT 150 NM SW OF BERMUDA EARLY
THIS MORNING MOVING RAPIDLY NE. COLD FRONT WILL EXTEND S
OF GALE CENTER TO __ MOVE TO NEAR 65W TONIGHT. ANOTHER
COLD FRONT _ W OF CAROLINAS WED AFTERNOON.

.TODAY... N OF 29N E OF 73W WIND NE 35 TO 45 KTS. SEAS 12 TO
18 FT. OF COLD FRONT WIND SE TO S 15 TO 25 KTS. SEAS 6 TO
9 FT. REMAINDER OF AREA WIND NE TO E 20 TO 30 KTS. SEAS 7
TO 10 FT WITH LARGE NE SWELLS. SCATTERED TO NUMEROUS
SHOWERS AND TSTMS OVER THE NE PART.

.TONIGHT... E OF 75W WIND NE 20 TO 30 KTS. SEAS 7 TO 10 FT
WITH LARGE NE SWELLS. W OF 75W WIND NE TO E 15 TO 20 KTS. SEAS 4 TO 6 FT WITH LARGE NE SWELLS. WIDELY SCATTERED SHOWERS.

.WED... WIND NE TO E 15 TO 20 KTS. SEAS 4 TO 6 FT WITH LARGE NE SWELLS. WIDELY SCATTERED SHOWERS MAINLY N PORTION.

.OUTLOOK FOR WED NIGHT AND THU... LITTLE CHANGE.

Shorthand often beats telex. The shorthand version above has picked up the garbled transmission of the telex which would have shown a second cold front moving SE from the Carolinas in the afternoon. Note I use subscript notation to indicate the word "of".

Thus R_α means **remainder of area**.

Listen to rebroadcasts from other stations just to double check your copy from the official weather service. You'll see how your shorthand improves. And how the rebroadcasters so often screw it up.

TRICKS UNDERWAY

No matter the boat, the rig or the crew, trade conditions call for efficient and s eamanly handling of chores underway.

SINGLE HANDED TRICKS
Advice to the Lonely from a Solitary Cruiser

I hate tennis. Probably because I play it poorly. Watching it gives me a crick in the neck. Except once when I sat mid court, and I watched Martina Navratilova play. My head never turned from her. She had what the Greeks knew about athletic beauty. When she left the court I sat silently as though in the wake of a stunning symphony. If you have Martina's physical power and endurance, you needn't read further. I doubt you do.

Still with me? Then you shall enjoy hearing about the other time I didn't get a stiff neck. I sat looking end court on, and watched an old man beat the caulk out of two young women while hardly himself moving. The elderly gent startled me with his play. He never wandered more than a step or two from center court. He lazily swatted the ball to exactly where he wanted it in his opponents' court. The young ladies dodged all over the place, straining to just get the ball over the net in fair territory, mostly within the senior's reach.

It came to me that I played the same game as a single handed sailor, and later, as a sea worn wrack. I substituted smarts for sweat. I had to. If you want to control both the ball and center court on your boat, I have some tips for you.

THE BOAT'S WAY

However you do it, whatever you do, do it the same way every time. And insist that guests do too. I call it "the boat's way".

While visiting in the U.S. I took friends for a day sail off Ft. Lauderdale. Both couples had long experience cruising blue water. One couple worked long distance deliveries for a blue chip yacht builder. Against my custom, I had let the delivery skipper raise sail on our way out. Returning to port I parked the boat in front of the causeway drawbridge and began to lower the main. I had a way of instinctively cranking rudder against current, mizzen against wind. We sat dead in the water like a duck while the other Sunday seabuoy sailors buzzed busily about in circles just to maintain controlled way.

I coil running line from bigger to smaller loops. I latch the coil to a cleat with a half hitch on a bight drawn up through the coil. They've held in hurricanes. To douse sail I simply lift the halyard off and drop it large loops down on the deck, and down zips the sail. This time I stepped to the mast, lifted the coil and dropped it on deck, and up zipped a snugly tied off *gasket coil* which jammed under the spreader. The half lowered sail bagged in the wind and the boat lost her balance. I stood dumbfounded and disoriented while my whole world gained way and trundled off toward the lowered bridge.

My guest had violated the first principle of boat handling: don't do it your way, *do it the boat's way*. He should have examined how I coiled my halyard before uncleating it.

I had a coffee cup whose handle had to stow toward a given corner of the shelf. Only that coffee cup, and only that shelf. I instructed my charter guest on this cup's peculiarity. "Men are all alike," said she. "You not only don't know how to organize a galley, but you are so petty about details on your boat." Just then the boat heeled sharply on a rogue wave followed by the sound of sundering crockery from the shelf in question. "Don't do it *your* way or *my* way," I ranted, "do it the *boat's* way. "

All my boats have used a full clockwise turn with a half hitch on every cleat. When freeing the line I easily push off the hitch, and I still have enough purchase to hold the Queen Mary. My coast guardsman son, though brought up sailing with me, got reprogrammed by his bosun to wind endless figure eights counterclockwise around the cleat. When Son One comes aboard I inevitably get Dacron burn after unwinding the last half turn of all those eights as the line under tension tears through my hand. He knows the boat's way, but he says it helps settle scores with me for a deficient upbringing.

ANCHOR DRILL

Make a slow ballet out of anchor drudgery — a sort of T'ai Chi. Don't "drop the hook", as they say. Instead, lower the anchor until you feel the crown gently kiss bottom, flukes downwind, just as the boat gathers sternway. When weighing anchor, keep slack in your chain, so you can let the *catenary* pull the yacht forward, not the *coronary*.

Morning anchor drill can mold the day in gentle accord with nature, rather than mark the onset of another 24 hour endurance test. When I weigh anchor, I sometimes have to make it a two-cupper: two cups of coffee while I let the chop unglue the anchor on its taut rode. Then I interleave the drill with a dozen other tasks. While I flake the chain out to dry, while I tuck in a reef, while I wake the cattle egrets and get them off their mangroves and to their jobs delousing the cows and salvaging their drool. Not all cruisers see anchor weighing as a quiet time with nature, however.

Once a guy they called Animal stormed aboard uninvited and rushed to the bow where I sat plucking up a few slack links at a time, a cup of coffee in my idle hand. "Here!" he shouted, shoving me aside, "Let me show you how to put some *ass* into that thing!" While I still tried to figure out what hit me, he popped the anchor up right through the teak grating on the bowsprit. Satisfied, he hopped back into his gofast dinghy beside his admiring surfer girl and sped off, waving at me over his 4 foot wake with a big grin on his stupid face, while *Jalan Jalan*, untimely loosed, drifted broadside toward a pier with her bowsprit platform in splinters.

Animal could really weigh anchor fast.

LINE HANDLING

Of course the single hander has to have all the lines ready to deploy before approaching a dock. Bow, stern and, just in case, both springs. Place each line eye-end outboard, the standing end led around stanchions or under life lines, clear of fenders and cleated. The body of the line lies coiled flat on deck, big loops down, smaller loops up, so the thrown coil doesn't foul. Secure the eyes to the dock, then tend all lines from onboard ship. Since you have no one at the helm, all this must get done while still beyond the entertainments of channels, sea marks and converging boat traffic near the dock.

I don't do docks well, but single handing forces forethought of current, wind, fenders and lines. If you pass a day drinking beer at a busy dock, you shall no doubt value the difference in deck preparations between crewed and single handed yachts. Though not necessarily so, the single hander at least *looks* more competent.

SPEED

Do everything in slow deliberation, especially in emergencies. When you turn aft from the pulpit, thinking all secure, and you hear 200 feet of chain burst clattering out the hawse pipe, as has happened to me once, don't race for the windlass. You may step in a bight of chain and have your leg chain-sawn off at the hip. Resign yourself to the problem and deliberate its solution. It shall always prove simple and easy, such as motoring up to vertically hanging slack before grabbing the running chain. Or perhaps an unplanned morning swim to recover the bitter end. Rushing around on deck stubs toes, if it doesn't break bones. And stubbed toes do lead to broken bones, because you tend to favor the toe instead of the deck work at hand.

Actually my chain once ran out in 100 fathoms. When the nylon appeared I managed to wrap it around the bitts where I brought it to a smoking, stretching stop. Then I spent a day adrift pulling back up 15 feet at a crack with sheet winch and chain hook.

You don't run horses to the barn, neither your sea steed. It pays to enter all harbors, even your home port, at dead slow. It certainly makes backing off ground a lot easier.

Similarly, never use reverse gear as a brake. This forces you to approach docks at a speed commensurate with stopping the vessel by hand. And with the momentum of my 52 foot LOA, 35,000 pound ketch, this meant s-l-o-w. Of course you've got to grin innocently at the crowd of monkeys on the pier screaming all kinds of raucous advice, because they don't think you know what to do. But you must get used to that, especially, sadly, if you belong to the growing class of female single handers.

EXHAUSTION

Passage making, the actual doing of a voyage, as opposed to a sail, requires prudent navigation, sea-readiness, competent seamanship and unrelenting vigilance. The last can destroy your mind. Exhaustion can and does kill. My sea crossings have taught me I need three good days of gaining sea legs before anything goes right. Now most people think the expression "sea legs" means getting your balance on a floating, pitching platform after habitual use of tierra firma. It does. But it also applies to sea habits, the trifling routines of checking the bilges, engine, rigging, scanning the sea state and wind, getting proper rest and diet and so on, which, when instinctual as walking while ashore, save your life at sea. You know you have your sea legs when you really don't want to see land. Island groups don't have crossings that big. Therefore I island hop, and harbor hop while coasting.

Both single handers and older sailors have a problem with stamina. Sleep can fall like the curtain of doom when least expected, but always at 04:30 in any case. In anything less than three days at sea exhaustion can creep up on little cat feet, even without any strenuous activity. Decisions which seem sensible turn disastrous. A while back a couple lost their boat because they hove to on a tack which fore-reached toward the reefs rather than toward open sea. Given the motion of the sea and the rigidity of their minds at the time, it seemed the right thing to do. It may seem sensible to fault them, unless you have experienced exhaustion at sea yourself.

HALLUCINATIONS

My favorite hallucination stood to his belly button in hip boots, fly fishing many miles off the Venezuelan coast. I spotted him way forward and followed him out of sight astern. Afraid of losing him, a startlingly realistic delusion, I didn't flinch an eyelid. I wanted to know just how much detail my brain would fill in, if I permitted it to do so. Yet a tingle of superstitious doubt lay under my curiosity. Suppose spooks really existed and he reached out and pulled me overboard? More probable, suppose my mental experiment drove me overboard to join him in his fly fishing?

The boat ghosted toward him until he stood within 15 feet of the beam. I carefully lifted the binoculars and peeked. Among the trout flies pinned to his hat he sported a button whose slogan I read in the moonlight. It read "Wilkie for President"!

Real passage making need not occur between North and South America nor among the Pacific's vast fields of island groups. You should sail these areas with relatively short hops, chiefly because passage making among reefs and islands draws a rhumbline to destruction. From Bimini to Venezuela you get only twice out of sight of land, and even then only for about six hours. Don't go hunting my fly fisherman. He and his like keep the gates of Hell.

Here you have a true gift of a tip. Carry a John Philip Sousa cassette or CD. Play it when you need to crisp yourself up, like approaching harbor. Really puts snap in your step. But when entering harbor, kill all music and talk. VHF16, of course, stays on loud.

PICKING WEATHER WINDOWS

Sailors new to cruising often become so hyped up on *getting out there* that they look for huge windows in which to do it. Long periods of balmy weather in light winds and seas rarely occur in nature. Like fish, large windows appear rarely, but the little ones swarm in their multitudes. They can get you from here to there a lot sooner than you shall find a big one. In other words, the shorter weather window you can accept, the more windows you shall net.

Considering the danger of passage making through reefs and islands, look for weather windows of 2-3 days. That's a day to ensure you really have the window, a day to use it at its most stable state, and a safeguard day. With today's ubiquitous forecasts no one island hopping needs to get surprised by the weather.

A truly golden tip: when you listen to a weather net, listen to the whole show, even if you think it doesn't pertain. You'll find that after you normally would have switched off, a fill for your area often comes by a later reporting station, or you get more detail of a situation to weather of you. Have you something more important to do? After all, you live and die by the weather. And, of course, copy your weather at the same time of day, every day, so as not to miss a beat and offset your sense of progression.

Many cruisers get enamored of long passages from reading the tales of Pacific cruisers. Single handing in the Caribbean I often pass these people by harbor hopping each day a few hours around dawn. Having giant stepped through reefy islands, they hole up in a lousy anchorage because they couldn't get any farther in their weather window. They of course passed by the best waiting hole one anchorage back. Then they express shock at their final destination when they find me already there at anchor, having slept all my nights and dawdled all my days at secure little coves.

In the larger islands along the coasts, you can find a couple of hours of calm, scraps of leftover night lee, each and every morning with which to hop to windward without strain — often during adverse forecasts.

A chain of islands makes a ladder. Skipping steps while climbing up and down a ladder you'll eventually break a leg. Why do it *"out there"*?

WHEN DO YOU?

The old sailor's query, "When do you reef sails?" has the answer, "The first time you think of it." Sailboat or trawler, you have hundreds of questions to draw from.

When do you heave to and sleep? When do you go below to inspect bilges? When do you eyeball the engine room? When do you stand up to scan the horizon behind a blind spot? When do you bear off from wind or sea? When do you let out more rode? When do you set another anchor? When do you put the anchor back down and stay in port for another day?

Answer? *The first time you think of it.* Never any deliberation here.

The guest aboard sneered when I tacked early coming into Isle des Saintes' harbor. I tacked because my mind had asked itself if I should. The narrow channel with close lee rocks, other sailboat traffic, tide set, wind funnels, and whatnot, all converged to a nano-uncertainty 100 yards into the future. I had to explain the principal of always leaving a spare tack between the boat and the rocks just in case you screw up the first tack. My guest's non sequitur response, "But how can you screw it up?"

Single handers sail their home, their whole world, past rocks a little differently than the Club team squeezes by the windward mark.

GETTING OFF GROUND

I would rather kedge off ground single handed than use all the resources of New York's harbor tugs. This simple exercise performed all alone in the wilderness of the tropic islands has Zenful beauty. But it outdoes a Keystone Cops episode when other cruisers rush to help out. Everyone has an idea, each of which, no matter how nutty, you must brook or get damned by the local cruising community. Should you have the misfortune to go aground while crewed, "You're screwed". Your crew shall flap about, asserting your incompetence to one and all, and your refusal to have listened to the sage counsel from the ranks.

God help you if you accept a speedboat's offer to pull you off. They'll pull out your bitts, or their own transom. And don't stand behind the strained nylon when they pull. Nylon stretches to near 33% of its length without damage, but it can do severe damage if it lets go. Little David never had such a slingshot. The transom cleat of a weekend fisherman took out all of Son Three's front teeth in this manner, on Son Two's boat.

Instead of outside help, just go forward every 10 minutes or so to take in another few inches. Another slow ballet, this process may take time, but it always works, *sweatlessly.*

If you've done a public grounding, recall the "centering" exercises at Yoga class — you know, the one you hoped would introduce you to sexy new crew candidates? You can practice the art of centering amidst the grand huzzah of a fleet of cruisers who "only want to help". Pretend with all your might you stranded solo on Hogsty Reef, but remember the guy in the paper hat working the crowd in their dinghies and selling beer.

First, find where deeper water lies and carefully plant a heavy anchor a few boat lengths into it a little aft of the beam. Though extreme examples can befall, no boat drags well aft nor forward, and you don't want to break your rudder. No matter your keel configuration, however, all boats like to *pivot.*

Second, set up strong and constant tension on the anchor from the foremost point of the yacht. Deploy chafe gear on your rollers or cheek plates as needed. If you have sturdy bow eyes, go through them. With all chain rode, take in a link or two at a time with each sag of the catenary using a chain hook, or a rolling hitch on Dacron line (not nylon or poly) led to your windlass, or aft to your halyard or sheet winch. Strong and constant tension means a bar taut chain, or dangerously stretched nylon rode.

If you haven't any chop, you need to make some. You need to get bights of slack in the taut rode in order to sweat some in. Set up rocking of the boat, even a 20 tonner, by madly running the beam back and forth, or churn about with your dinghy in snowplow mode. If you have a 2 hp hard dink, you can't do this. Take the lesson and get a gofast inflatable before you do the islands of the trades.

Speed boaters who normally wake you and roll your gunnels into the bay on a Sunday, shall now march at funereal half step past your predicament. Your contortions communicating the tidal waves you want them to produce shall get read as commands to go dead slow. If your eager salvors still mill about in their dinghies like Dodg'em Cars, they'll love the exercise of making chop. If you hear snatches of sage counsel from them between the oaths and alarums they bandy during their collisions, ignore it, stay cool and carry on.

Tremendous forces hide in wave action, time and tide. Your quick response in laying out a tense kedge to pivot you toward deeper water should not have waited while you examined tide tables. You wanted to do that whether the tide rose or fell, so go look at your tide tables *after* setting the kedge. Reckon both the tide and any expected change in current or wind. Mayhap you shall get saved by tide and time. If you draw a falling tide, assert tension in the slackening rode every inch you get. At low tide, go below and read a book. When the tide again rises you shall gradually pivot toward deeper water without lifting a hand, provided you kept the rode humming tight while it went down. If high tide doesn't get you off, redeploy the kedge and go again. You'll read two books and get that much smarter for next time.

When finally laying fair to wind in good water, take an icy gin and tonic and go to bed. Deduct the day from eternity. Never try to recover it by hurrying on or planning a larger leg the next day. That probably answers why you went aground in the first place. And don't forget the guy in the paper hat. He owes you a commission.

THE AGING CRUISER

"There are old pilots, and there are bold pilots. There are no old and bold pilots." This old saw applies to pilots of the sea as well as to the aerial sort. No matter your age, if you want to get older, take a lesson from the old tennis pro in center court. Deliberate, planned moves. No rush. And if you don't worry about something, ask yourself what you forgot. You should worry.

I suppose more mayhem has come to crews by the stubbed toe and the torn toenail than by any acts of nature. Favoring your toe while trying, in the dark and on a pitching, yawing and rolling deck, to lasso a parted stay, a broken halyard, a loosed boom, or worst of all, a snatching chain, will do you in for sure. The simple cure? Don't go to sea favoring anything but your boat. Hold center court and command the game.

And oh, yes. Take this old pilot's word for it: always wear deck shoes on deck. They call them deck shoes just for that reason, funny enough.

Simply because they have no one else to depend on, single handers depend on things going wrong, and then see to it that they don't.

> **Managing alone, single handers often have the best of the cruising life -- just therefore.**

This old cruiser's favorite bar in the mangroves.

MOTORING & MOTORSAILING

Handle your sailboat as a motorboat that can sail, and your motorboat as a boat that may have to sail!

Tricking the trades not only has lots of motoring opportunities but today's yachts have lots of motor to do it with. Motoring to windward, however, boils a different kettle of fish than motoring out to the sea buoy on a Sunday afternoon. Half the time you shall run close to all out revolutions. With no genset, the other half gets used on low revs generating zaps or running an engine driven compressor for your refrigerator.

You can buy many good books to help you with diesel problems and their prevention. I've got some tips how to avoid problems, or to plan for the inevitable ones when they come because you motor in the wilder seas of the trades.

Sail	Power and Sail
Switch the motor on when you need it to maintain the minimum average speed you had assumed in planning your landfall.	Trim ship for comfort and accept the easier destination.
Keep the jib up only if it helps you point better	With the engine up to temperature make a flashlight tour of the engine room. Look for spotting from oil or water leaks and fog from exhaust leaks. Check the bilges at the same time. Repeat every hour.
Always have the main up, usually reefed. Tack a bit if dead into the wind.	
Ensure the exhaust outlet stays above water while the engine cools. Following seas or heeling may cause sea water to get drawn into the exhaust, flooding a cylinder and seizing the engine.	Heeling: you can suck air through the raw water intake, causing an airlock in the cooling system which shall overheat the engine. You can siphon sea water into the engine after you switch off, while the anti-siphon valve remains tipped under sea level.
For downwind passages in the trades, install a ball valve at the exhaust outlet. Remember to open it when the engine cools! Tie the start key to the valve handle.	Let the engine idle to lowest operating temperature before killing it.
	Ensure a goodly air supply to your engine by opening hatches if you have a tight installation. Ducted fans may not carry enough air to the engine.

Any vessel can use a window with which to see into the fully lit engine compartment.

Sailing purists hate to switch on the engine, when sailing to windward or even when drifting in a calm. Typical enthusiasts start out for an island which they see just poking up over the swell with a "Yeah! Right On! Let's go for it, man!" charge. But toward lunch the locker room banter begins to mellow. After an exciting morning's beat into 4 to 7 foot seas with 10 foot breaking rogues, our heroes, refreshed by a lunch of soggy egg salad sandwiches, return to a grueling afternoon's beat into the same conditions worsening. After following the carefully crafted and posted watch schedules a couple of times the crew begins to realize they won't have any clubhouse showers at the end of the day, nor shall they go to any prize banquets and parties. Just the sour bunk to return to, sodden by the sea water spurting through the crack caused by separation of hull and deck

As the challenge of the whole thing melts into a funk with expensive repairs at the end, Captain Courageous flicks the starter switch and goes over to motorsailing. If he can. The incessant pounding has sloshed up the muck at the bottom of the fuel tank and the engine won't start.

Now, Leisure Sailors of the trades not only select their passages and their weather windows for short and easy legs, but they know the following basic rules of motorsailing and don't cavil at applying their auxiliary.

MOTOR MAINTENANCE

If you can't maintain your own diesel motor, stay home. You shall find few marinas and most of the "help" available might leave you worse off than if you had done it yourself while reading a shop manual. You have an engine shop manual, of course?

BEFORE YOU LEAVE HOME

If you have accustomed yourself to leaving the car for maintenance at the corner garage because you never had the time to do your own maintenance, you now have the blessed opportunity to change. If you really want to sail leisurely, you've got nothing but time. Get a shop manual before you leave home, and do your own maintenance. When you screw up, you at least learn something and won't do it again. If you let someone else do it, you will pay for the same screwup time after time. Review the next few pages. You may want to do some refit before leaving home.

Take a course in diesel mechanics. Manufacturers such as Ford, Perkins and Detroit, offer simple short courses, as does your local adult education center. Think of it! You can get independent of mechanics simply by going to your local high school one evening a week for 8 weeks. Some courses last only a single day. If you don't incline mechanically, don't think you can't do it. Nothing simpler than a diesel engine. Patience and logic, assisted by a new part or two, can follow down and cure any problem.

THE SAD SYNDROME

An engine simply running out of fuel gives a resigned klunk-puff-puff and dies, just like when you use the kill switch, which, by the way, works by strangling the fuel input to the high pressure pump. An engine killed by something stronger than itself coming along and stopping its rotation, like a huge cargo net wound up in the propeller, dies with a squawk and a bang, and perhaps the sound of rushing water.

The infamous Surge And Die syndrome (SAD) occurs when a diesel gets starved for fuel. Air gets into the lines because the desperately sucking fuel pump succeeds in breaking the fuel line seals. When this happens the engine surges (fast RPM-ing), making a panicky scream. Engine death inevitably follows its fibrillations.

The vast majority of engine problems in the tropics come from contaminated fuel. You can finesse most of these problems by using a Baja Filter (see Glossary), using a good fungicide (not too much), and by preparing your installation with adequate filtration. Adequacy at home turns to insufficiency between the tropics. Besides the manufacturer's engine mounted canister filter and the engine's lift pump screen filter, you should have at least one other filter and a water separator mounted between the tank and the engine. Ensure the fungicide you buy doesn't decompose the filter elements you use.

You can mount a switchable fuel pump to get a few more hours of engine life when clogged fuel filters cause SAD. This also gives you a way to bleed your fuel lines without getting spasms in your thumb from the lift pump lever. It also gives you a way to clean your fuel tanks without having to bucket out the fuel and strain it through tee-shirts.

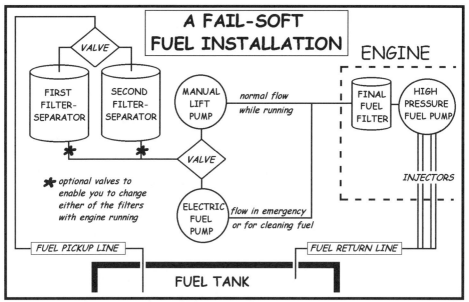

Keeping Your Fuel Clean

Not only does this installation give you better protection but the electric fuel pump gives you the ability to overcome clogged filters in order to make port. When you hear the engine start to surge, put the fuel pump in-line and switch it on. Once in port, you can also use the installation to clean your tank.

Spare Parts

If you have recently installed a new engine you may consider saving key elements of your old engine for spares: head, high pressure pump, water pumps, injectors, delivery pipes, exhaust elbow, starter motor, alternator and instrument senders. However, you should have the following minimum spares aboard before leaving home. Minimum motor spares to have aboard when starting out

Sail and Power	Also for Power
vee belts (3)	alternator
complete gasket set	heat exchanger
starter	oil cooler
fuel filters (6 each)	raw water pump
oil for 6 changes	fresh water pump
fungicide for 1500 miles fuel consumption	short vee belt to go between the crank-shaft and the fresh water pump (a mock alternator)
oil filters for 1500 miles motoring	fuel lift pump
full gasket kit	2 motor mounts

Minimum motor spares to have aboard when starting out

THE DIRTIEST JOB IN THE WORLD

Nothing beats changing oil on a diesel engine for nasty. Thorough preparation before starting makes the job somewhat easier. In other words, flip the settee cushions looking for the new oil filter *before* your hands get covered with black goop.

Invest in a filter wrench and lots of 3-ply garbage bags. Also have a good stock of old newspapers, and save those plastic gallon jugs with which to dump the old oil. If you don't have a scavenge pump, have a funnel standing by (a cut off plastic bottle top works fine). Even better, install a petcock in place of your pan's drain plug.

Scavenge pumps get most of the old oil out but they don't get the gunk in the bottom of the pan. Accumulation of this stuff can ruin your engine. Get the last of the old oil out through the drain plug in the bottom of the pan. You can also flush the engine from time to time with diesel.

If your installation has an angle which prevents complete drainage, flush the sump each time you change oil by using more oil than necessary. After draining the old oil, and before replacing the filter, add a quarter sump of fresh oil. With the engine kill switch on, run the starter for 20 seconds, pause a few minutes and do it again. Drain the engine again, change filters and add the new oil. This procedure costs you a little oil every time you change, but it may add thousands of hours to your engine's life.

As with many engine jobs, you have an easier cleanup if you start the job with a little Joy dish soap rubbed under and around your fingernails.

MOTOR FAILURES

Skippers have their own styles going to windward, and every boat performs differently. Some sailboats motor more than others. Some trawlers motor faster than others. Some crash into it or corkscrew down from it, others tack and wear. Broken engines litter the tropics, because their skippers didn't wait for good conditions to prevail. They bucked right into short, steep seas for dozens of hours with the throttle wide open. Some boat manufacturers may not anticipate this use of engines in their boat design, and most installers for sure don't when they install them. Neither do power boat owners generally ask much of their engines until they meet trade wind conditions week after week. Motor mounts, shaft alignment, fuel feed, cooling setup, transmission bolts — you name it — none have gone through the rigorous tests that continuous rough use gives. Not by puttering about home waters or running in idle 20 minutes each week in a marina.

I've listed below the usual engine failures. You can either modify your installation before leaving home, or don't leave port in the conditions for which your engine has not come prepared. A truly Leisure Sailor will do both.

FUEL SYSTEM

Motoring into heavy chop emulsifies whatever the fuel tank has in it besides pure fuel. It also gives your fuel pump a good gulp of air between sloshes in a near empty tank. The SAD syndrome described earlier will come from air getting sucked into the system as well as from clogged filters and water in the fuel.

If running dangerously low on fuel, you can supplement diesel with mineral spirits from your lamp oil supply. You can throw in some transmission oil to thicken the brew if you use more than a couple of gallons. I know a German ship's engineer who made port on his yacht with a mixture of cooking oil, engine oil and gasoline. Shake well before using. And don't forget the oregano if your engine's Italian.

You shall buy dirty fuel everywhere, so plan on having it. Have an installation which combats the problem. And use a Baja Filter and a fungicide when adding fuel.

Do not let your tanks sit half empty in the tropics. Condensation and heat will start the microbes crawling on its walls. If they don't clog your filters and fuel pump with mucous gook. Without full tanks and with fungicide, even if you win, you lose. The fungicide, if it works, shall produce a black residue along with dead microbes, which shall plug everything up with soot. Keep full, fungicided tanks.

EXHAUST SYSTEM

Intrusion of the sea through an open exhaust port into a cylinder can ruin the engine. Water gets into your exhaust manifold several ways, not limited to those already discussed above. You shall not notice corrosion in the exhaust elbow's water injection jacket from the outside, and with some installations, water can drip back into the manifold this way. Know how they build your elbow, and check it before leaving.

If you have a water muffler such as the wet exhaust Verna Lift type, make sure it has a tank large enough to hold all the water from a full exhaust swan neck plus a good gulp from the through hull on a big roll. Reckon the volume of water in your swan neck as the length of hose to maximum rise multiplied by half the inside diameter squared:

$$\text{volume} = \text{length} \times \pi \text{ radius}^2$$

Make sure that you have a high enough swan neck to motor heeled in high seas and that your outlet won't spend a good deal of its life under water. The bane of the windward yacht, chafe, can hole your exhaust hose. While not mortal, it sure makes a mess. Always idle your engine until the operating temperature bottoms out before cutting it off.

Throw away that bronze anti-siphon valve and replace it with a plastic one, or rig a simple hose out to the deck. While you do it, raise the anti-siphon valve and its U fitting higher than the level of sea can conceivably come without your boat turning turtle.

COOLING SYSTEM

Your engine can overheat for hundreds of reasons, but motoring to weather in tropical heat exposes you to all of them. When it happens, which it shall eventually, check:

1. weed clogged raw water through-hull fitting
2. gulping air with raw water while heeling and pitching (airlock)
3. clogged raw water strainer
4. raw water strainer too small for flow volume
5. water pump impeller going or gone (salt or fresh)
6. water pump belt slipping or gone
7. heat exchanger clogged
8. thermostat jammed
9. water pump bearings gone

Most raw water pumps have a weep hole in the shaft housing between the pump seal and the engine oil seal. Some manufacturers make weep holes too small, or they get mounted them so that they point up or sideways rather than down, where they can drip freely. Salt and corrosion will seal them up, and they won't weep. If you don't have one at the bottom of your shaft housing, bore a quarter inch hole to permit weeping. This will prevent water from getting through your oil seal and ruining the engine.

They designed the lip seal on the engine side of the pump shaft to keep oil in, not water out. Yet a physical phenomenon can force water through the engine oil seal when the pump water seal breaks down. Water on the rotating pump shaft clings to the shaft in a spiral and accelerates axially toward the oil seal, striking it with great pressure. One does tend to think engineers ought to have figured that one out before specifying the pump on their engine design. I gladly note that some now have.

Powering off sandy ground can etch pump shafts and undermine the seals. Volvo motors have high pressure raw water pumps guaranteeing an effective sandblasting of the shaft.

Water in your engine's oil, due to blown pump seals or gaskets, will show up as milky streaks in the jet black dirty diesel motor oil. If it just started, look for drops of condensed steam clinging to the inside of the oil filler cap after running. If you waited until you had a gully washer pouring into the oil galleries, watch for a fountain of hot gray oatmeal-like stuff to come foaming out of the blown oil filler cap. Better you check for the water droplets on the filler cap before it happens.

If you attempt to start your engine and it doesn't budge, count your blessings. The attitude of the stroke when it stopped meant that the flooded cylinder compressed before another one fired. Water having incompressible properties, your starter can only sit there and hum a tune. Had a dry cylinder fired, you'd have scrap for an engine.

Many of these problems occur on yachts on their first extended cruise, what really amounts to their first real sea trials. If you elect to bash into it and cause these problems, they shall happen sooner or later. If you continue in the same style, the next few months shall give the *coup de grace* for your engine.

If you have sea water incursion do the same thing you did when you dropped the outboard motor overboard. If you haven't done that yet, not to worry, you shall soon.

1. Take off all the injectors to expose the flooded cylinder(s).
2. Crank to expunge the water through the injector holes.
3. Pour in some diesel or mineral spirits through the holes, and crank again. If the water got to your oil supply as evidenced by gray streaks on your dip stick, drain the oil, pour in a quarter sump of diesel oil, crank briefly and drain again. Now add oil, crank lots, then change oil a final time.
4. Put back the injectors, bleed the fuel system and get underway.

Different from resuscitating an outboard, you don't have to change the gear oil in the lower unit. A diesel hasn't got one. But check the sump oil for water.

ELECTRICAL SYSTEM

You can find many fine reference works readily available to thoroughly confuse you. I intend to only give you warning of pitfalls unique to cruising in the tropics. You shall for sure see charging problems and more charging problems. You can have wind generators, solar panels, automated battery charging systems and generators separate from the main engine. You'll still have charging problems. Especially if you have an electric refrigerator with less than 6 feet of insulation and more than one cube's ice making capacity. The wind won't blow, the sun won't shine, all your charging connections will corrode and generate more heat than they carry electricity. Certainly your diodes will blow.

You've heard of Ohm's Law. Well I have one too ...

> **Bruce's Law: electricity use expands beyond the boat's capacity to supply it.**

Carry a spare alternator, and get the burned one fixed or rewound as soon as you can.

Painting your boat white, instead of dark blue or whatever, shall instantly triple your ice making capability.

Chafe and corrosion cause most failures. Before you leave home do a thorough review of all wiring runs. Invest in good metal jawed cable ties and tie them everywhere. Make a wiring diagram of the whole boat including motor and instrument panel.

Have a good multimeter and know how to use it to debug the system. If you rewire anything use one or two gauges of wire heavier than called for, and use tinned stranded wire. Label everything and turn square corners with the runs. In short, failures shall happen. Have a system that you can quickly debug. Have aboard as many reference books as you can carry.

Here's a gift: while cleaning up your engine's wiring, install a momentary switch on the hot line to the starter solenoid where it runs through the engine room. You'll use this for bleeding the fuel system at the injectors.

FISHING
Tricks for cruisers most disdained by professionals.

You can buy from a plethora of pamphlets, books, fish identi-kits and even dowsing tools at any gas dock or bait and tackle shop. You'll find useful and serious information in all of them. Some tips follow which, though not at all unique to the trades, I've nonetheless not seen them elsewhere.

1. First you have to decide if you shall fish for fun or to feed yourself
   — *hunger catches more fish than diversion.*
2. You can't catch fish without a hook in the water
   — *hook time catches more fish than fancy lures or luck ever did.*
3. Don't listen to the crybabies who whine someone has fished out the whole world
   — *the fish swim where you find them.*

SKIN DIVING

You should view fishing underwater as primarily a hunting expedition. To hunt, you have to take time. You have to watch the fish and learn their habits. You have to let them get used to your presence. If you missed a shot and spooked the fish, give them time to get unspooked. All that adds up to time with you in the water just like hook fishing requires lots of time with the hook in the water. Wear a wet suit, even in the summer.

Some fish have extremely tough skins, hard to penetrate with a spear. Before starting out make sure your spear tips get freshly sharpened. Coral rock shall dull even your stainless points. Use a sharpening stone to shape a triangular point. Always the same triangle.

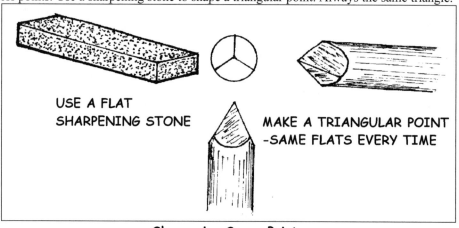

USE A FLAT
SHARPENING STONE

MAKE A TRIANGULAR POINT
-SAME FLATS EVERY TIME

Sharpening Spear Points

Good tasting fish like grouper and snapper usually hide under something. Sometimes you can spear them through a hole above, like a skylight to their living room. More often than not you have to get them through a side door down near the bottom. If they run into one door expect them to leave from another. If they go around a rock, creep over the top and prepare to shoot down on them. With time in the water you shall observe and learn their habits, and you can anticipate their responses to your shots.

Only with many shots can you become good at it, so shoot lots. If you can't get that fat grouper you have chased, and you feel close to hypothermia, shoot a couple of small grunts or a trusting trigger fish. You should always come home with bait at least. If you just began spear fishing it shall surprise you to learn that you need to get quite close to the fish to kill it. The tip of your spear should generally get no farther from your prey than the length of the fish itself. Even closer for a pole spear or a Hawaiian Sling.

For lobster, conch and whelk, swim low along the undercut shore ledges at the time of day when the sunlight slants in under the ledge and lights it all up. For lobster around rocks and coral heads, swim around the pile with your cheek on the sand, looking into every crevice and hole. Wear gloves to protect yourself against skin reactions to various corals when you pull yourself along by grasping rocks.

The good eating, such as grouper, snapper and lobster, doesn't always swim around coral heads, rocks and ledges. Often enough you can see sizable grouper playing 'possum in the branches of a bush while lobster are hidden in the roots. When all the jocks go roaring off in their Zodiac Grand Raids to dive the forty feet on the windward side because the harbor got "all fished out", leisurely peruse your own anchorage and get ready for surprises. No one fishes the anchorages, and yet they seem just the places where fish thrive due to the edible detritus falling from the boats above. This assumes a clean anchorage with good flow, of course.

Take a catch immediately to the surface. Hold the thrashing animal still with both hands, or hold it above the surface of the water, until it safely lies in the dinghy which you always keep nearby. Shark and barracuda get unjustly blamed for mythical mayhem to swimmers. Yet you cannot hold them responsible for instinctual behavior. Especially the barracuda. The barracuda acts as a territorial garbage collector. He owns the reef and when something dies and goes through the vibrations of extremis, the barracuda has the task of darting in and cleaning it up. You can get away with letting your dying catch slide down the spear and rest against your fist and never have an incident. But with low luck your catch shall someday meet with a set of flying teeth which may, wholly unintended, carry away a few knuckles. Let the fish trail away from you until it's clear of the water. And, of course, wear no shiny objects.

A pleasant way to fish a reef and ensure that you have the dinghy always handy, just have the dinghy painter in hand or tow it around with the anchor and chain looped around one arm. When you see something interesting plant the anchor noiselessly and pursue your pleasure. To fish an island's seaward reefs this way wait for slack low tide plus one hour. Then ride the tide back into harbor with dinghy in hand. The reef community all come to meet the incoming nutrients from Mother Ocean with their mouths agape, and won't they get surprised by you and your spear instead.

CORAL CUTS

> **For coral fungus that won't heal, try monosodium glutamate (MSG).**

As a boy I ran away to Cuba. When I slunk back I could only show a sore foot as my reward. I'd scraped the top of it on some coral. Working through high school as a bellhop, I had to wear black socks and shoes all night. I could never go barefoot to dry it out. For

129

three years I paid dermatologists and slept with bags of gentian violet and other muck on my foot. And the wound leaked sticky, smelly lymph all that time. Surprisingly, I didn't grow up a serial killer. My mom's boyfriend, a professional diver, suggested MSG (monosodium glutamate, a meat tenderizer and notorious flavor enhancer in Chinese restaurants). I sprinkled some on, and five days later I had a new foot. And a lifetime of healthy distrust of medical doctors began.

For cracked lips, try Preparation-H . . . but keep two separate tubes on hand!

I could free dive to 40 feet, and all my dinner swam or crawled well above that. I didn't need scuba gear, but I tried to get clever. I bought a tank, just to clean my bottom. The tank never lasted a full bottom cleaning operation. Gliding around playing a murky rerun of Jacques Cousteau documentaries, you can get close to an hour out of a tank. Professionals perhaps more. Scrubbing the bottom of a full displacement, long keeled boat takes muscle, not brain, and muscle takes oxygen. Furthermore the tank had to get fills at stations, usually fancy resorts, where persnickety attendants insisted upon seeing my certificates, reconditioning and recertifying the tank, and always selling me new gear. Creeping around third world waterfronts looking for a tank filler without scruples, I felt like a junkie needing a fix. In short order I sold the rig to someone who didn't know better, although I tried to tell him, and went back to healthy free diving to maintain the bottom coat.

If you have the space and the money to have a refilling compressor aboard, I still don't envy you. Unless you have professional reasons to have scuba tanks such as research, teaching or salvage, in less than three years of trades cruising your scuba tanks shall come in about as handy as snow skis in Florida. That doesn't keep some sports in Palm Beach, however, from nailing ski racks on their BMW's, just to show the girls what gallivants do.

An onboard oil-less compressor built for diving makes a fine investment. They come in DC as well as AC, and as yet anyway, bear no post purchase controls by governments in league with industry lawyers, i.e., you don't need permits to use them. You can build them in to the boat with a quick connect air hose fitting on deck. Fine mesh stainless filters in the hose prevent any material due to mechanical decay of parts to get through to your lungs. Even the simplest rigs will take two people to 40 feet, a single person to 60.

I installed one of these in my ketch, and I transferred it to my trawler. In more than a dozen years of trouble free operation, this device has done more than cut the time of my bottom scrubs by 60%. My haul out expenses have further shrunk by 33%.

You may have taken that PADI resort course, fallen in love with your instructor, and loaded up on neon colored gear that makes you feel like a million. But faddist parapher-nalia has no place onboard a boat. A cruising buddy of mine, a professional diver who spent a good part of his life at down to 300 feet or more, never cruises with anything but flippers and snorkel. He says his dinner swims within free dive reach, and you can't see well below 30 feet anyway. He says if you really want to see the depths, do it on vacation in the Red Sea at Raz Mohammed, or more reasonably, buy a good coffee table book with pictures. Professional photographers can use devices your eyes haven't got in order to show you the beauties of the deep, which anyway get more sparse with depth.

In my own years cruising I've seen many go cruising with tanks, few return with them and if they did, they went unused. They discovered that Ocean, a lot bigger than the flickering blue screen, just doesn't follow the Cousteau scripts.

TROLLING

When you have fed all your expensive lures to the lure monster, try making your own for free. The corner of a plastic garbage bag with appropriate slits can make an excellent squid, or skirt. So do small translucent tubes of shampoo or whatever. Do you remember how to make those little yarn dolls that you hung on the Christmas tree as a kid? Make one out of the yarns from an old piece of nylon 3-strand rope. Wind the head of the doll around a 3 ounce oval lead and leave off the arms. Let the hook just shimmer below the skirt. Keep your hooks sharp and rust free.

You don't need fancy equipment. The Cuban reels (plastic doughnuts, or yo-yos) work great. Instead of a drag to alarm you to a bite, or more likely, seaweed, put a bight of the line through a clothespin spring and then around the clothespin. Then clamp the clothespin to a lifeline with a couple of yards of slack line behind it.

Use stainless clamps to fix an old reel to the pushpit. Surprisingly, I have got 10 years of maintenance free operation out of an old reel exposed continuously to salt and sun.

Use 80 to 100 or more pounds test line. Have lots of large swivels and use lots of heavy stainless leader and big hooks. Run a line on each side of the boat. Four, if you like. Two short and skipping, two long and deep. Don't make sharp turns with the boat, though.

Now tend those lines. Keep them free of seaweed — a frustrating and monotonous task. People who complain they never catch any fish usually wait until they sail in open sea before they put out a single puny line. Then they tow seaweed around and reel it in when they first sight their landfall.

Have your lines (plural) out while going through cuts or entering and leaving harbors. If you get a strike while going through a cut, ignore it, of course, and tend to your boat first. When you do reel in your catch it may have drowned, saving you the trouble of dispatching it.

Fishing the Shoals and Heads

Many places you can dip your lure right into fish living rooms. For example, when you see a series of coral heads in front of you, don't automatically tack around them. Instead, trail a line for grouper and wigwag your way around the shoals, dipping the lure onto them. To dip your lures onto heads and shoals have about eighty yards of line out. Maneuver the boat, or use the wind, to get the lure over your target. Now put slack in the line by turning upwind or, for sailboats, by putting the helm hard over in both directions several times to lose way. When the line drops almost to the bottom, fill sail or thrust throttle and run away with the lure. You can do this on ketches and yawls by just playing with the mizzen sheet. It gives you the feel of rod fishing in a way.

131

BOTTOM FISHING

Save the cadavers for bait after cleaning your fish. Save the heads for making soup. The eyes work as a thickener. Swap your lure leader for a leader with bare hook and bury it in a fist size, or larger, hunk of bait. Before your second SG&T, walk to the bow with the baited line. Using large coils, hold a good boat length of line in one hand and, with the other, swing the baited hook in wide circles. Let go of the whole mess and the wind should bring it back to a boat length off your beam where the bait shall rest on the bottom.

Sometime between your second SG&T and four in the morning your drag will go off like a siren. Nocturnal types, like grouper and snapper come out at this time to graze the anchorage. Sometimes you'll get a shark, but more often a good eating bottom fish.

If you got some BBQ chicken or ribs ashore, keep the bones to use as bait that night. They perform great. Just work the hook into a joint, or if chicken, through the bone.

A GOOD FINISH

I lost many fish trying to board them until I began to stun the fish with rum. Now I use my aftershave lotion, a squirt bottle of alcohol. You might also invest in a water pistol filled with alcohol, even a super squirt. You shall need lots, so buy lots when the drugstores have sales. Squirt a goodly shot into the gills. This shall immediately stun the fish. Hit the other gill while he's out to ensure he stays out. Now board the fish without drama.

For a humane and healthy way to sacrifice the fish, perhaps even a *kosher* way, you must dump all its blood, a vehicle for toxins, at one gush at the same time you sever its spinal column. If you don't use an ax, you'll have to have a sharp, large Bowie type knife or short machete. Insert the knife downward in the soft spot behind the dorsal edge of the gill, cutting edge up, and give it a good hard karate chop. Do the other side. The spinal cord shall part and the blood dump, all while the animal lies out cold and still. Decapitate, slice from anus to throat, scoop out the guts, chop off the tail and fillet with a good boning knife.

The head on bull dolphins has much meat, as do the jaws on a grouper. Both sites give gourmet gobbets of a delicate white meat for *chichorones*, or fried fish fingers, for the hors d'oeuvres to go with your Sundowner Gin and Tonics.

Keep the cat busy with the scraps, and bag other remnants for bottom fishing bait.

ANCHORING
An art without veterans.

I spent some time interviewing a family who had sailed 15,000 miles round the world in under three years to end it all on the edge of a cut through a reef. They motored to a waypoint given to them with great care and precision by a friend, to a waypoint smack in the center of the channel itself, equidistant from each reef edge. Approaching the cut in dead calm on a clear, moonlit night, their oblique angle to the cut caused them to strike the reef rather than enter through the cut. A simple lack of proper GPS procedure cost them everything but their lives. They had many years winning races at their home yacht club. The skipper had even done the Whitbread world race. How can it have happened to seasoned "round the worlders", to seasoned seamen like these?

Well, it didn't happen to seasoned seamen. These folks had no more sea seasoning than the bright brass of their port lights. After talking with them for a couple of days I learned that they had anchored less than a dozen times since learning to sail. They took long legs and hung out for long periods for work to refresh their kitty. This family unfortunately typifies many cruisers. Many people who have sailed a bunch have not anchored much. They may not realize they lack such elementary seaman skills. They might have gone round the world, but in doing it, they learned little more than they had when they left.

Sharpen your anchoring habits before you leave. Don't learn the hard way later.

THE GOOD NEIGHBOR

Good neighbors remain silent while you anchor or weigh anchor. Let the new boat anchor in peace. I sometime get gratuitous complaints that I'm too close to someone's boat while I start to lay my first anchor. Then the guy sees the second anchor deployed and my boat lays on a wide vee 100 feet off his quarter. He thinks I did it for him.

Anglophones particularly worry about Francophones whose sensitivity radius comes much shorter than theirs. I personally prefer Latin closeness to Anglo aloofness. Anyway, Anglos have a perception problem. The French may anchor closer, but I notice they usually do a good job of it, if not better. All should fear Charterphones, and with good reason.

A good neighbor does not call you on the radio nor dinghy over to talk to you while you work your anchors. Often I would go to the shortest possible scope, hoist the mainsail, then haul anchor when the bow pays off the way I wanted her to go. People often dinghied over to chat just as a gust took the sail and the boat started to move. I try to stay civil at times like these, busy maneuvering under sail in a crowded anchorage. I suppose I sound rude by shouting, "Couldn't you have come by during all the days we've been in harbor?"

A good neighbor doesn't offer help or advice unless asked. I take my time. I don't strain myself or my boat. Sometimes I do a "two-cupper": two cups of coffee to let the chop unglue the anchor while I flake the chain out to dry. I don't need anyone's help.

BRIDGE COMMUNICATIONS

This subject ought to come under a heading of Marriage Counseling. Mom and Pop on their retirement cruise have never stayed so close for so long in forty years. Now they stand farthest apart only while anchoring. Only thirty feet or so.

Pop stands at the wheel for his technical skills, while Mom stands at the bow anchor because she has stronger hands. Some prefer to reverse the roles. One or the other signals and the miscommunication begins.

It can take another forty years to develop hand signals and the divided responsibilities needed to choreograph the delicate ballet of anchoring successfully in all conditions and in front of the usual audiences who pretend to look the other way. If you can't do it alone at least follow these rules.

The bowman (-woman) should do all signaling from the same position always and with the same hand always while holding the forestay with the other hand to ensure its immobility even more than to ensure Bowman's stability. Signals needed?

left · hard left · right · hard right · center wheel

ahead · astern · more power · less power · stop · @^$*%>#!!!

Treat the last command as optional, since it might destroy harmony in the more untested relationships. And to avoid nasty equivocation keep all fingers together.

Boats under 50 feet handle best with one person. You haven't the Queen Mary. Knowledge of what got done while anchoring should not reside somewhere between the wheel and the pulpit with neither station having all the facts. This can save marriages as well.

The person who selects the spot and lays the anchor should prepare the boat to fall off in the proper direction, not someone who stays at the helm and doesn't quite know where the spot lies nor how the anchor may soar to it. It also calls for knowledge of the boat's characteristics of way, its momentum, and how easily she faces or crosses the wind.

While anchoring single-handedly, maneuver to station the slowly swinging bow over the spot selected such that the walk forward from the helm to the pulpit goes with a certain seaman like decorum, rather than a headlong, cursing rush.

LAYING ANCHOR

Yachts that drag into you in the tight anchorages invariably seem to pay more attention to sailing than to seamanship. Any idiot can make a boat go. Ninety-five percent of seamanship lies in the art of keeping the boat from moving. The below aphorisms, when taken together, go some distance toward describing the art of anchoring in the trades.

Don't anchor near boats with damaged topsides.

No explanation necessary.

Don't anchor near boats with performance hulls or rigs.

Likely these five-percenters have only five feet of chain. They dance all over the harbor in any breeze. I watched one hull-sailing full circles all night long. He had two anchors, thank goodness, and the boat wound itself up like a cuckoo clock and took off on the other tack for another fifteen circles.

Set anchors by wind and current first (when you have them).

Not by someone behind eighty horses unable to see the tension on the rode. Burying types such as Bruces and plows, dig in by wiggling and worming with the action of the sea and tug of the chain. If you apply full tractor power to them before they've set, they will revert to kind and plow a furrow. Watch for drag by picking a range (not other boats)

134

perpendicular to the extended rode. Also, a grasped rode can telegraph dragging to your hand. It may prove difficult to set any anchor in mangrove mud in windy conditions or hard marl. Arrive in those harbors early, *before the trade wind comes up*. Otherwise, try to motor into the wind at low revs so as to maintain slow enough sternway to permit the anchor to set.

Anchors like to get laid, not dropped, thrown or swung.

All anchors benefit by proper *laying*, but especially Fortress and Bruce types. *Laying* an anchor implies touching its crown to the bottom, gently *laying* it biting side down, and controlling a smooth backward drift in the direction of the expected flow of wind or current, while *laying* the chain in a straight line behind the straightly *laid* anchor. *Lay* enough chain to ensure pull on the anchor directs itself along the bottom, which you gently hook. Pay out more rode and dig it in again. Pay out 30% - 50% more rode than your final scope, and test with motor, gently at first. Sailors who routinely talk about *dropping* the hook often do have little hooks instead of proper anchors, and they usually simply drop them, heavily trussed in a bundle of rope and chain.

Let the yacht come to rest before setting scope.

Snug in to your final scope only after securing the yacht and tidying up the deck. That will ensure more time for her to reach rest condition. The seaman who takes longest to get his yacht settled on her anchors probably does the best job of anchoring.

Dive on the anchor, if possible, to check it.

If necessary, set it by hand. While down there check your neighbors' as well. I cruised in company with a good friend, a professional diver on the oil rigs. In deference to his skills (and my taste) I started on the SG&Ts while he dived on our anchors. He found a neighbor's CQR lying sideways on the bottom. "Impossible!" shouted the salty-whiskered downeaster while posed cross-armed and bantam-like on his taffrail. "I set that anchor with 55 horses!" My friend set the fellow's anchor for him in order to protect our own boats.

Select your anchors for bottom and boat.

See the tables in this chapter which demonstrate the holding power of some anchors, ground tackle strengths, and data which you can use to figure the loads generated on your anchors and rodes while riding out a Class 1 hurricane in a protected hole. The data may surprise you.

Use about a pound of anchor for every foot of the boat. A 45 pound Danforth would suit a 41 foot boat, but not as a single anchor if wind or current can switch. Danforths, while capable of tremendous holding power, do not reset themselves well and the stock can easily foul. Heavy burying type anchors such as the CQR or Bruce work well on most all bottoms and tend to reset themselves. Use Danforth types, CQR or Deltas in mud or grassy bottoms, making well sure the points dig in. In a blow, Danforths hold best pound for pound, but no matter what the Danforth folks say, don't use a short length of chain. It may function in theory but, in the tropics, any nylon rode less than one inch shall most certainly chafe through on the bottom, if not by coral, then by broken rum bottles.

For rocky bottoms use a heavy prayer.

In coral rock, whatever you put down may just break off a bit of coral and come loose during the night. If you mange to set an anchor on smooth, hard rock, it shall scrape and bounce across the bottom as soon as wind or current changes and it dislodges. In boulders you may ride safely through the night but lose your anchor in the morning.

Use enough chain: long enough and big enough.

Consider first that the chain's catenary must never reach the anchor itself so as to exert upward drag on the shank — even in the most violent conditions — especially in the most violent conditions. Second, ensure that any fiber rode attached cannot come into contact with the seabed or obstructions on it (coral heads, rocks, wrecks and broken rum bottles).

Take care that chafe at deck level does not occur, or consider using all chain. The catenary of an all chain rode makes a good shock absorber. If you use all chain, attach a half inch 3-strand nylon snubber as long as necessary to quiet the action. Use absolute minimum chain length of five feet for every sixteenth of an inch of chain size, i.e., twenty five feet for 5/16 chain, thirty feet for 3/8, etc. Another rule of thumb: use a boat length. These rules assume you anchor in water no deeper than triple your keel depth.

For full displacement boats, add a sixteenth of an inch in chain size for every ten feet of boat's length above twenty feet. Thus, for LOA's 20-29 feet use 5/16 inch chain, for 30-39 feet use 3/8 inch, for 40-49 feet use 7/16 inch, and for 50-59 feet use 1/2 inch.

For all chain use a scope of three to five times the depth of water added to the distance from sea level to anchor roller.

For chain and fiber rode use a scope five to seven times the depth added to the distance from sea level to anchor roller.

To reduce the amount of scope required in tight anchorages, consider extending your anchor snubbers from a rugged bow eye you build in at the water line.

Use two anchors when in doubt.

You'll find few actual uses of the Bahamian Moor, one anchor against each expected change of current direction: tidal bays, coves, creeks or rivers, places where currents can become strong and regularly reverse with the tide. Most anchorages don't have these effects, so why else use two anchors?

Because everyone around you does, and if you don't you'll find your bow poking into someone's bedroom in the middle of the night.

Because you expect a switch in the wind or a front to come; or worse, because you don't expect it.

Because the harbor goes absolutely calm at night and you want to prevent the boat from walking around your lone anchor, droodling chain all over and under it, so that when the morning wind rises you drag onto the beach, towing a ball of tackle.

Because you come first in a harbor used by the charter companies, and you expect 40 partying bareboaters to plunk balls of chain all around you in the middle of the night and you want to keep your elbows tucked in.

Because you don't want to wind your rode around a coral head.

Because you're in the anchorage for the first time and you don't feel quite sure about that wide open fetch to the southwest.

Because you're leaving the boat unattended.

BUT, if everyone else swings to one anchor, go with the flow and set only one yourself so they don't bash you.

And, oh yes, always set your anchor to the direction of the trades.

I don't care what direction the boats lay to when you arrived in harbor.

WEIGHING ANCHOR

The following may seem old hat. But sit any morning in harbor and watch the scene while folks up anchors. Before observing too long, you'll want a tot of rum in your morning coffee.

When weighing anchor, keep the chain vertical.

Doing this ensures two things. First you shall approach the anchor along the chain's lie and in a pace commensurate with safety and the proper stowing of the tackle. Secondly, you unlay the links of chain right up to the anchor's shank, ensuring that you don't dislodge the anchor until ready and it won't skitter and roil around the seabed fouling things like other people's rodes. Keep the chain vertical under the bow by never powering beyond the catenary. Instead let the catenary pull the yacht forward, not the coronary. And use the windlass only to pull up slack links, not to pull the yacht.

Keep station until the anchor clears the water.

The bane of all anchorages, the morning clod who, upon sensing the anchor has broken loose, turns his head aft and yells "She's up!", and off the yacht drifts downwind, with a giant grappling hook beneath her soaring a few inches off the bottom, headed almost surely for *your* rode. Even bane-ier: the knuckle head who powers about the anchorage with an acute angle of chain stretched behind the bow while the crew tries to wrestle up the taut chain and anchor before they snag — you guessed it — *your* rode!

Mangrove anchorages have a colloidal mud bottom which makes the anchors-up drill a messy, sweaty job. Best you should, as noted in the section on staging, do the cleanup the day before leaving. Wherever possible, depart fresh and rested from a clean, short rode. Ground tackle cleanup should never have to upset your departure timing.

> **Set or weigh anchor before or after the trades blow, never *while* they blow.**

OPEN ANCHORAGES

Know your criteria for choosing anchorages while passage making. If your weather window starts to close on you earlier than you thought it would, you may get stuck in your anchorage for a considerable time doing another wait for weather. One wants a good hangout. Ditto, fishing and diving. Consider comfort as well, but not to your detriment.

No one wants to suffer a rolly anchorage, but landlocked anchorages don't always suit passage making by harbor hops. You tuck into anchorages *enroute*, you don't set up winter camp. In the trade wind belt the wind direction stays rock steady. This makes for minimum roll in even wide open lee anchorages. Open anchorages in the lee of an island, a reef or a headland can make daysails out of overnights in settled weather.

Ideally, a lee anchorage on a weather beach should have deep sand with lots of productive coral heads or rocks under keel depth. The skipper can anchor to windward of a good fishing spot and let out rode until the stern sits over his dinner. Plans for an arrival during favorable light conditions, often over the shoulder light, should of course consider the light needed underwater to skindive up your dinner from the bathing ladder, usually while you still have a high sun. That way the dinghy can stay in the davits.

Often cruisers on downwind passages among islands get so enamored of their progress they continue right past ideal sandy beach anchorages on the lee sides of the islands, then find themselves sailing among reefs and islands in the dark. It only would have taken a few minutes to have loosed sheets and rounded up into these well protected lees, and anchor in their deep sand bottoms. The idea that the boat would lie open to ocean on three sides haunts the skipper new to the trades. So they don't stop. Nor do the trades in their relentless easterly flow, making such lee side beaches ideal in settled weather.

ANCHORS AND GROUND TACKLE

You may come from the Chesapeake Bay or the Los Angeles area. Though capable of holding your 38 foot boat quite happily at home, a twelve pound Danforth Deepset and a half inch nylon rode with 6 feet of chain, as recommended by Danforth himself, will not suffice in the coral strewn tropics. If the sun doesn't melt such thin fiber rode then chafe from the bottom or the bow will surely set you adrift some night.

I've seen many cruisers with too light and too few anchors. They usually use no swivels and favor undersized nylon rode behind too little and too small chain. Many came from home ports where they spent years of recognition as knowledgeable boaters. All of them leave the trades with big anchors and heavy chain.

Use Danforth type anchors for grassy and mud bottoms. Heavy burying type anchors work better on coarse sand bottoms or hardpan, clay and shale. Both types of anchors can hook or wedge fast in rock and coral bottoms, but a heavy plow type will dislodge the easiest when you go to get it up in the morning, and it will have less chance of getting bent if a you get caught in a high chop. I've come to prefer the Bruce for all but grass, and there I use the CQR. Both heavy.

My Fortresses wait in the bilge and lazarette with all my old chain for use in hurricane season. A 20 pound Danforth works as an occasional lunch hook to keep the boat comfortable in swell when out for the day with friends. Counting the dinghy grapnel, I have aboard at least five anchors, and I have had as many as nine aboard. You can never have too many anchors or too much used chain, because if you don't use them for moorings, you can always make money selling them in hurricane season to the goofs that have too few.

Below I've listed some facts from my logbook, gleaned from too many sources to recount. I give them for the reader who, like me, can't easily find the data compiled in one place. When time comes for refurbishing my ground tackle, I make my purchasing decisions for my boat from these notes and calculations. But, like all statistics these numbers can tell different stories to please the tale teller.

The following table shows pounds of cable tension necessary to drag different anchors when set with a 5:1 scope in soft mud before getting well silted in (which could take weeks). Note that this differs from some holding powers which may imply breaking strengths of the gear. Multiply by 5 to obtain figures for hard sand.

138

INCH DIAMETERS	1/4	5/16	3/8	7/16	1/2	5/8	3/4	7/8	1"
BBB CHAIN '3B'		1,700	2,320	3,160	4,120	6,300			
PROOF COIL 'G3'	1,250	1,900	2,650	3,520	4,500	6,800			
HIGH TEST 'G4'	2,600	3,900	5,400	7,200	9,200				
STAINLESS CHAIN	2,000	2,850	3,550	4,300					
GALV. FALSE LINKS	1,400	2,000	2,800	3,720	4,750	7,250			
GALV. SHACKLES	1,000	1,500	2,000	3,000	4,000	6,500			
GALV. SWIVELS	850	1,250	2,250		3,600	5,200	7,200		12,500
NYLON 3-STRAND		240	340	470	520	620	1,380	1,880	2,460
DACRON BRAID		230	330	500	640	700	1,600	2,300	2,800

Safe Working Loads in pounds for Ground Tackle

- Safe Working Loads (SWL) for chain runs about 40% of the load under which chain links begin to elongate prior to breaking. If you find elongated links, chop them out and splice with false links, also called connecting links.
- You may exceed SWL of galvanized chain under shock load without permanent damage, but the chain should get replaced when elongation begins to occur. All galvanized chain will elongate up to 15% before breaking.
- You should never exceed SWL of shackles and swivels.
- Proof Coil chain has already had tests to 200% of SWL.
- High Test chain may have from 2 to 3 times the SWL of Proof Coil, but High Test chain breaks in a shorter time after elongation than does Proof Coil and BBB.
- Ultimate Breaking Load (UBL) of Proof Coil and BBB chains run 4 times the SWL.
- UBL of High Test chain runs about 3 times SWL.
- UBL of galvanized shackles and swivels run up to 6 times their SWL.
- UBL of stainless shackles and swivels run double their SWL.
- Dacron Braid has no stretch and its UBL runs up to 5 times the SWL.
- Nylon 3-strand will stretch up to 33% and its UBL runs up to 10 times the SWL, making it ideal anchor rode.

TYPE of KNOT	% REDUCTION in UBL
EYE SPLICE (4 tucks, 3 tapers, unfinished)	15
CLOVE HITCH	30
ROUND TURN and TWO HALF HITCHES	30
ROLLING HITCH	40
BOWLINE	50
OVERHAND KNOT	60
SQUARE KNOT, (REEF KNOT)	60

Effect of Knots on Nylon Rode

The above values show the percentage reduction in Ultimate Breaking Load (UBL) in 3-strand nylon rope tied with the indicated knots.

In addition, the strengths of nylon ropes reduce by up to 15% when wet.

WEIGHT OF ANCHOR IN POUNDS	10	20	30	40	50	60
BRUCE	110	180	230	280	330	370
CQR (plow)	160	250	330	400	470	530
DANFORTH TYPE	460	730	960	1,160	1,350	1,500

Lbs. Cable Tension to Drag in Soft Mud at 5:1 Scope

		TRAWLER				CENTER COCKPIT			
		DOUBLE CABIN		SEDAN		SLOOP		KETCH or YAWL	
LOD (feet)	LWL (feet)	wind on the BOW	wind on the BEAM	wind on the BOW	wind on the BEAM	wind on the BOW	wind on the BEAM	wind on the BOW	wind on the BEAM
28	23	1,578	3,595	2,623	5,246	1,150	2,890	1,610	3,520
30	25	1,812	4,122	2,978	5,991	1,310	1,310	1,830	4,020
32	27	2,046	4,692	3,351	6,786	1,490	3,770	2,070	4,560
34	28	2,280	5,262	3,723	7,582	1,660	4,220	2,300	5,100
36	30	2,558	5,890	4,146	8,478	1,860	4,740	2,560	5,710
38	32	2,835	6,577	4,586	9,426	2,070	5,280	2,840	6,360
41	34	3,274	7,600	5,263	10,882	2,380	6,110	3,260	7,340
43	36	3,595	8,375	5,771	11,965	2,620	6,730	3,570	8,070
45	38	3,946	9,178	6,295	13,082	2,870	7,380	3,900	8,830

Lbs. Wind Drag on a Yacht in a Category 1 Hurricane (up to 80 knots)

The table above shows pounds of drag exerted on various yacht configurations in 80 knots of wind, both on the bow and on the beam while the yacht sheers.

✓ Sailboat data includes spars, standing/running rigging, stanchions and lifelines.
✓ Trawler data includes spars, stanchions and lifelines.
✓ Data assumes you stowed all canvas below.
✓ Data assumes hull streamlining efficiency of 20% (30% = maximum for a yacht).
✓ Data does *not* consider the effects of seas or shock loads while sheering.
✓ Data assumes you put the yacht in a secure hurricane hole with *no wave action*.

Since load increases with the square of the velocity of the wind, and wind gusts to 50% of its average, you should notice the complete futility of riding out a severe hurricane at anchors. "Hurricane moorings" exist only in fiction. If the mooring holds, either it or other boats shall beat you into the bottom. If the pennants hold, they'll saw your bow off.

You can see the stress on a yacht's ground tackle gets brutal indeed. After yanking around with great shock loads you should inspect each link of chain for elongation. Rodes subjected to severe and prolonged stretching should get replaced. See also the table on the weakening effects of using various knots on your nylon rode.

USING THE RADIO
First read your manual, then apply common sense.

VHF

FM Radio Telephony, or VHF, has reached an interesting stage of development. Rules for using the VHF got developed for poor reception. When Alpha wants to call Bravo, Alpha should say "Bravo, Bravo; Alpha" and Bravo should reply "Alpha, Bravo; nn", where *nn* means the number of a working channel to which they both repair.

Now that VHF provides high quality reception at a cheap price, every boob has one into which he speaks as would Thomas Alva Edison into the ear of Victorola's dog if he had expected the dog to speak back to him. Worse, Bravo has invented a lottery in which he asks Alpha to "Pick a channel". Although they call each other several times a day, they will usually pick channels which neither has. Then they talk in International Signals Code over the telephone. These guys also call themselves "THE Bravo", or worse, "This is the sailing vessel Alpha". Sheeesh!

These same guys play CAPCOM MCC (Capsule Communicator, Mission Control Center) and say "Affirmative" and "Negative" and "Roger That" three times each to a boat two hundred yards away. Deke Slayton took endless ribbing when he slipped up on acknowledging a complex transmission from space with "Roger ... uh ... that". He never did 'that' again. But today a whole new generation of Captain Videos repeat it and other airwave eating clichés — endlessly. Myself, I like to play Glenn Ford at the controls of his screaming Saberjet calling to his wingman . . .

In most anchorages VHF users lay in good hail of each other on low power. In remote harbors without telephone they may have 200 land stations and 50 boats. Worse, in some yachting centers they may have 50 land stations and 400 boats. Just following the normal rules with power down shall reduce traffic and hasten communications.

DOs rarely DONE	DON'Ts DONE frequently
turn your power down	Don't call yourself anything but your name, Red Ryder.
find an idle channel before calling	Don't talk HAM or CB, good buddy.
talk normally, and out of the wind	Don't eat your microphone.
wait thirty seconds for Bravo to answer before calling again	Don't repeat everything twice.
get off the hailing channel with minimum chatter	Don't use channels permanently assigned (e.g., Coast Guard, hotels ...)
use your mother's language	Don't sit on your handheld's transmit switch, blocking all traffic for hours, while the whole harbor listens to your muffled grousing about your spouse.
make each transmission brief and use a minimum of words	Don't chastise non-English speakers without understanding them.
repeat only if asked	Don't deputize yourself a Radio Nazi.

Radio Nazis sit by the radio and bust in with chapter and verse of the Law of the VHF. They take up more air time than casual abusers because their dictates get followed by storms of support from the Good Citizens around and Bronx cheers from the Outlaws and the Rowdies in the harbor. Unless duly authorized officials of the country whose air they use, you can tell the Radio Nazis to take their Barstool Regulations and . . .

VHF B UDDY C HANNELS

> **CAUTION : never use "buddy channels" to the exclusion of Channel 16.**

I recall two yachts which crossed the steel cables of a 1500 foot tow at night, while the tug's skipper bawled on Channel 16, and I desperately dialed around to find their buddy channel. The hawser could have sawn the boats in halves, sintering fiberglass and flesh in a heartbeat. It took instead a small bite from a skeg. Until the cables bit into the second boat's skeg, the two yachties sailed blithely in the night unaware of the approaching guillotine. They stood tuned to buddy channel 66 without a dual watch or a scan to 16.

SSB, OR HF

I took a weather window on an exposed coast that I knew had a certain risk of collapse. I heard a yacht radioing a friend that he intended to use the first of two open anchorages. I had that intention as well, until I heard the 6 p.m. weather. The window would collapse. A stalled front had begun to move quickly. I headed directly to the second anchorage, thinking to rest and look again at the weather. If the front continued I had just enough time to boogie around the end of the island into a safe refuge, something I couldn't do from the first anchorage.

Stupid me, I did what one must never do. I offered gratuitous help. I called the yacht behind me and advised the skipper of the weather changes and of what I intended to do. He said he hadn't listened to weather all day or the night before. Stupid him.

I arrived at the second anchorage and promptly went to bed, knowing I might get chased out early by a bad weather report. The alarm woke me at the appointed hour and I turned on the SSB. The other guy now lay next to me, gabbing on a close by frequency. His interference made it impossible for me to receive weather reports by either telex, fax or voice. I stayed awake for the next 6 hours trying to get weather. Each time I began to get a report the guy started blabbing with relatives on nearby HAM frequencies or with cruisers over marine SSB. I couldn't raise him on VHF. He had turned his off, though security precautions would have it on. I finally got pieces of a report through his noise. The advancing front had slowed. My normal departure time now only 2 hours away, I just couldn't get back to sleep. While I raised anchor, the guy doubled the insult. He popped up and wanted to know what I'd heard on the weather!

> **If you use a manual tuner, tune up low power 6 KHz away from a used channel.**
> **If you use an automatic tuner, tune well off a net frequency, not right on it.**
> **Don't use a frequency near half or double that of an in use weather net.**

EMERGENCY PROCEDURES

Use VHF 16 for all emergency traffic as well as for initial contacts. Leave your VHF on channel 16 when not in use. Use these levels of safety broadcasts on whatever radio:

securité (say-CURE-it-TAYE, French for *safety*) Broadcasts of navigational hazards come after the word securité said 3 times. For example, a sea mark out, or off position, or a tow restricting passage in a channel.

pan (PAHN, Greek for *everywhere*) Broadcasts of lookouts for personal safety follow the word pan said 3 times. For example, when the Coast Guard has lost contact with an overdue boat, or when you have lost the ability to maneuver, but life threats do not exist.

mayday (MAY-day, kind of French for *help me*) Broadcasts of imminent danger to life proceed from the word mayday said 3 times. Use mayday if sinking, if on fire, if someone has gone overboard, or for any immediate threat to life. Do the following:

1. Set the VHF to 16, and the SSB to USB 4426, 6501, 8764, 12788 or 13089.
2. Clearly and slowly pronounce, "mayday, mayday, mayday".
3. Say your boat type and name, "[sailboat, or trawler, or motor yacht] Boatname".
4. Clearly and slowly give your position: "latitude 1-8-0-4, longitude 6-5-2-8".
5. Repeat the emergency simply, "sinking, sinking", or "man overboard" or "fire".

If you can't stand by your radio, repeat the mayday several times, hammering on position and type of distress. Force yourself to speak clearly, slowly and with a minimum of words. Everyone shall understand "man overboard" even with bad reception. No one can grasp the nature of a rapidly shouted "my husband was looking over the stern and fell in the water and I can't find him". See also the chapter on *Security Afloat.*

FINDING THE BOAT

As with most things in life, we spend too much time and effort looking for stuff in the wrong places.

PROJECT PLANNING
Defining the problem by owning up to illiteracy.

Although I have bought, sold and traded many boats, I found myself on this occasion forced to make a change while, as usual, strapped for funds. I decided this time I would make it a hardheaded business project. Project control got computerized from the first, for which reason I have the first detail account of one of my boat deals. And perhaps therefore, the most successful. I offer its history to you as a model.

Whether you want to trade up or stand pat, go to power or sail, new or used, the following experience can help you evaluate what you have versus what you want, and that versus what you should have, for cruising the islands of the trades.

For me the problem defined itself easily. Forty-five years of sailing had to end, however grudgingly. Skin cancer, a stroke leaving me with bouts of vertigo and a foot that dragged, missteps at night while working on deck single-handing a big ketch through the islands. Clearly, to continue running the island chains, I had to get off the deck, get under cover and get inside something I couldn't easily fall out of.

Jalan Jalan

Several "millimeter pads" got used up sketching houses to put on my classic clipper, *Jalan Jalan*. Whatever I sketched amounted to her total rebuild. Anyway, the extreme ugliness of anything I could design for her eclipsed any worry about time and cost. *Jalan*, the apotheosis of a lifetime's boats, should have sailed with me until the end. Heart in my boots, I began to look for a trawler to continue our blue water passages.

First I needed an education in trawlers, just as when I upgraded from racing boats to my first liveaboard, and as when I switched from coastal to ocean navigation.

146

EDUCATION

I read books and talked to owners. I found that sail and power have many differences, most of which seem driven by demands of the market and the outfitters rather than those of the sea. They also use different terminology. For instance, power boaters call a shoe a skeg. I still don't know what the motor crowd call what a sailor calls a skeg. Whenever I described one, I got dumbstruck stares. I learned that power boats, motor yachts and trawlers differed in their owners' perspectives even more than did sloops and catamarans. Incredibly, power people called those sheltered back porches that I much admired, *cockpits*, even though one couldn't steer from them nor get wet in them. I had a lot to learn, but as one confirmed trawler man told me, "It's like riding a bicycle." I wished for a trainer like I got with my first liveaboard sailboat.

TRAINING WHEELS

I had a pittance in my "get well" fund, the money I would need should all come down the chute at once. Money which would let me go from life raft to shore, pay a few months' rent, get a car and a job. An *inviolable* account. I violated it to invest in a fixer-upper from a charter fleet. Profit from the enterprise would go toward the costs of simultaneously selling the sailboat and buying a trawler, a neat trick if I could swing it. Just the cost of getting *Jalan Jalan* to the Florida market, and keeping us there, me in beans and her in polish, until she sold, loomed tremendously over me.

The tired 35 foot charter queen, looking more like a giant sugar cube than a boat, gave me a home in the event *Jalan Jalan* sold. I could then use it to cruise around, with lots of time, and more money, to look for a more elegant solution.

Since *Jalan Jalan* means "aimlessly wandering", I named this sun deck trawler, *Tingal*, Malay for "I'm staying put", which I would have to do until one of them sold. Though a single screw, she was not a full displacement. To get speed from the power of her 6-cylinder engine her designers gave her a semi vee entrance and a hard chined dead rise configuration aft. This subtracted from the hull's downwind tracking ability, but she rolled less than a full displacement sailboat. The ride was nonetheless rougher. When I first experienced *Tingal*'s snappy chined roll in seas, I finally learned why they call full displacement hulls "sea kindly". Her additional speed, however, permitted a wide range of motoring tactics to control the tossing.

I made the delivery of *Tingal* alone. Running downwind in strong trades, I paced along with 8 to 10 foot cresting waves. This would have seemed exhilarating stuff with my sailboat, but my eyes never left the RPM gauge. For the first time in my life I had no sail to bail me out of my usual gross misjudgments while motoring. Reefs close abeam had never concerned me while running before the wind. I could always kick the helm over and reach on out of there under sail at the first contrary heave of a ground swell. Now I stayed two miles offshore. Only that Perkins stood between my soft body and destruction on the reef, an end not unlike that of a carrot's in a juicer. I began to think only insane people leave sail for power of any kind.

After a few hours of those conditions a sense of relative normalcy came over me. One eye still on the RPM, I speculated on performance tests one could make. The heavy sea conditions appeared perfect for discovering her points of instability. I'd heard that chined boats had an instability problem, a discontinuity in the smooth transition from stable to unstable. In 15 years operating *Jalan Jalan* I hadn't found any critical angle at all in the same conditions we now had.

Cautiously, at first taking shallow turns, I zig-zagged her down waves too monstrous for a Sunday picnic sail, but normal for fresh trades. I steadily increased the angle between zig and zag, having a great time, and glad my wife hadn't come with me. Tingal gave a nice progression of roll which, if drawn as a curve representing max roll angle versus zig angle on the seas, would have shown a gentle function indeed — clearly not even quadratic, let alone exponential, and much less roll than a sailboat. It turned out, however, her *instability* curve gave a chaotic function, discontinuous, and quite nearly disastrous.

At almost beam on to the seas she suddenly went unstable. Real sudden. I found myself looking down through the port door's window at the face of a cresting wave. The wave's crest rose closer to the fly bridge than its hollow came to the gunnel. She hung there in a freeze frame with the engine screaming to me that the prop had come out of the water. I confirmed the rudder had bitten air as well by sawing away at the wheel with no resistance. I must have kicked her to starboard just before the rudder dried out, for she had enough starboard momentum to get some part of her to bite into the sea in the right direction. She righted and skidded and damned near repeated the performance on the other side. Humbled and scared, I hunched over the RPM meter once more and steered a die straight course for *Jalan Jalan*'s harbor.

Tingal

PROJECT MANAGEMENT
Lotus 123™, the boat buyer's guide.

I use marine surveyors for insurance since they demand it, but for me, I do my own surveying. I crawl all over a boat with a mirror and mini light, a pencil and a checklist. Then I compare the results to my requirements list and to others surveyed. To make rational and economic decisions with no emotion involved, I created a computer spreadsheet template which I could apply to any boat I looked at. With the spreadsheet as a tool I traded off advantages and disadvantages between candidates. With a key stroke I could model the impact of making wanna-dos into hafta-dos, a neat method of setting value on emotional choices when they arose.

CROSSFOOTING THE CANDIDATES

All costs imaginable went on the spreadsheet. They fell into the following structure:

Fixed Costs:	commissioning and repairs to bring vessel to standard
	acquisitions for new refit items required
	cost of capital used (lost opportunity, interest)
Risk Costs:	*possible others* to come up on survey
Recurring Costs:	annual maintenance and operation

Cost of commissioning and repairs to bring vessel to standard:
Replace or dutchman where rotted
Haulout, scrape, paint
New cushions & carpets
Power distribution system
Revise engines, gauges, telegraphs
Recondition windows/frames
Clean, sand, varnish/paint
Replace corroded fittings
Review and renew all wiring

Cost of possible others (risk):
Overhaul engine/transmission;
Windlass replaced;
New refrigerator; Renew hydraulics;
Blisters on hull; Hull-deck join;
overhead leaks; etc., etc.

Cost of acquisitions:
Radios: SSB, VHF, AM/FM, antennas
Depthsounders (I have always put a sounder in the boat's forefoot)
Aluminum propane tanks
Autopilot
Genset if required
Fuel transfer/cleaning system
Batteries and controls (I like gels)
Solar Panels
Wind generators
Inverter/charger
Dinghy and outboard (gofast)
New engine or rebuild
Fixtures and furnishings (especially for work station)

Surprisingly, I could quite often generate the value of a particular wanna-do on a particular boat using data available on its spec sheet alone: LOA, LOD, LWL, displacement, horsepower, tankage, genset wattage, fuel consumption, (sail area) and so on. Though only numbers, when plugged into the spreadsheet they directly yielded values such as relative density which manufacturer's use to estimate the costs to build, or boat speed specific fuel consumption, a design efficiency ratio.

149

SETTING REQUIREMENTS

From my experience with *Tingal* I now knew my number one requirement:

FULL DISPLACEMENT.

Nothing less in trade seas. I sold *Tingal* after fixing her up. She made a great Virgins cruising boat, but I had two to three thousand miles a year in bluewater trades to do, half of it downwind. Her net proceeds gave me a marketing fund with which to sell *Jalan Jalan* and find the new vessel.

Having had a career managing complex projects, what more natural thing for me to do than develop a formal Functional Requirements Document? Right? Well, almost. If clear requirements and objectives help corporations and governments to allocate their resources with care, they might lead an aging sailor toward a sensible use of his dwindling purse.

Most of my initial ideas for a new boat came from what I had learned the hard way, messing about on sailboats for half a century. After 55,000 miles, mostly single-handed, *Jalan Jalan* and I talked a lot together. She had become a sentient mortal to me. I began to make lists, a shameful activity at first. I shoved them deep in my left pocket where she couldn't see them, and the lists grew slowly. Before long, however, I found myself jumping up in the middle of the night to jot down an idea. Even so, the hot items of midnight didn't always survive the cool of morning.

Any time I had for reflection, such as sucking a beer in the beach bar, out came the list for mental juggling and revision. When my pocket notes threatened to deteriorate from beer stains and pocket lint, or they became too greasy to write upon, I transferred them to the computer. While editing the computer file the week's penciled ideas met the much vetted digital ones, and that started a new round of shuffling and cutting. In theory, only important and feasible ideas made it back into my pocket in the serious form of a computerized list printed in Times New Roman.

Eventually I had a stable list of prioritized requirements above a cut line. Below the cut line I also had dozens of ideas for a refit. This began to get as exciting as all the times I had changed sailboats in the past. I felt full of plans for the future.

Priority	REQUIREMENT	RATIONALE
1	Full displacement	sea kindly, tracking, survivability
2	Single screw	low central ballast, F.D. hull can't use more power
3	Sedan superstructure	more accommodation, less exposure to sun and wind
4	flat roof, no flybridge	solar panels, wind generators, simplex steering
5	One forward stateroom	forehatch breeze at anchor, rare guests use saloon
6	Single head	no double trouble, only friends come aboard anyway
7	Walk-in shower	we have a home aboard, not a weekend camper
8	Large work station	area convertible to an office — with a real chair!
9	Long range	if I must burn fuel, let me find it at bargain rates
10	All round visibility	on deck a sailboat gives you 360°; plus, after living half my life below, in a cave, I needed the view.

Cost of capital:

For each candidate I also included its BUC market value before and after repairs and refit, adjusted for the Caribbean area according to BUC rules. The difference between what the sailboat would fetch and what the trawler would cost I played off against the difference between the apparent market value of the refitted vessel and the final cost estimate on the spreadsheet. This later became a bonus in negotiations, since I could graphically and rationally demonstrate to an owner my potential offer. Negotiations became business as usual rather than emotional haggling.

Annual maintenance and operation costs:

Finally, I calculated M&O costs at 3000 miles' usage for each candidate. This included fuel, oil, haul out, insurance, and of course, the spreadsheetist's friend, 'Other'. Note that most of this data can get generated automatically from hull LWL and engine horsepower given for each candidate.

A slam dunk on all 10 requirements didn't seem likely. For sure I would have to modify any candidate vessels in order for them to come up to these requirements and "meet spec". But a "fixer upper" would expose the project to time and cost overruns as well as quality risks. I needed to make rational and economic decisions within a sea of confusing choices, with no emotion involved. I needed numbers with which to calculate the true cost in time and money for any boat that aspired to take *Jalan*'s place.

I looked for ways to trade off time, labor and quality against 100% requirement fulfillment at the time of purchase. For example, I placed an upper limit of two years on any upgrade work. If forced to do a major refit, I based the cost estimates on three months in the States working on seaworthiness items, three months to drag her to South America for cheap labor, and 18 months work there — maximum.

CAMPAIGNING

I launched two marketing campaigns, one to sell my ketch, *Jalan Jalan*, and one to identify and buy the vessel to keep me running free in the trades.

First, I had to have a base from which to operate, and I had no doubts that Fort Lauderdale made the market. Most advertisers require copy and payment up to two months in advance, but you can change telephone numbers in the ads pretty much at the last minute, meaning I didn't have to solve my slip and phone problem until I got to Florida. I produced a full color brochure of *Jalan Jalan*, and a full spec sheet with picture and layout. I also placed ads under the "Trawler Wanted" category.

In Ft. Lauderdale I rented dock space at Hendricks Isle which had good access to interstates, airports and lay smack dab in the middle of the yacht market. I bought a boater's special beat up Toyota, ordered a phone and rented storage room. And I acquired my most important business asset at Office Depot, my secretary, a $90 US Robotics computer modem card. I programmed it to respond from multiple voice mailboxes. I also did a page on the Internet, got lots of hits, but not one serious inquiry. Overall, I found the Internet, as a marketing channel for private sellers, more hype than help. That may have changed by now, though hype probably still reigns over help.

With my voice mail fax modem, callers responding to my ads could key in whether they wanted to offer me information on a trawler or needed details on my sailboat. "Press 2 if you want to hear about the ketch for sale. Press 3 if you want an immediate fax back of its detail specifications. If you want to fax me data on your trawler, press 'send' now." And so on. I even sold the dinghy and motor separately through key 4. This computer tool permitted me to answer inquiries specifically and immediately with faxes, or with letters or phone follow-up later.

This simple to set up fax and voice mail system freed me to wander the State during the day surveying candidate trawlers and visiting brokers. In the evenings I processed a full in-basket of faxes and voice messages. I answered them all, or scheduled the computer to answer them by next morning, when I again set out by car. On the way to visiting brokers and inspecting trawlers, I carted my belongings off to the storage room. Nights, when I finished working with my computer 'secretary', I worked at putting my sailboat in show condition. She became a hotel suite, where I lived out of a suitcase, always ready to show her off to anybody that came by.

I credit this onboard automated office with the actual outcome of the campaign: three months after arriving in Florida I walked off *Jalan Jalan* and walked right onto *Tidak Apa*. I also hit the ground running, as they say, and worked without stint. In other words, I treated this business of selling and buying a boat as a business! A big one for me.

A cruiser who had come to Fort Lauderdale to sell his boat at the same time I did, met me as I prepared to leave.

"Congratulations!" he cried as he pumped my hand. "Our boat will move any day now. Any number of hot prospects. It's a continuous boat show aboard!" He had moored his boat on the upscale side of the island, where he had a swimming pool, patio bar, barbecue and bikinis. "Your boat is a significant investment, and it needs to be well represented," he had told me, as his exclusive listing broker must have had told him. It took him, or I should say, his broker, a year and several price reductions to sell it.

DANCING WITH BROKERS
Only at arms' length, and you do the leading.

I called upon a raft of yacht brokers, more than half of which required exclusive listings. Already doing my own marketing, I only took *open listings* under *my* terms. Nonetheless, all brokers received me as courteously and helpfully as possible, and I gave each a list of my 10 requirements for a trawler and the color brochure for *Jalan Jalan*.

Regarding my list of requirements, the need for a single screw became the hardest to explain. Most brokers, even the salty whiskered *yar* types, saw two engines as necessary for security. Several fellows made it clear that only a fool would set to sea with a single motor. When possible, I simply pointed skyward at the biplanes towing banners over the beach, suggesting he notify them to land their ships immediately. Designers add a second engine for more *speed*, not necessarily for more reliability.

The quest for speed and the acculturated security need for twin screws causes some to place an enormous iron dumbbell of two engines athwart-ships, a coupled force ballast which only ensures a good roll. A comfortably lower center of gravity of a single mid-ships engine and sea-kindlier speed doesn't sell on the waterway, however. Some brokers handled only waterway queens which never passed the seabuoy. They pursue a legitimate and lucrative market, but not for where the trades blow.

These guys usually asked, "How much do you want to spend?" before looking at what I wanted. Twice I got instructed by brokers that single-screw, single-stateroom boats did not exist above 35 feet LOA. Amazed at such assertions by professionals in the field, I asked, "What about the Krogen 42 or the Marine Trader 40 Sedan? What about the Lord Nelson Tug? The Schucker 440? The Nordic Tug?" No answer.

Most brokers fed parameters like price and hull type into a computer and reeled off a sheaf of Multiple Listing Service (MLS) spec sheets. At first this looked promising, but it didn't take me long to realize that these listings commonly represented the wallflowers of the fleet. The way it worked, brokers with an exclusive listing kept it off the MLS until they had a few months' crack at it. Since they already had to split the commission with their office, they would try to sell on their own before splitting it again with a faceless broker, someone who did nothing more than show a client a computer listing. Often the brokerage partners would give a senior broker a crack at it for another two months when the boat didn't attract interest, and they thought it ought to have. For these and other reasons it might take five months to get your boat listed anywhere but with your exclusive broker.

Don't blame the brokers. They often have to split a commission three times, or, in other words, settle for one eighth of their target. 12½% (or one-eighth) of 5% yields only 0.625%, or only $625 on a $100,000 boat. I got the impression that many of the brokers I met owed their soul to the local Jaguar dealer, while they lived in a fourth floor flop on dog food. Any system, no matter how good at first, suffers over time from too intensive development. Like states or really large corporations, brokerage businesses could benefit from revolution or renewal. But also like states and corporations, that won't happen easily.

As the Coast Guard says, "Be advised:", by the time your boat wends its way through the broker underbrush into the MLS outback, it shall become unpopular through no fault of its own. Better you stay on top of it yourself, or resign as much as 20% of its value.

Discouraged by the responses I got in my hunt for a trawler, I began to include work boats and fixer-uppers in my sweep. Within a week I received more relevant spec sheets faxed from owners than all the brokers could deliver from their computer networks.

FRIENDLY ADVICE

Norman Churchill, a dear friend who had preceded me in converting to power after many years cruising under sail, listened to my requirements. He suggested I give a look at the Schucker. Jim Schucker had built 250 of the boats in Cape Coral, Florida from 1977 to 1980. Designed as motorsailers, 20% sold as trawlers with a fly bridge instead of a sailing rig. The Schucker fell on my eye, it's stout construction and commodious layout notwithstanding, as something Goofy and Clarabelle ought to drive. After decades dinghying out to classically lined sailboats, I couldn't stand the idea of coming home each night to a comic satire. It seemed I had my own acculturated tastes to overcome.

"You need a Schucker," Norm patiently insisted. I surveyed one that needed work just a week before it sold. Another came on the market and, as quickly, left. It had a fly bridge which I would have had to have cut off to achieve my flat roof.

When a third Schucker appeared on the market, a 440 motorsailer without its mast, I looked at it for Norm's sake. It had 400 gallons of fuel, 200 of water and a Perkins 4-236, which at 85 hp burned only 1.25 gallons an hour at 6 plus knots, or 5 miles per gallon for a 2000 nm range. The previous owner had removed the sailing rig and made her a trawler. She had a head and walk-in shower forward which, like some cruising sail designs, aptly solved the problem of the unusable fore peak. She had scads of space for storage around and under the queen bed which lay under a 4 square foot hatch for at-anchor ventilation. Flat roofed with wide overhangs, she carried a long keel, 18 inches wide and flat on the bottom. A huge bronze shoe kept lines out of the prop -- or should I, as a trawler man, call that a skeg?

An added bonus, her barn door rudder could turn her while making way without power. Something I found with panic that motorboats don't do. The first time I drove my training trawler, *Tingal*, in a tight marina I found myself inches from tee-boning a megayacht, probably owned by a lawyer. It didn't occur to me at all naturally to do what one must do with power boats about to tee-bone another boat: apply full revs right at the guy with full helm on! While most power boats turn by throwing prop wash over the bitty deflectors they use for rudders, sailboats maneuver on the rudder's slipstream, even while reducing way. The Schucker had a schooner hull with a schooner size rudder.

FINAL DECISION

A buyer made a date certain to take *Jalan Jalan*. My trawler education nearly complete, and the sailboat all but sold, doubts began to nibble. What if I had to move to an apartment, spending my boat capital like a farmer eating his seed corn? Homeless shelters and employment offices which I had not before noticed now seemed placed about town with undue prominence.

While in the bilges seriously surveying a prodigally well built Marine Trader 40 Sedan, comparisons with Goofy and Clarabelle's boat kept tugging at me. On my back and upside down, in the heat and excitement of penciling the refit of that dream of an MT40 onto my pocket list, the comic satire of the Schucker tacked in and out of my mind. The MT40 had a long list of tradeoffs and refits, which I happily anticipated. I ticked off each

one of my original requirements under the flashlight's beam. The MT40 had me really excited, though it met only 70% of the requirements. Goofy and Clarabelle's boat met each requirement 100%. To boot, both fixed and recurring costs spreadsheeted in at grass level along with risk.

No emotions involved, I told myself. Did I have a frivolous requirements list?

I couldn't get to the bank fast enough. Afraid this third Schucker would also not last long on the market, I arranged to wire a deposit. Three weeks later I walked off *Jalan Jalan* and took possession of the Schucker 440, which I named *Tidak Apa*, my fifth Malayu boat name. *Tidak Apa* means "it doesn't matter anymore" and "it doesn't make any difference". And I hoped with all my soul it wouldn't.

SEA TRIALS

A real shakedown cruise before hitting the trade belt.

You can't take a run around the seabuoy and expect you've made ready for the trades. A full local sea trial shall net you enough re-dos to keep you busy awhile. After that the real sea trial should encompass a thorough cruise: long enough to run out of stores, water, fuel; rough enough to bust a sail, a cooling hose, your favorite coffee cup; enough sea time to slacken motor mounts, engine alignment, hose clamps; and enough to chafe through some wiring, deck lashings, or your wife's favorite blouse. Chafe especially finds the errors in all those slick little solutions you made in your stowage schemes. A sea trial cruise must really un-gang the shiny new or refit installations until they've passed their burn-in failures, and they happily chug along with each other on their normal life cycles of service. More on this later under Equipment Reliability, and back for now to my refit.

I quickly replaced hoses, converted from electric to propane, loaded the roof with wind generators and solar panels, plumbed in fail-soft fuel and lube systems, added a 44 Bruce and a 45 CQR with lots of chain, and sailed for the Bahamas to begin a real cruiser's sea trial. I had the tools and the spares to do it without returning. The gizmos and doo-hickeys would get taken care of on the passages south from the Bahamas.

I used the 1200 mile windward route through the islands with which I had 20 years of experience. I didn't sweat it. I figured a trawler should like to go against sea and wind more than across it, just not too much of either. I can find lulls in the trades, but after that near suicide on *Tingal*, beam seas without sail now worried me, so did strong downwind trade seas.

Another friend, who had already made the switch from sail to power, got only as far as the Dominican Republic before turning back to fit on flopper stoppers. I did not want the expense and bother of gantried paravanes. A tangle of cables and spars would only complicate the basic job of learning to motor a boat at sea without a sail. If they became necessary, they'd come later. For the nonce, I intended to substitute their cost and nuisance with more careful navigation planning.

As it turned out, I successfully avoided beam seas all the way down islands and back by simply following the advice in *Passages South*, and doing what I did with my sailboats: wait for favorable conditions. From Florida to Tortola I had nothing but kindly seas under three feet. As for seas astern, my concerns evaporated the day I turned downwind. With each wave *Tidak Apa*'s egg shaped schooner stern lifted as certain and sure as with a hydraulic ram, then settled dead in line with the run of the seas. A real full displacement, long-keeled action.

I've found that I tack less than I would have under sail, but still I tack. Many of my trawler colleagues so concentrate on headings and bearings, on getting from point A to B, that they accept discomfort rather than tack (or wear, downwind). The action of sea, current and wind lies in my bones. I go for comfort always. I find myself burning margin-ally more fuel than I did with my sailboat, and I don't have to amortize the costs of sail and rigging replacement.

I can truthfully recall no tears shed in the transition, and none of the heartbreak I had expected in parting with, *Jalan Jalan*, my faithful and beloved partner of 15 adventurous years. She had, after all, written my top ten requirements for me, and the trawler *Tidak Apa*, though a sort of funny valentine, exceeded by miles each one of them.

OUTFITTER'S TRICKS

When you see your first single hander sporting a man
overboard pole, you shall know the mercantile pit from which
some cruisers learn their seamanship.

EQUIPMENT RELIABILITY
A knowledgeable look with a jaundiced eye.

My old boss, Dick, calls me in Göteborg, Sweden, at 3 a.m., 8 p.m. for him at Houston's Mission Control Center. He tells me Apollo has just exited the back side of the moon, and safely got reacquired by earth's computer systems. On a post crisis high, he just has to call. I don't know Apollo still flies, let alone that this one has troubles. I now work in Sweden at Volvo. I hadn't thought of NASA for three years.

He tells me the Mission Control Center's computers crashed five times in a row while the crew, with their own problems aboard, flew the back side of the moon incommunicado. If MCC failed hard at that point, ground systems around the world could not reacquire the ship. It would truly have become lost in space.

It made me think of getting lost at sea with my children aboard last Sunday while we sailed among the Skagerack islands.

Dick says that each time a computer had failed, another diagnosed the problem, successfully doctored it and took over the mission. But then another, unrelated failure happened to the fresh computer. This went on five more times giving the human controllers five quick visits to controller hell. Several years back we had integrated all the systems. I recalled our worst nightmare, a sick computer playing doctor on a healthy one. But that hadn't played out on this Apollo.

We talked, he and I, of old times at NASA. The early Scandinavian sun painted my drapes shiny gold. While he talked, I flashed to the 1967 reliability task force where I smart mouthed the brass. I told them they could only increase reliability by decreasing the Mean Time to Repair (MTTR), and only computers had the speed to do that. With the flippancy of youth I said we had to teach NASA's man rated mega-computers to diagnose and repair their own failures. They shut me up. They made me computer systems reliability manager. Somebody else worried about systems aboard the spacecraft itself — thank God!

Through integrating the hardware systems and doing some pretty sophisticated computer programming, we dragged down the MTTR of the Apollo computers to near zero. That stuff eventually migrated into mainframes, and now you can find updated versions of it in your laptop computer.

During Apollo I sailed around Clear Lake and on Galveston Bay. I used to dream how reliability innovations such as ours might work on my retirement sailboat, 30 years in the future. I envisioned myself sailing the world by waving a languid hand at dimly lit controls. How does it look now, several decades later? Any better?

Well, despite the current fad for integration of electronics, most boat gear still comes in fail-hard individual components, and they don't respond well when I wave at them. Can you configure them for total systems reliability? Look at the problem.

THE BATHTUB CURVE

As a software geek I've had to learn some engineer-speak to get along with hardware guys. Engineers have expressions as neat as those of the computer nerds. Take the Bathtub Curve for an instance.

Each software hunk, once it finally works, never wears out. Hardware, on the other hand, not only burns *out*, but it burns *in* as well. While the occasional gizmo might fail during the burn in test immediately after its manufacture, given enough time, all the gizmos shall burn out, as shall anything built by man, which includes engineers.

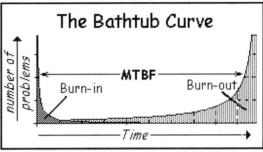

Engineers picture this life cycle of a gizmo with what they call the Bathtub Curve. Gizmos typically have a high infant mortality rate, but if they survive into childhood, they generally hang around through the graceful decay of maturity, perhaps even mislaying their reading glasses. This means that you shall likely have more trouble when you first install a device on your boat, if it doesn't fail outright, than in its subsequent daily use. And years later, when it goes terminal on you, it shall likely put you through a series of headaches before you chuck it over the side and buy a new one.

If you plot the number of problems you get with your boat over time, you'll get a Bathtub Curve for the whole boat as a complex system. We'll look at that, but for now look at one device at a time. Each gizmo leaves its characteristic ring in the bath tub at the tub's mean high watermark. Call it the Mean Time Between Failure (MTBF), or the time that the average gizmo in a large population of gizmos takes to burn out. Once done with its illnesses of infancy your equipment travels a risk curve that shows, at least at first, that the longer it runs well, the longer it shall continue to run well. Sounds like your life insurance man's statistics, doesn't it?

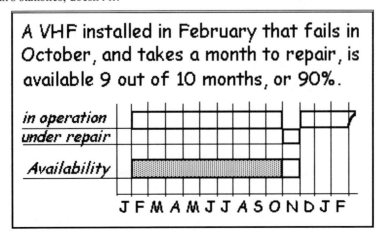

KISS VS. RAS

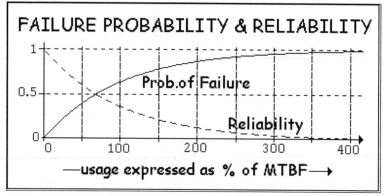

For most of the twentieth century sailors, and trawlermen alike, used the watchword KISS, for Keep It Simple, Stupid! Only glitzy megayachts could afford to high-tech it. But like Englishmen proud of their warm beer only until they got affordable refrigeration, even small craft sailors now forsake their KISS principle. With today's cheap electronics and information systems anyone can afford to get complicated. Even me.

Take the reliability engineer's trinity: Reliability, Availability and Serviceability (RAS). If you want to flood your boat with high-tech stuff at max reliability, max usage and most ease of fix, then you have a desperate need to know the RAS relationship. Note, though, that world cruising boats with high RAS values come neither cheap nor easy, since repairs come both slow and dear in Tierra del Fuego.

Availability refers to the amount of time you have a gizmo available for use without failures. You express availability as a percentage of the total time both in and out of service. Engineers, quite unimaginatively, call the total time a box lies out of service, plus the time to repair and place it back in service, its Time to Repair, or, in its mean state, MTTR.

One would think that high availability means high reliability. Not necessarily. Reliability comes from a low probability of failure, not from high availability. In addition, reliability also relates to the number and size of system components more than it does to availability.

COMPLEXITY

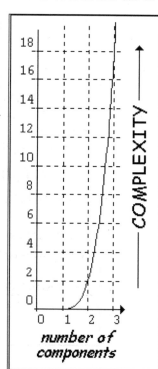

Humans have built quite a complex world since they first started messing with it. We built computers because the other stuff we've built in the last 100 million years or so grew too complex for the solitary naked human to handle. Now we build black boxes to coordinate and manage today's complicated nav systems.

You can make giant strides in both availability and reliability by taking aboard multiple copies of needed systems devices, but not without an unintended consequence. Doubling up on equipment can double your trouble.

In fact it can expand your troubles exponentially.

When you interconnect navigation gear, or install alternate power switches, you really proliferate system components, and therefore you increase failure points — drastically!

REDUNDANCY

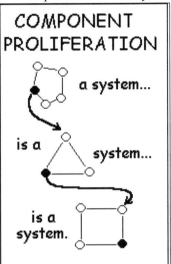

COMPONENT PROLIFERATION

a system...

is a

system...

is a system.

It seems our boats' components proliferate fore and aft with the arrival of each new marine catalog, and complexity soars. While complexity rides the waves, reliability wallows in the troughs. Calm this troubled sea by structuring the components.

Each component of a system itself has a system of subcomponents. For example, a VHF radio makes a system of power source, power cables, breaker switch, the radio itself and its antenna. The radio itself has controls, a display subsystem, receiver, transmitter and amplifier boards, and a speaker, each of these subject to shock, chafe, corrosion, lightning induced currents and, certainly in my case, user stupidity.

The more components you serially arrange, the less reliable the system. Your anchor chain, for example has a system reliability vastly lower than any one of its links, as the figure shows. But don't go shortening your chain for that reason.

Well, then, how about parallel devices?

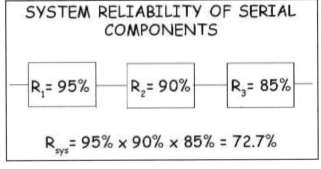

SYSTEM RELIABILITY OF SERIAL COMPONENTS

$R_1 = 95\%$ —— $R_2 = 90\%$ —— $R_3 = 85\%$

$$R_{sys} = 95\% \times 90\% \times 85\% = 72.7\%$$

As a blow boater I never understood the stink potter's love of redundancy. While fitting out my trawler, *Tidak Apa*, in Florida, most of my newfound trawler buddies crowed over their dual VHF and GPS installations. I got it figured out.

Most motor boaters cruise coastal waters where a VHF can get you a tow when you need it. While they short-hop narrow entrances on a lee shore, a GPS becomes a prime navigation tool rather than just a confirming navigation aid, the way I always use it.

A boater with three VHFs to select from would essentially have them available in parallel, and therefore have a damn near perfect VFH *systems* reliability.

I must perversely point out, however, that I bought the cheapest of the West Marine VHFs, and I have had it on 24 hours a day for 5 years without a single failure. But I expect that from a VHF, actually. I dual it only in the sense of having a handheld. What shall I expect of new and different gear, however? In deciding what to dual, triple or quadruple, you could use the manufacturers' MTBF estimates, but you'll never get them. Some bathtubs apparently have too much grime on their waterline ring.

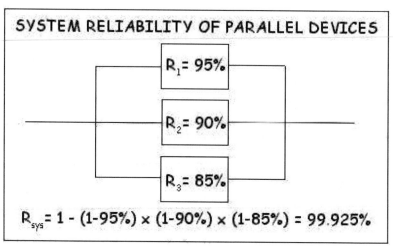

SYSTEM RELIABILITY OF PARALLEL DEVICES

$R_1 = 95\%$

$R_2 = 90\%$

$R_3 = 85\%$

$$R_{sys} = 1 - (1-95\%) \times (1-90\%) \times (1-85\%) = 99.925\%$$

SWITCHING

To raise your proliferating components' availability and your system reliability you can use much more than serial and parallel structures. You can break systems into switchable components which shall increase reliability and manageability as well. Consider the reliability of the ultimately switched VHF's shown here.

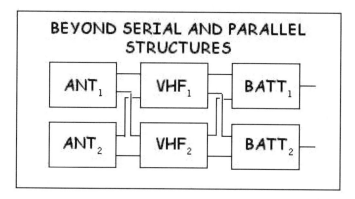

BEYOND SERIAL AND PARALLEL STRUCTURES

ANT_1 VHF_1 $BATT_1$

ANT_2 VHF_2 $BATT_2$

RECONFIGURATION

Consider a stack of batteries arranged through a crossbar switch. You can select any battery, any group of batteries or all batteries to participate in any function you define. And you don't have to crawl around in the engine room with a voltmeter to test an individual battery.

Some years ago I built a 2x3 switch like this for three 8Ds using flattened 5/8 inch copper tubing and the Hella battery switches rated at 100 amps continuous each. The switches' red flag handles which show either horizontal or vertical, made the crossbar switch easily readable against their teak panel even from a distance. How about a dozen group 27 gel cells stuffed all over the boat and run through a 3 by 4 crossbar?

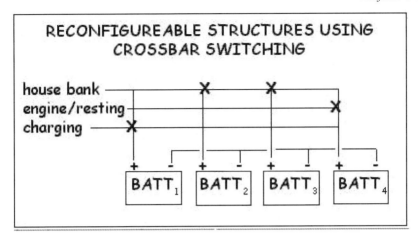

RECONFIGUREABLE STRUCTURES USING CROSSBAR SWITCHING

AVAILABILITY

Can you have too much? There exists for every boat and every skipper a unique performance envelope of max reliability for max availability. Trying to go beyond the envelope may increase availability, but it shall reduce reliability, since reliability inversely relates to the number of components by the quadratic.

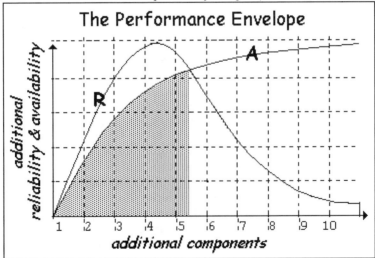

The Performance Envelope

So where do you belong in the envelope? I have an answer that works for me.

The 100 fathom line should separate **KISS**ers from **RAS**ers. Knowledgeable skippers that continually cruise blue water should still lean to **KISS**. Long-range, long-term cruisers, even if from trawlerdom, often prefer not to double up on some systems, but to double up on unit quality and on spares. So what if the VHF may fail when you don't have anyone to talk to within fifty nautical miles? Much less a Seatow. So what if the GPS goes blank, as it did the night Clinton bombed a Sudanese aspirin factory, and I lay between islands? I just threw a little more windward into the helm, going back to the normal navigation strategy of making intentional errors to windward, so that when you arrive at the coast you know you have to work it downwind to find your harbor. Technology won't in our lifetimes, nor those of our grandchildren, discount the need for knowledge of the sea nor of its navigation.

New gizmos shall always get invented to give us fun with failures. Imagine leaving your VHF on for 5 years when it first came out with radio tubes. It would probably have failed later than if you had turned it on and off lots, but it most probably would not have worked continuously for 5 years. Occasional, marina-hopping cruisers who can afford to push the RAS envelope brought about that reliability revolution as they shall the next revolution of integrated systems. Offshore long distance cruisers who some day shall simply wave a finger at a collective control shall owe them for it. For now and for me, I have most of the modern gizmos installed but rigidly separated. That way systems reliability doesn't worry me, nor does the reliability of most of the boxes. I use them, but I don't rely on them. I do rely on the fathometer and the bilge pumps, however. I have three of each, and each independently switched.

RASers should go for higher reliability navigation systems the nearer to shore they cruise. KISSers should go for redundantly installed and redundantly switched fail safe bilge pumps the farther offshore they cruise. But cruising the trade winds belt, power or sail, you need to load up on spares and the know-how to fix stuff.

GANGING

After some years of continuous cruising you stop having so many failures anyway. An effect I call *ganging* plays havoc with marina bound weekend cruisers and intermittent passage makers. You know the ganging effect well if you cruise to the Bahamas only to anchor several months in Marsh Harbor, then cruise back to Florida to hole up in Stewart for more months.

It works like this. When you fit out a yacht the first time, you have all new or renewed systems. From sea trial to somewhere way down the islands, you perform essentially what the engineers call Field Test. All your gizmos have started the teething stage of their burn-in. All their little bathtub curves have their faucet ends tucked up against the y-axis, ganged together like stock cars at the start line of a demolition derby. Once they all have gone around the track a few hundred miles, they'll sort of spread out evenly, but anywhere near the start, just like stock cars, the trouble incidents pile up.

When you plunk down your anchor in Marsh Harbor, you set yourself down to several months of sorting out all the bugs discovered enroute. Three months and three hundred (thousand?) dollars later you've got it all in hand, and you up anchor for Florida. You guessed it. Ganged again! Well, pretty much anyway. But you use the marina that lies so close to the marine store just for that reason, don't you? With intermittent cruising the ganging never stops.

Over all my cruising years I've seen many times more cruisers who gave up the game and went home than I have those that stuck to it. They first suffered through their ganging problems, then they fuss at every new incident until everything's all shiny new again, guaranteeing a slide back up the curve to a new set of ganged incidents.

By the third year after a refit my incidents usually settle down to one a month. Take the typical ground wire corrosion problem. I reach deep into the locker, jiggle the wire on its terminal block, and I get back into business for another three years. Lord help me if I empty the locker and set about fixing the problem.

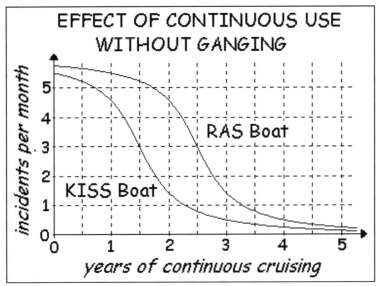

A tenet of reliability theory says that any tampering with working systems causes some regression along the RAS curve. It can reinitiate some level of ganging depending on the number of incidents needed to adjust to the change. This holds true even for factory upgrades specifically intended to increase reliability. If you ever down loaded so-called fixes from the Internet, or upgraded your computer's operating system, you'll understand this effect. It has got to do with Poisson distribution of incidents and such, but I don't understand that. I do understand "If it ain't broke, don't fix it!"

Confirmed intermittent cruisers can sometimes simulate continuous cruising. I had an old radar whose picture got jumpy if it didn't get run warm at least twice a month. If I found myself on the hook too long in one place, I ran the radar each time I cleaned my rode. It turned out that both the rode and the radar had similar service cycles.

Too little simulation, and too much preventive maintenance, can backfire on you. I knew a guy who only used his boat for dockside entertainment. He ran his old Perkins 4-108 diesel 20 minutes every Saturday for three years. "To keep resale value," he said. When he sold the boat he had to do a rebuild. The engine always ran cold and without load. Its cooling airspaces sucked in fresh salt air every time he shut it down. It sat 99.8% of the time with salt air licking into it and pitting its wrist pins.

On the other hand, I once asked a man on a Micronesian island how long his village's electric generator, also a Perkins 4-108, had continuously run. "Five years," he said, "excepting the time I got drunk and didn't pump fuel up into the day tank." That's 43,800 hours! And they built the 4-236 for continuous use, not the 4-108.

The insurance-required surveyor for my trawler's 4-236 looked at the Hobbs meter's reading of 2,350 hours and reported it soon should have a rebuild. It had seen regular intermittent use only while loaded. I look forward to somewhere between 12,000 and 20,000 more hours from the engine. The factory will say I can get them, but many experienced Fort Lauderdale mechanics will say, "Not a chance!" Of course. Most of the engines they see come from waterway queens like the dockside entertainment guy.

THE ANSWER

When you understand the RAS problem, you may opt to KISS a little more, but don't replace your head with a bucket. Some devices merit their troubles. How far you KISS your RAS really has to do with the ganging phenomenon and your style of use. I know this from several decades of cruising in which I've fit out new boats and refit used ones, starting in Sweden, not long after the call from my ex-boss about our reliability successes in Apollo.

He talked in a computer programmer's caffeine and nicotine rush. I felt as pleased as he did with the success of the reliability software. We had put together a hell of a team, and we had licked the problem. He had other calls to make, and the bird still had to get out of the woods. Nonetheless he asked, intrigued with my having, as they say, *gone foreign*, "What are you up to over there?"

I listened to the morning birds outside the window and thought about the epidemic of computer crashes Volvo thought I could fix or prevent. I peered out the window down to my *Snipa* moored way below, under the cliff in Hovås Hamn. I already had a list of equipment for the new boat which I saw at the Earl's Court boat show in London. Lots of gear to install, little time. And 62° latitude makes for a short sailing season.

"I'm thinking of getting a bigger boat and going cruising permanently," I told him. "In the tropics," I said.

And I did.

WHAT YOU REALLY NEED
Versus what the marine store thinks you need.

Magazines and marine equipment dealers make elaborate plans for you to acquire stuff. You can not dispense with some gear, such as appropriate navigation aids. But some equipment, as you shall see, may actually lead to failure of the expedition, despite their claim to support ship's reliability.

Most cruisers consume themselves with getting to a certain place at a certain time. For this they heavily invest in all sorts of navigational equipment. The real art of navigation, however, lies in staying out of the wrong place at the wrong time. Use that as your criterion for choosing navigational aids.

CHARTS AND GUIDES

The problem of too much information confronts modern skippers as more devices come on the market. Years of cruising in the Third World with few documented navigation aids, and Europe, where they have too many, have led me to make the following recommendations, *listed in priority order.*

YACHTING GUIDES

Guides become out of date the moment they get printed. Look for guides that give you less tips on where to do your drinking, dining or dancing and more detail on anchorages, landfall marks, sea conditions, etc. The fathom lines rarely change but, bartenders, cooks and bands change frequently. The more guides, the better, since each author has a slightly different viewpoint.

MEDIUM SCALE CHARTS

These charts get you between cruising areas. For instance, if you already have a guidebook, you only need charts which show clusters of islands. When you have only ocean and no islands, you only need a plotting sheet or Pilot (Routing) Charts.

PILOT (ROUTING) CHARTS

The U.S. Pilot Charts (Routing Charts in the U.K.) have pages sized to a yacht's chart table for each month showing 150 years of average conditions for every patch of sea. I kept a pilot chart on my chart table at all times. I used it only occasionally for plotting crossings, tracking Tropical Storms. and planning passages with the current and wind data it provides. However, it got used every morning to plot the weather features from the various forecasts. Covered with pencil marks and coffee rings it became the single most used chart aboard. Aboard my trawler, the Wx chart sits behind Plexiglas on my refrigerator door. No coffee rings, just tracks and doodles of 3 colors of wet-erase pens.

LARGE SCALE CHARTS

These charts cover small geographic areas. You need these charts for areas where keys and reefs lie densely packed, or if you explore areas not shown in available guides.

SMALL SCALE CHARTS

These charts cover large geographical areas. They make great wall decorations. At sea, you only need those to plot ocean passages. Pilot Charts usually do nicely.

ALMANACS

Of great use as reference works aboard. (Who knows the breaking strength of 5/16 BBB chain, anyway?) I have found that a single copy of Reed's Nautical Almanac from any year provides more useful information than Chapman's and Bowditch's combined.

TIDE TABLES

In the English Channel I never sailed without my tide tables and current guides. The tides, after all, went to 34 feet at my moorings, and the currents reached 9 knots! In most places in the trades you need nothing outside the Pilot Charts which don't vary year to year. Many places the daily tides get broadcast several times a day on standard AM broadcast radio. Tidal differences rarely exceed one half hour from the reference stations in open anchorages, and tidal anomalies, such as on banks, all call for local knowledge the tide tables don't have. I've found tide prediction software sufficient and accurate for open anchorages.

> **Most places you can assume high tide at 8 o'clock local time everywhere near open sea on the day of a full moon. You can add 52 minutes a day thereafter and do without tide tables forever!**

THE BARE MINIMUM

COMPASS

I sailed for years with only a compass and a log. After a while I found even the log a luxury. Knowledge of your boat's speed settles into your bones after only a few weeks of cruising. You can navigate surely and safely forever with only a compass by careful and frequent position plotting, attention to leeway, current and tidal currents, and by introducing intentional errors in order to ensure which side of a feature you make your landfall. Even the compass needn't have all that much accuracy, since who can hold a perfect course anyway, what with all that bobbing around?

Old fashioned binnacles look nice and get used for taking bearings of ships. But you can't see them from comfortable seated positions. You should mount your compass where you can see it comfortably from your position on either tack while cruising. You rarely sit bolt upright behind or beside the wheel! The cruising steering position has a little more Zen in it. For instance, I always sailed scrunched up on a beanbag in the same corner of the cockpit on both tacks, never behind the wheel. Therefore I used a bulkhead compass. Occasionally I steered with my feet from the beanbag. Today I trawl around in a pilot's chair, but still with my feet hoisted up on the wheel. At night I spend some time on a futón instead of a beanbag. The compass therefore mounts on the overhead instrument panel.

The compass should have a rapidly damped large, legible scale, well illuminated, not just bright. Some compass lights illuminate everything but the card's scale.

Swing your compass from time to time, even though you compensated it, to adjust your compass' deviation table, and make sure you are using this year's variation.

LOG

Use sumlogs, taffrail logs, or any device which keeps a digital track of miles run only as a double check on the navigator. They all fail, and the skipper ought to know intuitively how fast his yacht goes through the water.

Before the impeller gets tangled in seaweed or a shark eats the rotor, take the time to calibrate your sense of the boat's speed by the old chip log method. Select a fixed length of deck viewed from your sailing position. Time bits of foam passing between perpendiculars that long, checking results with actual speedo readings. Get speed in knots by:

$$\frac{2 \times \text{Meters}}{\text{Seconds}}$$

Count seconds the same way you do to determine a light's characteristics. You can use either "one-Mississippi, two Mississippi ... " or "one-thousand-one, one-thousand-two...", whichever works for you. But either way, you must speak the words to have them work, and you must revert to "one" when you get to ten. Practice makes perfect and eventually you can tell with a glance how fast you go in any condition.

An old principle of navigation says that the more regular and frequent you plot your position, the more sure your course. If you have no sumlog, you should plot in shorter intervals. Shorter intervals average out errors in speed estimates.

SEXTANT

It seems sextants have gone the way of the slide rule. The last time I used my sextant I crossed the Atlantic in 1979. If you really know how to use them on clear and starry nights, then you might use one between widely spaced islands. I have a friend who could pull off a three star fix faster than my Satnav did one. He couldn't beat a GPS, however. Solar and lunar sights don't usually provide the kind of precision required to navigate among islands. But island hopping

short distances you have unmistakable and inevitable landfalls. And even if you do cross the sea, you won't require great accuracy, but the sextant can confirm set and drift.

You better spend your time and money on chart work and a good compass. You don't want to emulate the *professional* delivery crew who gave up their charge on a reef, having spent all their time playing with their sextants and none of it pinching to windward to avoid a lee reef. The day after the paid crew of three deserted their ship, by the way, a lone salvor took it off the reef whole by using the boat's own ground tackle. He turned the key and motored off with the boat.

The lesson here: just as with GPS, don't confuse position fixing with navigation.

ELECTRONICS

> **You can't buy safety at sea with expensive equipment or fancy calculations. As Eric Hiscock loved to say, "The price of safety at sea is eternal vigilance".**

If I only really need a chart and compass, then why should I spend the money on fancy electronic navigation aids? Because the older I get, the mistakier I get. Once I entirely missed an island group because a pair of pliers left under the compass gave me a deviation of seventeen degrees. Dumb? But as I recall, I littered my youth with mistakes as well.

Buy things which make checks possible on the dumb things you shall inevitably do.

In general, the more navigation aids, electronic or not, the better. Bless you for becoming affluent enough to afford them, clever enough to select the right ones from the welter of black boxes on the market, and patient enough to maintain them. Which devices will serve you the most in the trade? This list follows, like the last one, in *priority order*.

DEPTH SOUNDER

The depth sounder, or fathometer, gets much under-used among yachties. I rate this navigation aid only second to the compass. You need a reliable digital depthfinder in the cockpit for coasting. Tack in to 10 fathoms, tack out to 20, and so on. Additionally, some evidence exists that sounders left on, even when off soundings, deter broaching marlins and whales from coming up under the boat.

Use the Chain of Soundings method (see Glossary) when lost off a coast where everything looks the same. Many of us use this method of navigation unconsciously while coasting in order to confirm the boat's position. With chart in hand, keep mental track of the soundings on the fathometer. If the readings of the fathometer do not agree with your expectations gained from the chart, you have reason to wonder about your position.

By sailing a straight line and taking soundings at regular intervals one can arrive at a "signature" of the bottom which usually identifies only that line over that bottom. For a somewhat complex, but unequivocal, way of doing it, plot the readings to scale on a piece of clear plastic or tracing paper. Then move the tracing about on the chart until you have a match. Of course the bottom must vary, and sometimes you get a long line, and you have to get it all done before you've left the area and become lost again. While on soundings I prefer to just make mental note of the fathom lines as I cross them, and I don't lose my chain of soundings. Anyway, I usually follow a fathom line while coasting.

VHF

Required. Only one will do, but you'll like having a handheld in the cockpit or dinghy.

AM/FM

Of course you have an AM/FM aboard with cassette or CD player. You should also have a hand sized portable with a rod type extendable aerial in the emergency locker. If you have to abandon ship you can listen to all the religious stations that dot the tropics. But more important, you can use it as a highly reliable radio direction finder, homing in on island rock stations. Reception gets loudest with the aerial perpendicular to the station. Perhaps the combination of direction and religion shall save you.

AUTOPILOT

I believe exhaustion has caused more accidents at sea than any other human factor, and like the "rapture of the deep", exhaustion takes its toll before you notice it. The autopilot has become an absolutely necessary piece of equipment on any cruising boat. The duties of a vigilant watch can tire one enough without having to face the tyranny of the wheel. You can buy autopilots today for ampere-poor sailing craft, which use only 3-5 amperes on duty, negligible current draw on standby. Most sailboats with a balanced rig can sail themselves when close hauled with the helm lashed, but the autopilot handles motor sailing better than a crew could. For long distance trade wind sailing you might want to snap on a self steering device such as the Aries wind vane.

SSB RECEIVER

For receiving the weather forecasts and the various cruiser nets you must have a radio capable of receiving Single Side Band. You can use a cheap portable with a "BFO" switch. Before you pay $300 for a SONY, however, look at more professional gear which may even prove cheaper in the long run and give much better reception. I had two of those small SONY units which corroded. An older Radio Shack model, however, lasted for years. To actually talk to the weather net gurus you need a transceiver.

GPS

They come in a variety of models. All GPS units seem to have the worst human factors since they eliminated spark advance from steering wheels. "Hoo-boy!", says the engineer, "if we connect the freemis to the gizzis, and you press these six buttons at once, you'll get the Gregorian date expressed in hexadecimal." "Grrreat!" explodes the marketeer, and into the machine it goes. The manufacturers make these do-hickeys to keep up unit price in an expanding market. Unless you have a commercial boat with repetitive routes, you only need a few waypoints: where you came from, where you want to go (with a couple of options) and the location of a weather feature on which you may want range and bearing. Yet they give you hundreds, free for them, costly for you.

GPS Cautions

Don't lose your nav skills. If you haven't any, get them quick. Despite your use of the GPS, while planning or executing a crossing, make estimated positions (EPs), not DRs (dead reckoning). EPs include current, leeway, tide, variation and compass deviation.

With the full availability of GPS cruisers have taken to giving each other precise coordinates of reef entrances and channel markers. Use these at your peril! Adjust all such arrival waypoints to give you:

1. a safe offing with which to proceed visually, and
2. a safe approach from sea at any reasonable arrival angle.

Take this example of a dangerous yet common practice. A helpful yachtie, the leader type with a radio voice the envy of every Pan Am Flight 001 captain, dinghied out to the red ball *inside* the harbor's entrance reefs. Holding the ball, he did several GPS clickety-clicks. Proud as Columbus, he told the cruiser nets of his adventure with the "seabuoy" and advised them to replace arrival waypoints in the guide book with his "more accurate" numbers. Three yachts approaching the harbor on an oblique course went onto the reef in the next two weeks, each bound die straight for the little red ball on the other side of the reef. That guy still cruises, by the way. Watch out for him.

You certainly have your stories too. When you use a GPS waypoint, do the following:

1. check that the chart's datum uses the same as the waypoint's
2. move the waypoint to a safe offing clear of all possible dangers
3. if uncertain of your chart's datum, calibrate it using a charted mark which lies near to hand before using it to create or check waypoints; then draw a difference vector on the chart (e.g., 0.35 nm at 350°)
4. proceed visually in all channels, cuts and harbors.

Steering a straight line across the bottom in tidal streams can create the longest path, for either sail or motor. Check it out before you do it.

While coasting, make your own fixes regularly by compass bearings and confirm with the GPS. This ensures your continuous recognition of land features.

Never believe claims of accuracy, nor confuse accuracy with precision, and treat all beacons and lights as unreliable, damaged or decrepit.

In other words, navigate the boat yourself no matter what aids you may have.

COMPUTER WEATHER FAX

The best solution for the cruiser combines Wx fax with a computer (as if you hadn't enough complications already). You can receive and store weather charts, satellite pictures, and even get the telex of the verbal weather reports to eliminate copying errors. Needless to say, the computer can do email, store charts, keep records — you need one.

Weather faxes represent some of the source materials of the reports you hear on the radio. The analysts studied for years and went on to earn an incredible buck reducing these macro plots of micro data to a carefully considered verbal report with which mariners can make decisions within local areas. To second guess their analysis seems dangerous. Don't exclude them for only charts.

SSB TRANSCEIVER

A transmitter helps you keep in touch with your friends while sailing in company and leapfrogging each other. It also helps you keep up with the rumor mill which grinds between the cruisers on your path so you don't feel such a stranger when you arrive. Take care with weather information received, however, as well as talk of piracy, revolutions, the sky falling in, and so on. You may use either the more powerful Marine SSB radio or a less powerful HAM radio which you can get modified to transmit on the Marine band.

RADAR

As with all electronics, think of your ampere usage and make sure you can handle it. Some can suck juice like a water maker. Normally the trade winds produce no fog. Radar gets used for confirming landfalls, finding seabuoys and, 'lordy, lordy', plying a windward coast so close you can shake hands with the natives. For the single hander, a well tuned eight mile radar with a "fence" function may help keep watch on crossings.

RADAR REFLECTORS

Marginally more effective than a tiki in avoiding collisions. Better to keep a good watch. Yachting Monthly showed the futility of anything but welded radar reflectors and the Japanese "goat's eye" solid type in a study done in 1978. We repeated their tests in Antibes the next year and got equally dismal results. Even the manufacturers produce reflectors that you can not mount in the proper "catch water" attitude. I had used a fender full of aluminum chaff once until I discovered my new mast steps offered a better target. Like reflectors, radar transponders depend on the ship's officers looking at their radar within the time you've got between acquisition and collision.

To calibrate your boat as a target, talk to seagoing tugs. They usually keep a good radar watch and the ones I've met will enjoy helping you.

RADAR DETECTORS

They work, but ships often don't use their radar in the open sea. If you find yourself coasting or in a shipping lane, you better darn well keep your own lookout. These things chirp at such distances the alarm goes off constantly despite no ships in sight. If you squelch them to eliminate ships over the horizon, with the controls so rinky-dink you may squelch out the guy about to run you down.

RADIO DIRECTION FINDERS

Though fine for simply homing on a port, unless you have a double loop, mast-mounted antennae tunable to any frequency, forget it. Fixes available from three senders on shore will have a cocked hat larger than the gap between you and the shore. I buried

172

my last RDF in the North Sea. Use a portable AM with whip antennae on rock stations.

HAM Radio

It certainly gets you invited to a lot of hamfests. Think of the telephone bills you'll save calling home. Whether a Rowdy or a Good Citizen, you will find a team to root for on the various Radio Nazi shows HAMsters run. During emergencies HAM ncts may help you. But far from home, you shall make your first calls on the marine SSB nets.

Cruisers on the coasts of the U.S. can quite beneficially use HAM radios since their communications encompass many land based HAMs and friends and family with telephones. After a couple of years in the tropics where they find a new compass of friends, most HAMs migrate to marine bands, and the HAM frequencies get used for long calls to family at home.

By all means get a radio able to communicate on all frequencies in an emergency, but prepare yourself to handle 99% of communications on marine band.

Electronic Charts

All the debate notwithstanding, this gets my lowest priority. Furthermore, screens at cruising helm stations give poor legibility. And shall do so for some time to come.

Think for a moment:

> You have a sheet in the prop and a jammed furling gear. The boat got bound on the wind, and you can't cross it. You have tumbling groundswells which wildly corkscrew the deck. A rising sun aft blasts into the chart screen. You hadn't planned to find yourself in this position. In fact, you had just got up from a catnap you took to shake off the illusions of extreme fatigue. You have only one chance to throw the helm hard over to enter a cut safely and avoid a reefing. You cling to the overhead grip and the fiddle of your chart table, hoping to construct a range on which to make the entrance. You realize you haven't got the correctly scaled chart with which to make transits on the distant points of land behind the reefs. You bounce back to the helm, cracking a rib before gaining foot- and handholds. In agony and panic you try to clear your brain with only a moment to spare. The glarey screen won't display the scale you need to see both the reef and the island features with which to make a range. You scrabble your fingers at the buttons with mere seconds left. It all goes wrong. Just as you have the display you want, you get thrown into the panel and lose the display. You gain it again. You peer through the glare. A flash of white dazzles the helm station, the reflection of the final groundswell breaking over you. With a terrific whump! the world rolls an instantaneous 90° and turns a dark, dark green. Your face smashes into the overhead and an excruciating seizure of pain tears down your spinal column. In the gloom, just before you pass out, the chart you wanted beams brightly on.

Still want to go with electronic charts as your only charts?

But, if you've got the wherewithal to play the game, why not play? But have backup on the navtable, and use a paper guide book in the cockpit.

> **The three pieces of equipment I see most regarded by cruisers headed to the tropics, and least used or discarded after a couple of years cruising there? Diving tanks, bicycles and sailing dinghies.**

GLOSSARY

All you never wanted to know but needed to dearly.

Air Pressure Think of it as the weight of air molecules stacked vertically above the place at which you measure it — between your ears. It weighs 14.7 lbs. per square inch at sea level. Actually it "weighs" sideways too, since the weight gets produced by molecules in Brownian motion colliding with each other. But I prefer to think of myself walking around with a 400,000 foot wobbly stack of air on my head.

Backing Wind counterclockwise shifting of the wind (e.g., from southeast to east)

Baja Filter A California invention for use in cruising the Baja. A funnel which has nested, removable filters of successively finer mesh through which fuel gets poured into the tank. The best will have a Teflon coated filter to separate water as well.

Beaufort Wind Scale Admiral Beaufort's Scale of Wind Speed, made to enable ships of the line to classify conditions from observations. It measures wind speed 10 meters above sea level and the corresponding sea effects for open sea far from land. Refer to the section entitled Think Beaufort to read the Beaufort Wind scale.

Blue Northers Colloquial expression for the arctic winds which scourge the plains of the continents, but not the scraggly tail ends of the fronts that reach the tropics.

Coastal Front Cumulus and cumulonimbus clouds created by the circulation of *sea breeze* (see below) and marking a zone of change at the margin of sea and land. In the islands these usually get pushed over the heated land by the stable sea air stream. Depending on the colors and textures of the land below these clouds can show mariners an outline of the coast before they see the coast. Particularly true where an island's colors and textures have uniformity. The island and any banks water behind a coastal front often get reflected in the lower surface of these clouds. On the larger islands, look for strong gusts and showers coming from *storm cells* (see below) spawned by the coastal fronts in the late afternoons. Don't make the mistake of forecasting sea conditions based on conditions in harbor beneath a coastal front, especially over an irregular coastline.

Coastal Report weather reports usually available on VHF stations. Historically, these reports got sent from coastal stations such as light houses and life boat stations. They report sea conditions in wave height and swell height.

Cold Front The zone of division between Tropical and Polar Maritime air masses which generally moves eastward with clear, colder air at the rear of a depression. May get preceded by squalls.

Coriolis Force discovered in the 19th century by French scientist Coriolis (of course) which causes anything moving above the earth's surface to curve right in the northern hemisphere (left in the southern hemisphere).

Culture Shock Reaction to sustained mismatch between cultural stimulus and response.

Deathtrap Any area which appears safe in most conditions but surprisingly unsurvivable when attacked by wind or wave from its not always obvious weak points.

DR Dead Reckoning: a method of establishing position of a vessel by projecting miles run from the simple product of average speed in knots and hours run along a stable heading. See also *Estimated Position* (EP) below.

Dangerous Semicircle The half of a developed depression with cyclonic winds which contains the quadrant of highest winds, i.e., those which lie along the direction of travel of the depression.

Diurnal Variation Daily variation. For wind, the strength and direction of surface winds near land during, and as a result of, the passage of the sun from horizon to horizon. *Sea breeze* (see below) becomes stronger as the sun gets higher, and weaker as the sun gets lower. Wind will usually shift somewhat to the right during the sun's transit. In offshore waters the *gradient wind* (see below) has small diurnal variation, none at all above 30 knots.

EP See Estimated Position

Equatorial Current In the North Atlantic Ocean the *North Equatorial Current* means the west going part of the clockwise circulation around the Sargasso Sea, and the *South Equatorial Current* means the current just north of the equator which runs counter to the earth's rotation. It runs along the coast of South America and into the Caribbean Sea. North of the Antilles the northern current blends elements of the southern current but the southern current runs much stronger off South America's north coast.

Estimated Position A method of establishing position of a vessel which biases the *dead reckoning* position with estimated leeway, expressed in degrees from heading, and the two vectors of tide and current whose values you show in degrees of set, with magnitudes of knots.

Force Beaufort See *Beaufort wind scale* above

Front The line of separation between cold and warm air masses.

GPS Global Positioning System, capable of providing 3-dimensional position data every few seconds with great accuracy (20 meters when not dithered by the military with a feature they call Selective Availability). A nearly indispensable device for confirming a navigator's *estimated position* which should get kept hourly in the old paper way.

Gradient Wind The wind forecast in the weather reports. The wind close to the surface (see *surface wind*) in the open sea. It will flow between pressure zones from high to low pressure, turning always to the right (left in the Southern Hemisphere) due to the *Coriolis Force* (see above). Weather maps get drawn with lines called *isobars* (see below) which correlate directly to the lines of equal altitude on terrain maps. Isobars close together give the appearance of a steep incline. Far apart, they show a gradual rise. Thus the term gradient.

High Pressure Center A dome of high pressure shown on weather maps as rings of closed *isobars* (see below). Really air stacked higher than average. When it slides off the peak of the dome it curves right (left in the Southern Hemisphere) due to the *Coriolis Force* (see above), thus setting up a clockwise (counterclockwise) rotation of wind around the center.

High Pressure Ridge A linear region of atmospheric pressure bounded by lower pressures on both sides, which on *isobar* (see below) charts gives the appearance of a ridge of terrain.

Hurricane From the Indian god who wreaked destruction by wind, Oricán [or-ee-KHAN]. Name given to the tropical cyclonic storms east of the Americas (Typhoon west). It also applies to Force 12 on the *Beaufort wind scale* regardless of cause.

Hurricane Games My name for the very serious business of posing all the "what if" questions when selecting an anchorage in the hurricane season. Draw a hurricane spiral to scale on a piece of transparent plastic and move it around on the chart.

Hurricane Hole An anchorage protected from the seas, if not the winds, of a hurricane.

Hurricane Warning A hurricane may approach within 24 hours.

Hurricane Watch A hurricane may approach within 36 hours.

Inshore Wind The wind inshore, or within about 2 miles of shore. The winds here mostly get steered by encounter with land features such as beach, river mouths, mountains and draws, where the seabreeze begins. It extends out to sea and over land. Nocturnal winds blow strongest in this zone, and wise coastwise passage makers angle coastward to take advantage of them on a clear night.

Isobars Lines drawn on weather maps which connect points of equal atmospheric pressure (see *air pressure*). As on terrain maps, these lines demonstrate the mountains and valleys, hills, cliffs and inclines of the sea of air stacked above us Thus terms such as *ridge, trough* and *high* and *low centers* describe the surface of that sea at some arbitrary altitude.

Joy The only detergent I know which works as well in sea water as it does in fresh.

Katabatic A wind that flows down slope, usually at night, due to the cooling of the upper level air which then becomes heavier and flows down hill. Along with land breeze, the katabatic wind creates the *nocturnal wind* (see below).

Land Breeze The opposite of *seabreeze*, and it occurs at night with a much milder circulation than that of a *seabreeze* (see below).

Line Squall So named for having sunk a ship of the line off the Needles, beyond the Isle of Wight. A sudden squall with violent blasts of cold air occurring at the point of a V-shaped depression, or derivatives of tropical systems (see below). Usually preceded by a flat black bar of cloud low to the sea. It can easily pack winds above 50 knots.

Low Pressure Center A depression in atmospheric pressure (see *air pressure*) shown as tight rings of closed *isobars* (see above) on a weather map, similar to a bowl shaped valley on terrain maps. Air falling into the center tries to fill it, but will rotate around it counter clockwise due to *Coriolis Force* (see above).

Low Pressure Trough A linear region of low pressure with or without closed *isobars* which gives the appearance on weather maps of a long valley of terrain. Called trough, as in the inverse of a wave. If the *isobars* close, the length of the trough renders circulation questionable. Nonetheless, winds ahead may veer slightly, and winds behind may back a bit. If the trough shrinks in length, or breaks into segments, it can become a rotating *low pressure center* and eventually a *tropical depression* (see below).

Murphy's Law Even looking at it optimistically, whatever can go wrong shall, in fact, go wrong (e.g., the toast always falls buttered side down).

NAVTEX U.S. Coast Guard transmissions on 516.9 USB in SITOR FEC mode.

Night Lee A lee from wind and sea at the margin of sea and land. Created by thermal effects caused by the land cooling faster than the sea. Significantly abetted by orographics on mountainous coasts. See *Island Effects: Playing the Island Lees.*

Niño [KNEE-nyo] Boy child. Also the name of a world wide weather disturbance brought about periodically by a reversal in the Humboldt Current (See National Geographic Vol. 165 No 2, February 1984, and Vol. 195 No 3, March 1999).

NOAA National Oceanic and Atmospheric Administration, a branch of the U.S. Government which regularly loses its weather satellites over the Atlantic.

Nocturnal Wind The night wind, a combination of land breeze which feeds the updrafts over the warmer water, and the *katabatic wind* (see above). The nocturnal wind begins after sundown and dies before dawn, reaching its strongest between midnight and 2 a.m. See also *seabreeze.*

Norther Colloquial expression for fierce and durable winter winds from the north. Used in New England, Iceland, Alaska, Lower Slobovia, but NOT between the Tropics!

NWS National Weather Service

Offshore -Waters, -Wind, -Conditions, -Passaging, whatever. Generally 8 to 12 miles offshore. Actually, as far from or as near to shore that gradient wind touches down and conditions go unaffected by land, the NWS Offshore Report's "more than 50 miles from shore" notwithstanding.

Passage Making The actual doing of a voyage, as opposed to a sail or crossing. Passage Making implies prudent navigation, sea-readiness and competent seamanship.

Pilot Charts Charts for each of the twelve months which give the statistics compiled of the weather, wind, current and storm tracks over a period of nearly 150 years (thanks to Lt. Matthew Fontaine Maury, USN). The British know these as Routing Charts.

Prevailing Conditions In the northeast trades, wind east northeast to east southeast at 15-20 knots. Rare extremes of northeast by east, southeast by east, and 10 or 25 knots briefly occur. Look for perturbing weather features when wind goes outside these limits. For detailed discussion of how these prevailing conditions vary seasonally, see the chapters *Island Weather: Weather Windows*, and *Trades Strategies: Wait for Weather: Think Beaufort.*

Rage Bahamian name for the condition of the seas when the wind has blown hard onshore for some time.

Range Two features, marks or lights coming into line, the rearmost positioned vertically above the foremost. One can make one's own range out of any objects in foreground and background in order to stay a course (see also *transit*).

Ridge see *high pressure ridge*.

Rule of Twelfths A rough rule for estimating the variable rise or fall of the tide, and therefore the tidal current if you know peak flow. The rule states that the first, second and third hour of tide rise or fall accounts for one twelfth, 2 twelfths and 3 twelfths, respectively, of the tidal range, whereas the fourth, fifth and sixth hours account for 3-, 2-, and one- twelfth(s), respectively. Thus, if you have a range of 3 feet, 3 inches will fall (or rise) in the first hour, 6 in the second, 9 in the third and fourth hours, and finally, 6 and 3 inches in the fifth and sixth hours, for a total of 36 inches, or 3 feet. Similarly, the current, as a ratio of peak flow, runs an average of one sixth, one half, 5 sixths, 5 sixths, one half and one sixth knots, for hours one through 6, respectively. For example, if the peak flow on flood runs 1.2 knots, then hours one to 6 of tide rise shall average rates of 0.2, 0.6, 1.0, 1.0, 0.6, and 0.2 knots.

Seabreeze The sun heats the land during the day. The land heats the air above it which rises to get displaced by more air from the sea. A circulation begins which can create wind of up to 20 knots with effects distinguishable as far inland as 10 miles and as far at sea as 20 miles. In the tropics seabreezes run year round, but they blow strongest in the spring and summer.

SG&T Sundowner Gin and Tonic. A mnemonic for any inflexible custom which makes the Leisure Sailor perform all passage planning so that late afternoons get spent at leisure in a safe anchorage with the yacht completely put away and ready for sea. This gives captain and crew a full evening of rest and relaxation with which to face the next day, or with which to face an anchor drill called invariably at 2 a.m. Any other custom at sundown doesn't classify as Leisure Sailing, but a mark of the anxiety driven working class.

Storm Cells Cells of rising or sinking air currents scattered, or occurring in lines (frontal thunderstorms). Thunderstorms from late summer afternoon *coastal fronts* (see above) can grow vicious, especially on large or high islands. Since winds can rotate around cells either way, you can tactically use these.

Sundowner G&T See *SG&T*.

Surface Wind In the open sea, the *gradient wind* (see above), the forecast wind, slows at the sea surface due to the force of friction. Lighter gradient winds, 5 to 15 knots, can curve 10° to 15° toward lower pressure as they brush the surface. Stronger gradient winds will bend less.

Thornless Path a way of *passage making* (see definition above) to windward which creates a delightful, relaxed experience.

Thorny Path a way of *passage making* (see definition above) to windward which tries the soul as well as the boat.

TPC *Tropical Prediction Center* (see below).

Trade Wind Winds which blow from the high pressure areas of the tropics to the relatively low pressure of the equatorial regions. They get bent with the Coriolis Force, becoming easterly by the time they pour over the islands of the western oceans. These winds continuously switch like a cat's tail between northeast and east southeast in the winter, and between east northeast and southeast in the summer.

Trades Short for the *trade winds*. One should always read this to include seas as well.

Transit Two features or marks, identifiable on a chart, coming into line (also *range*).

Tropical Depression A bad weather system characterized by closed *isobars* of barometric pressure, precipitation and mainly ascending air in which the gradient winds can get quite strong and will flow counterclockwise (clockwise in the Southern Hemisphere) and toward the central low.

Tropical Disturbance any large area of disturbed weather in the tropics not yet, nor perhaps ever, classified a *tropical depression* (see above).

Tropical Prediction Center The Tropical Analysis and Forecast Branch of the U.S. National Weather Service located in Miami, Florida

Tropical Storm A *tropical depression* which has developed into a full cyclonic storm on the *Beaufort wind scale* with winds from 48 to 63 knots.

Tropical System Any of the summer weather systems in the tropics: see *tropical wave, tropical disturbance, tropical depression, tropical storm, hurricane.*

Tropical Wave Atmospheric pressure waves forming in the tropics of the eastern ocean in the summer. These can stretch up to a thousand miles long and move between 10 and 20 knots toward the west. They usually have associated precipitation and spawn *storm cells* (see above), but like *fronts*, regions of the wave can pass relatively clear.

Trough See *low pressure trough*.

Veering Wind Clockwise shifting of the wind (e.g., north to east)

Wait for Weather Read the section, *Trades Strategies: Wait for Weather*. This, and the *SG&T*, quite seriously form the nucleus of the *thornless path* concept. If you can afford to wait for the appropriate *weather window*, and you always lay to anchor in a snug harbor with a ready boat and getting lots of rest by late afternoon, you rate absolutely as a Leisure Sailor of the first order.

Weather Window The period during which wind, wave and swell conduct themselves favorably for completing a leg of a passage in safety and comfort.

Xenophobia Suspicion, fear or hatred of foreigners or things strange. Usually an infirmity of the French but can reach virulent degrees in Homo Americanus when found aboard between the tropics.

10/23